Sports Economics, Management and Policy

Series Editor
Dennis Coates

For further volumes:
http://www.springer.com/series/8343

R. Todd Jewell
Editor

Violence and Aggression in Sporting Contests

Economics, History and Policy

Springer

Editor
R. Todd Jewell
Department of Economics
University of North Texas
Union Circle 1155
Denton, TX 76203-5017, USA
tjewell@unt.edu

ISSN 2191-298X e-ISSN 2191-2998
ISBN 978-1-4419-6629-2 e-ISBN 978-1-4419-6630-8
DOI 10.1007/978-1-4419-6630-8
Springer New York Dordrecht Heidelberg London

Library of Congress Control Number: 2011934247

Printed on acid-free paper

Springer is part of Springer Science+Business Media (www.springer.com)

Contents

List of Figures

List of Tables

Contributors

Vassiliki Avgerinou University of Peloponnese, Sparta, Greece
vasavg@uop.gr

Marcel Battré University of Paderborn, Paderborn, Germany
marcel.battre@wiwi.upb.de

David J. Berri Southern Utah University, Cedar City, UT, USA
berri@suu.edu

Stephen B. Billings University of North Carolina at Charlotte, Charlotte, NC, USA
sbillin2@uncc.edu

Ross Booth Monash University, Melbourne, VIC, Australia
ross.booth@buseco.monash.edu.au

Robert Brooks Monash University, Melbourne, VIC, Australia
robert.brooks@monash.edu

Dennis Coates University of Maryland, Baltimore County, Baltimore, MD, USA
coates@umbc.edu

Trevor Collier University of Dayton, Dayton, OH, USA
collier@udayton.edu

Craig A. Depken II University of North Carolina at Charlotte, Charlotte, NC, USA
cdepken@uncc.edu

Christian Deutscher University of Paderborn, Paderborn, Germany
christian.deutscher@wiwi.upb.de

Stefanos G. Giakoumatos Technological Educational Institute of Kalamata, Kalamata, Greece
giakoumatos@teikal.gr

Janice A. Hauge University of North Texas, Denton, TX, USA
jhauge@unt.edu

R. Todd Jewell University of North Texas, Denton, TX, USA
tjewell@unt.edu

Andrew L. Johnson Texas A&M University, College Station, TX, USA
ajohnson@tamu.edu

Afsheen Moti University of North Texas, Denton, TX, USA
afsheenmoti@gmail.com

Ryan M. Rodenberg Florida State University, Tallahassee, FL, USA
rrodenberg@fsu.edu

John Ruggiero University of Dayton, Dayton, OH, USA
ruggiero@notes.udayton.edu

John Solow University of Iowa, Iowa City, IA, USA
solow@uiowa.edu

Peter von Allmen Skidmore College, Saratoga Springs, NY, USA
pvonallm@skidmore.edu

Part I
Introduction

Chapter 1
Violence and Aggression in Spectator Sports: A Prologue

R. Todd Jewell

Background

As the title of this book suggests, the chapters it contains deal with the relationship between aggressive and violent play and spectator demand. This is not the first book to examine this issue, as the topic of violence in sports has been the subject of psychologists, sociologist, and other social scholars who are interested in explaining the behavioral motivations of players who engage in aggressive and violent play in contests or who are interested in understanding the behavior of consumers who watch these aggressive and violent games. For instance, sport psychologists are concerned with the individual traits that motivate violent behavior in sport, under the assumption that such violence can be mitigated with appropriate behavior-modification strategies (Abrams 2010).

The reader may well ask: "If an expansive literature already exists on the topic of violence in sport, why does this book exist?" Primarily, this book exists because the lens of economics has not been systematically applied to violence and aggression in sports, with the notable exception of ice hockey as shown in Chap. 4 of this book. Following this introductory chapter and a chapter devoted to the history of violence in spectator sports, this book contains seven chapters that empirically analyze aggression and violence in various worldwide sports leagues from an economic viewpoint. Highlighted in these seven chapters are the incentives, in terms of costs and benefits, that drive the behavior of athletes and teams within contests and the incentives that influence whether a league encourages, punishes, or outright bans aggressive and violent play. The costs and benefits of aggression and violence in sports imply that leagues, teams, and athletes must make tradeoffs when determining the appropriate level of aggression and/or violence in their league or sport. In addition, this book contains two chapters on violence outside of sporting contests

R.T. Jewell (✉)
University of North Texas, Denton, TX, USA
e-mail: tjewell@unt.edu

R.T. Jewell (ed.), *Violence and Aggression in Sporting Contests: Economics, History and Policy*, Sports Economics, Management and Policy 4,
DOI 10.1007/978-1-4419-6630-8_1, © Springer Science+Business Media, LLC 2011

that influence the sports industry. These final two chapters concentrate on the impact that violence around sporting contests can have on the sports industry and the games themselves. All chapters include historical background and relevant policy-related implications of the empirical findings.

From the perspective of an economist, violence in sporting contests is an outcome of the forces of supply and demand, and violence and aggression exist because fans respond positively to them. Spectators may directly demand violence and aggression because these elements of sporting contests are entertaining. Teams and leagues that wish to maximize profits will optimally respond to spectator preferences by ratcheting up the aggression level. In addition, spectators are clearly entertained by seeing their favorite teams win, and there may be a relationship between aggressive play and team success. If violence and aggression help a team be successful, then fans will demand more violent or aggressive play to produce more wins.

The economic viewpoint also helps us to see other connections between violence, aggression, and the behavior of leagues, teams, and athletes. Thus, a secondary reason that this book exists is to stimulate further thought and research on violence and aggression in sports. Consider, for instance, the issue of injuries and head injuries specifically. Recently, information has come to light concerning the real impact of concussions on the health of athletes during their careers, the length of athletic careers, and the health of athletes after they retire. In recent months, high-profile athletes from a wide variety of sports have been sidelined with concussions: Aaron Rodgers, quarterback of the National Football League (NFL) champion Green Bay Packers, suffered two concussions during the 2010–2011 season (AP 2010); Sidney Crosby of the Pittsburgh Penguins of the National Hockey League (NHL) suffered a concussion in January 2011 that kept him out of a substantial part of the season (AP 2011a); professional skier Lindsey Vonn suffered a concussion in a training accident in February 2011 (AP 2011b); and Chris Paul of the National Basketball Association's New Orleans Hornets suffered a concussion in March 2011 (AP 2011d).

The cases of Sidney Crosby and Aaron Rodgers are especially relevant to the issues examined in this book. Among popular North American sports, ice hockey and gridiron football are possibly the most violent. Ice hockey is, arguably, not an intrinsically violent sport, but the NHL has a history of "the enforcer" whose main role is to physically intimate the opposition and protect his team from being intimidated. Further, evidence suggests that NHL fans get enjoyment from aggressive and violent play (see the literature review in Chap. 4 of this book). Crosby is one of the brightest young stars of the NHL, and losing him to injury of any kind will dilute the product, thus reducing the revenue-generating potential of games involving his team. The NHL clearly has an incentive to protect "assets" like Sidney Crosby, but the league also must respond to fan demand for aggressive play in order to maximize revenue. It is this sort of trade off to which economics is uniquely suited as an analytical tool. Furthermore, the NHL has recently seen some publicly aired backlash from an important sponsor regarding violence in the game. In a letter to the league, Air Canada asked the NHL to crack down on violence or risk losing them as a sponsor (Klein and Belson 2011). Clearly, violence and aggression can influence the NHL's bottom line in a positive as well as a negative manner.

Gridiron football, on the other hand, is clearly a violent sport, since aggressive hitting is fundamental to the game (see Chap. 3 of this book). Given the importance of the quarterback position in determining game outcomes, the concussions suffered by Aaron Rodgers could easily have ruined his team's chance to win the 2011 Super Bowl. That he was able to recover and lead his team to victory over the Pittsburgh Steelers only serves to illustrate the importance of regulating the inherent violence of gridiron football, especially as it relates to hits on the quarterback. Furthermore, the NFL has made headlines for an overall increase in injuries to current players, including head and brain injuries (Wendell 2011), and for health problems suffered by retired players, including Alzheimer's disease and dementia (AP 2009).

For the NFL, the issues of aggression, violence, and injury are now central to the relationship between players and management, as seen in negotiation for the most recent collective bargaining agreement (Pasquarelli 2010). As players get faster and stronger, and if the NFL is able to convince the players to extend the number of games in the regular season, injuries resulting from the violent nature of gridiron football will no doubt increase in the NFL. In a reaction to recent events and increased knowledge of the damaging effects of concussions, both the NHL and the NFL have chosen to change the way concussions are managed in game situations (AP 2011c, e). No doubt these decisions will affect all facets of the game, from the way management negotiates with players on salary and other issues, to the number of games that injured players miss, to the revenues generated by game-day attendance and TV viewership.

Finally, and lamentably, the recent deaths of NHL veteran Bob Probert and NFL veteran Dave Duerson clearly illustrate the personal cost paid by some professional athletes in violent sports. These tragic events also should sound a warning to the NHL and the NFL about the importance of dealing proactively with violence and injuries in their respective leagues, especially head injuries. A veteran of 16 NHL seasons playing for the Detroit Red Wings and the Chicago Blackhawks, Probert died in July 2010 of heart failure at age 45, but an examination of his brain tissue revealed a degenerative brain disease (chronic traumatic encephalopathy, CTE) also found in the brain tissue of almost two dozen deceased professional gridiron football players. Probert is the first ex-professional ice hockey player to have CTE confirmed after death. During his career, he was well known for his pugnacious style; he was even chosen by readers of *Hockey News* as ice hockey's best-ever enforcer (Schwarz 2011b). If Probert's life had not been shortened by a heart ailment, he almost certainly would have seen his quality of life diminished with symptoms similar to that of Parkinson's disease (Ziegler 2010).

Dave Duerson was an 11-year NFL veteran who played for the Chicago Bears, the New York Giants, and the Phoenix Cardinals. Duerson played one of the most violent positions in football, that of linebacker. If gridiron is a "collision sport," as the all-time great coach Vince Lombardi is credited with saying, then linebacker is the definitive "collision position." In February 2011, Duerson ended his own life at the age of 50 in a manner that would not damage his brain, which he asked to be donated to a long-term study on brain injuries (Schwarz 2011a). He had spent the past several years working with the families of ex-NFL players who had dementia. A few months after his death, researchers at Boston University examined Duerson's brain tissue and found that he did indeed have CTE (Schwarz 2011c).

Overview of the Book

This book is split into five sections. The prologue in the present chapter and a discussion of the history of violence in spectator sports comprise the introductory Part I. While the remaining chapters of this book deal with economic analysis of issues related to demand and success in sports and their relationship to violence and aggression, the discussion in Chap. 2 gives some historical background and evaluates the reasons why demand for violence in sports exists. The main thesis of Chap. 2 is that that violence and aggression have always been a part of spectator sports because fans derive pleasure from such behavior. To support their thesis, Todd Jewell, Afsheen Moti, and Dennis Coates give a brief overview of the history of violence and aggression in spectator sports, with special attention paid to bullfighting in modern-day Spain.

Parts II through IV of this book contain a series of chapters devoted to analysis of specific sports and leagues. Part II of this book is composed of three chapters on popular North American team-sports leagues: the NFL, based in the USA (Chap. 3); the NHL, based in the USA and Canada (Chap. 4); and the National Basketball Association (NBA), also based in the USA and Canada (Chap. 5). Chapters on two North American individual-sports leagues make up Part III: North American Stock Car Auto Racing (NASCAR), which holds most of its races in the Southeastern USA (Chap. 6); and the Ultimate Fighting Championship (UFC), an organizer of mixed martial arts (MMA) competitions (Chap. 7). Part IV contains two studies of international team-sports leagues: the English Premier League (EPL), the top league for association football (soccer) in England (Chap. 8); and the Australian Football League (AFL), the only fully professional league of Australian Rules football (Chap. 9). The final section of this book, Part V, is devoted to two chapters on violent behavior of nonparticipants: Chap. 10 is a study of hooliganism in Greece; and Chap. 11 analyzes crime around sports stadiums in Charlotte, North Carolina.

Part II: North American Team Sports

The most popular spectator sport in the USA is NFL football, and it could be argued that the NFL is also the most violent and dangerous sport for players. In Chap. 3, Janice Hauge analyzes the relationship between in-game penalties and success in the NFL, where success is defined as team-level winning percentage and postseason success. It is interesting to note that Hauge's study is the first to analyze this relationship. Hauge begins by examining the history of NFL rule changes, especially those designed to increase player safety in the face of the inherent violence of gridiron football. Using data from the 1995 to 2009 seasons, Hauge discovers some evidence that penalties are negatively associated with team success. Although Chap. 3 is unable to directly connect attendance demand to violence and aggression, the relationship between winning and attendance implies that in-game aggression will likely impact game-day attendance in the NFL.

Another North American sport with a reputation for in-game violence and aggression is hockey. In Chap. 4, Dennis Coates, Marcel Battre, and Christian Deutscher analyze the relationship between physical play and success in the NHL, and the authors compare their NHL results to data on leagues from Finland and Germany. Coates et al. find evidence that penalty minutes and fights are negatively related to NHL team success in terms of points and attendance, but no relationship between aggressive play and points is found for the European leagues. Further analysis indicates that the negative effect of penalties on points in the NHL is due to minor penalties and the negative effect on NHL attendance is due to major penalties. Revenue data are available for the NHL, and the authors find limited evidence of a positive relationship between penalty minutes and team revenue. Taken together, this study indicates that more aggression leads to less team success on the ice (at least in the NHL), but more aggression might lead to more success at the ticket office and greater profitability. Here is clear evidence of the tradeoff that must be made when a team or league chooses to address in-game violence and aggression: reductions in physical play may lead to more wins, but such reductions may also lead to fans receiving less entertainment value.

Although the game of basketball is clearly a less violent sport than American football or ice hockey, violent play in the NBA can potentially influence the economic situation of the league and of individual teams. In Chap. 5, David Berri and Ryan Rodenberg investigate the relationship between violent and aggressive play and NBA salaries, on-court success, and team revenues. The authors first examine the role of referees in regulating the sport and in influencing outcomes. Using meta-analysis, Berri and Rodenberg find that referee "bias" has little or no effect on outcomes in the NBA. Next, the authors turn their attention to the relationship between personal fouls, salaries, and team success; using a similar meta-analysis, Berri and Rodenberg discover that players who commit more fouls earn lower salaries and generally lower their team's odds of winning. Finally, the authors use the career statistics of Shaquille O'Neal to illustrate the impact that personal fouls (and an inability to shoot free throws) can have on wins and revenue. In sum, Chap. 5 illustrates the complex series of tradeoffs made by NBA teams when deciding their optimal level of aggressive play. For most NBA teams, it appears that more personal fouls are a net negative, but against certain teams (e.g., any team that has trouble shooting free throws) aggressive play may be a winning strategy.

Part III: North American Individual Sports

Aggressiveness is an intrinsic component of the sport of auto racing, since winning any given race entails a driver taking substantial risks. In Chap. 6, Peter von Allmen and John Solow analyze aggressive driving in NASCAR's Sprint Cup Series and the role that it plays in the demand for NASCAR. Using a unique data set on television ratings, von Allmen and Solow find that aggressive driving is an important part of the NASCAR viewing experience. Specifically, the authors find evidence that the number of crashes is positively related, in a large and statistically significant manner, to the size of NASCAR's television audience, with an increase of one crash per race predicted to increase TV audience by about 6%. Again, we see the tradeoff between the risk and reward of violence and aggression in sports: Crashes make for great spectacle, but crashes also present a real risk to the "stars of the show," the drivers. NASCAR clearly understands this tradeoff, since it has taken numerous precautions to minimize risk to drivers, crews, and fans.

MMA is a violent fighting sport that combines the disciplines of traditional martial arts, boxing, kick boxing, and wrestling. In Chap. 7, Trevor Collier, Andrew Johnson, and John Ruggiero analyze data from MMA competitions, concentrating on individual-fight data from the UFC. The authors begin by discussing rule changes made by the UFC to rein in the more violent parts of the sport. Fighting is about violence, and MMA spectators are fans because of it, but the UFC has a significant financial stake in keeping the violence at a level that is publicly acceptable. Collier et al. then analyze the relationship between the use of aggressive fighting strategies and the probability of winning an MMA bout. Interestingly, the authors show that the type of blow landed influences judges in matches that end in decision. Specifically, violent and potentially harmful strikes appear to sway judges in the direction of the fighter who lands such blows. Furthermore, knockdowns and damage inflicted on an opponent have the largest marginal effect on judges' decisions. Although the preferences of judges do not directly reflect the preferences of fans, there can be no doubt that fighters who win, and who are best able to land violent and harmful blows, will also be the fighters who draw the largest audiences.

Part IV: International Team Sports

Aggressive play is a strategy that has a long history in English association football. In Chap. 8, Todd Jewell estimates a demand curve for the EPL with an emphasis on the effect of aggressive play on match-day attendance. Jewell uses information on the number of fouls and the number of yellow and red cards to measure aggressive play. The author discusses the tradeoff that a team must make when choosing the optimal level of aggressive play; more aggressive play may lead to a higher probability of winning a given match, but too much aggression can lead to player expulsion and a lower probably of winning. This tradeoff is further complicated by spectator preferences for winning and for aggressive play independent of winning. The results presented in Chap. 8 show that aggressive play by EPL teams influences match-day attendance and this relationship varies by team quality; for the best EPL teams playing at home, normal fouls lead to lower attendance and yellow cards lead to higher attendance. The relationship is just the opposite for teams at the bottom of the EPL. Jewell also presents estimates of the elasticity of demand with respect to aggressive play, finding that attendance demand is highly responsive to normal fouls but much less responsive to red and yellow cards. Perhaps the most interesting result from Chap. 8 is that EPL estimated attendance demand is statistically unrelated to red cards given for clearly violent play.

Although Australian Rules football is played in several countries around the world, the only fully professional league exists in Australia itself. Like some other sports analyzed in this book, Australian Rules football is characterized by intense physical contact, and players who are tough enough to dish out and take physical punishment are held in high regard by fans. In Chap. 9, Ross Booth and Robert Brooks evaluate the history of violent conduct in the AFL, with an emphasis on recent attempts by the league to limit such conduct. The authors begin their analysis with a discussion of AFL history and details of the game (a great help to those of us who have little knowledge of the sport). Booth and Brooks then take a look at recent AFL data (2000–2009 seasons) to investigate the relationship between the league's attempts to mitigate violent conduct, the actual level of violent conduct, and the resulting impact on attendance demand. The authors discover evidence that the AFL's attempts to reduce violent play have been successful. In addition, the extent of violent play appears to have little influence on attendance demand in most of Booth and Brooks estimates. However, in the authors' final estimation, they look at attendance demand before and after changes designed to reduce violent play; in this case, they find that pre-change violent play had a negative impact on demand, while violent play is positively correlated with attendance after the changes.

Part V: Spectator Violence and Crime

Changing the focus of the book from on-field violence to off-field violence by nonparticipants, Vassiliki Avgerinou and Stefanos Giakoumatos analyze the effect of spectator violence on Greek football demand in Chap. 10. The authors begin their analysis with a discussion of the history of fan violence, often referred to as hooliganism. Using detailed information on incidents of spectator disorder in and around Greek stadiums from 1986 to 2009, Avgerinou and Giakoumatos find that the most egregious acts of spectator violence are negatively related to game-day attendance, with a 1% increase in serious violence predicted to result in a 1.7% decrease in average attendance. Since attendance is so responsive to changes in violence, the Greek Super League clearly has an incentive to adopt strategies to reduce spectator violence. Interestingly, the authors discover that most violence can be attributed to home fans, which further suggests that Greek clubs could increase attendance and revenue by reining in their own fans. The authors also find that less-serious incidents of fan disorder have increased in recent years, but these incidents do not appear to significantly influence demand for game-day attendance in Greek football. In addition, the most violent fans appear to be those of the five biggest Greek clubs: Olympiakos, PAOK, Aris, AEK, and Panathinaikos.

In the book's final chapter, the focus further shifts from fan violence to violence perpetrated upon fans. The relationship between crime and sporting events obviously is of concern to the fans themselves, and it is also an important component of the monetary cost of hosting a sporting event. In Chap. 11, Stephen Billings and Craig Depken investigate the pattern of crime around two stadiums on game days in Charlotte, North Carolina using data on all reported crimes from 2005 to 2008. The authors show that although total crime in the city does not increase on the day of a sporting event, crime around the stadiums does appear to increase when an event occurs. Thus, Billings and Depken show that crime is shifted closer to the stadium when an event occurs without an overall increase in criminal activity, suggesting that criminals simply move their activities closer to the stadiums when potential victims are present in large numbers. The results from Chap. 11 illustrate yet another tradeoff that team and leagues must make when trying to draw spectators; if large sporting events draw criminal activity as suggested by Billings and Depken, then leagues and teams will be forced to increase resources spent on security, which will negatively impact the bottom line.

References

Abrams M (2010) Anger Management in Sport: Understanding and Controlling Violence in Athletics. Human Kinetics: Champaign, IL.

Associated Press (AP) (2009) Ex-NFL Players Report Higher Rate of Memory-Related Disease. NFL.com, last updated September 30. Accessed online: http://www.nfl.com.

Associated Press (AP) (2010) NFL Sees Spike in Reported Concussions. ESPN.com, last updated December 13. Accessed online: http://www.sports.espn.go.com.

Associated Press (AP) (2011a) Sidney Crosby Out with Concussion. ESPN.com, last updated January 6. Accessed online: http://www.sports.espn.go.com.

Associated Press (AP) (2011b) Lindsey Vonn Sustained Concussion. ESPN.com, last updated February 3. Accessed online: http://www.sports.espn.go.com.

Associated Press (AP) (2011c) Standardized Concussion Tests Coming to NFL. NFL.com, posted February 24. Accessed online: http://www.nfl.com.

Associated Press (AP) (2011d) Hornets' Chris Paul Out with Concussion. ESPN.com, last updated March 8. Accessed online: http://www.sports.espn.go.com.

Associated Press (AP) (2011e) NHL: Doctors to Check for Concussions. ESPN.com, last updated March 14. Accessed online: http://www.sports.espn.go.com.

Klein JZ, Belson K (2011) NHL Faces New Scrutiny for Hockey Violence. New York Times, posted March 10. Accessed online: http://www.nytimes.com.

Pasquarelli L (2010) Injuries Give Players Leverage in Labor Talks. FoxSports.com, last updated September 15. Accessed online: http://www.msn.foxsports.com.

Schwarz A (2011a) A Suicide, a Last Request, a Family's Questions. New York Times, posted February 22. Accessed online: http://www.nytimes.com.

Schwarz A (2011b) Hockey Brawler Paid Price, with Brain Trauma. New York Times, posted March 2. Accessed online: http://www.nytimes.com.

Schwarz A (2011c) Duerson's Brain Trauma Diagnosed. New York Times, posted May 2. Accessed online: http://www.nytimes.com.

Wendell T (2011) The NFL Lockout's Health-Care Data, Revealed. Esquire, posted January 27. Accessed online: http://www.esquire.com.

Ziegler T (2010) Chronic Traumatic Encephalopathy. SportsMD.com, posted October 14. Accessed online: http://www.sportsmd.com.

Chapter 2
A Brief History of Violence and Aggression in Spectator Sports

R. Todd Jewell, Afsheen Moti, and Dennis Coates

> *Serious sport has nothing to do with fair play. It is bound up with hatred, jealousy, boastfulness, disregard for all rules, and sadistic pleasure in witnessing violence. In other words, it is war minus the shooting... Most of the games we now play are of ancient origin, but sport does not seem to have been taken very seriously between Roman times and the nineteenth century... Then, chiefly in England and the United States, games were built up into a heavily-financed activity, capable of attracting vast crowds and rousing savage passions, and the infection spread from country to country. It is the most violently combative sports, football and boxing, that have spread the widest.*
>
> – Eric Arthur Blair, British author and journalist, commonly known by his pen name, George Orwell (1945)

Introduction

Sporting contests have provided mass entertainment throughout history. Ancient Mesoamericans had their ball games, the Greeks had the Olympic Games, and the Romans had many spectator sports such as gladiatorial contests and chariot races. As pointed out by George Orwell in the mid-twentieth century quote above, present-day versions of these ancient sports provide entertainment for passionate spectators, and they tend to be heavily influenced by financial issues. However, it is unlikely that Orwell could have foreseen the economic impact that this "heavily-financed activity" would have in the twenty-first century. Plunkett Research (2010) reports that the US sports industry generated over $400 billion in gross revenues during 2010, with the big four US professional leagues generating almost $22 billion. As a point of comparison, the entire US movie industry generated less than $10 billion in revenues in 2010, making it only slightly larger in gross revenues than the National Football League (NFL).

R.T. Jewell (✉)
University of North Texas, Denton, TX, USA
e-mail: tjewell@unt.edu

R.T. Jewell (ed.), *Violence and Aggression in Sporting Contests: Economics, History and Policy*, Sports Economics, Management and Policy 4,
DOI 10.1007/978-1-4419-6630-8_2, © Springer Science+Business Media, LLC 2011

One commonality among many ancient and modern sports is the existence of violence and aggression in contests. Compare a modern stock car race with a Roman chariot race: only the technology has changed. In addition, violence and aggression are the hallmarks of the most-popular, modern spectator sports. When Orwell mentions "football" as being one of "the most violently combative sports," he is referring to association football (soccer), but he would not be surprised that the NFL is the most popular sport among US sports fans (Leahy 2011). No doubt, Orwell would argue that the NFL is popular because of the inherent violence in the game (see Chap. 3 of this book). Although his point could be debated [consider, for example, the issue of NFL parity and the success of the league (Hamlin 2007)], there is little doubt that the aggressive and violent nature of the game is an aspect that attracts fans.

Violence in Modern Sports

Ancient combat sports live on in modern-day professional wrestling, boxing ("prize fighting"), and mixed martial arts (MMA). Modern professional wrestling is more a circus than sport, with its mock violence, dramatic staging, and soap-operatic side stories. Nonetheless, professional wrestling has an ardent fan base in several countries; witness the drawing power of World Wrestling Entertainment (WWE) in the USA and the cultural significance of "Lucha Libre" in Mexico. Even the most ardent WWE fan would admit that this is theater instead of competition. In contrast, professional prize fighting is seen as a true sport, but demand for boxing entertainment has been on the wane for some time.

A comparison of modern boxing and professional wrestling might suggest that, at least in North America, there has been a shift in demand away from "real" violence in sports toward cartoonish depictions of violence. However, one only has to look at the recent rise in popularity of MMA competitions to see that there has been no such shift. MMA combines the disciplines of wrestling, boxing, jiu-jitsu, and kickboxing. One of the draws of MMA is that it allows fighters from these different disciplines to meet on a level field. The biggest promoter of MMA, Ultimate Fighting Championship (UFC), presents a spectacle that is a raw competition among fighters (see Chap. 7 of this book).

In 1993, when the first MMA matches took place, Senator John McCain of Arizona referred to the sport as "human cock fighting" because of its brutality. Although this statement was extreme and clearly incorrect given that MMA participants were rarely if ever killed by a competitor, it is true that MMA in its original incarnation was fairly brutal. At the time, the rules of the match allowed for anything except for eye gouging and biting, and the fight ended when an opponent was knocked out or by a judge's decision. In response, the competition was banned from all but three states. After regulating its matches by introducing more than 31 fouls and 8 ways to end a bout, the UFC found its way back into the public spotlight. In 2008, *Forbes* magazine reported that the UFC promotion company was worth close to $1 billion, a significant number by any standard, but especially when compared to the price paid for the company in 2001, $2 million (Miller 2008).

Ice hockey, the modern cousin of a variety of ancient games played with a ball and a stick, is another modern sport in which violence and aggression plays an important role (see Chap. 4 of this book). The North-America-based National Hockey League (NHL) believes that violence in hockey is unavoidable, but therapeutic and cathartic in minor forms (Eitzen 1985). Nonetheless, ice hockey "has been called the only all-human sport in which physical intimidation outside the rules is encouraged as a customary tactic: very nearly a blood sport, in fact" (Economist 1975). Although calling ice hockey a "blood sport" is a stretch, evidence suggests that violence is an intrinsic part of the game. Academic research suggests increases in violence tend to increase NHL attendance, so that the league and teams have an incentive to keep violent play a part of the game in order to maximize attendance (Jones et al. 1993; Jones et al. 1996; Paul 2003). However, Stewart et al. (1992) show that although violence leads to greater NHL attendance, it also leads to a lower probability of winning. Thus, NHL teams are forced to make a trade off when considering violent play. Specifically, violent and aggressive play may increase attendance directly, but it may also decrease attendance indirectly if attendance is positively related to winning.

Unfortunately, the violent and aggressive nature of the NHL game sometimes leads to egregious acts of violence by players against their opponents. In March 2004, Todd Bertuzzi of the Vancouver (Canada) Canucks sucker-punched Colorado Avalanche's Steve Moore which led to Bertuzzi's indefinite suspension. He was not reinstated until August 2005. NHL Senior Vice President Colin Campbell spoke of Bertuzzi's punishment, but did not comment on changing the rules to prevent this kind of behavior, effectively implying that this type of violence was a part of the game. Later, NHL Commissioner Gary Bettman repeated Campbell's message and did not deny Campbell's core message about violence being a part of hockey (Gillis 2004).

Chris Simon is another example of an NHL player who took the violent part of the game too far. In early 2007, the New York Islanders' Simon used his stick to whack Ryan Hollweg of the New York Rangers in the face. Simon received a 25-game suspension that covered the end of the regular season and the playoffs, and went into the 2007–2008 regular season. Soon after being reinstated, Simon once again got into an on-ice incident, this time with the Pittsburgh Penguins' Jarkko Ruutu. Simon pulled Ruutu's legs behind his and skated over his right knee. Simon received a match penalty and was ejected from the game. His punishment as a repeat offender was a 30-game suspension, the eighth suspension of his professional career and the second longest suspension in modern history of the NHL. Simon played one more game with the Islanders before being traded to the Minnesota Wild. He now plies his trade in the Russian professional league. It seems that there is a limit to the on-ice violence that the NHL, and its fans, will tolerate.

If one accepts the thesis that the violent and aggressive nature of modern sports is a factor to which fans respond, then we are still left with two important queries: (1) Why are violence and aggression a part of many popular sports? and

(2) why do fans respond to the violence and aggression in the games they watch? From the perspective of an economist, the answer to question (1) is straightforward: Violence in sporting contests is an outcome of the forces of supply and demand, and violence and aggression exist (and have always existed) because fans respond positively to them. If spectators demand violence and aggression and are willing to pay to see such behavior, then teams and leagues will provide it. An economics-based answer to question (2) is not so clear cut, and the traditional economist will not give much consideration to answering it. For the economist, preferences for or against violence and aggression are idiosyncratic, and understanding the mechanisms by which preferences are created does not generate sufficient scholarly interest. Instead, the economist is intrigued by the way preferences are expressed in demand relationships and the ways in which incentives influence the way in which preferences are expressed.

Answers to question (2) normally fall under the purview of other social sciences, such as sociology, anthropology, and psychology, which are more concerned with the causes of human behavior. In the case of NFL football, a sociologist may be interested in explaining why fans demand violence and aggressive play, while an economist would be interested in explaining how violence in the game affects a team's attendance, revenues, or on-field success. Furthermore, an historian may be interested in examining the historical factors and social processes that have led to the development of modern sports, especially the development of violent and aggressive sports.

Most of the chapters in this book deal with an economic analysis of issues related to demand or success in sports and their relationship to violence within sports. However, the chapters also include historical perspectives on each specific league or sport. As a means of providing some general background for the studies in this book, this chapter takes a quick look at social science research that attempts to explain fans' demand for violent and aggressive play, and especially the behavioral justification for the appeal of violence and aggression in spectator sports. This chapter also gives a brief overview of the history of violence in spectator sports. This brief historical review suggests that the most-popular spectator sports have always had violence as a component, a conclusion that George Orwell came to nearly 70 years ago.

Why Do Fans Demand Violence and Aggression in Sports?

Humans watch sports for many different reasons. For some spectators, sporting events simply provide entertainment in the form of unscripted drama and tension. Alternatively, the entertainment value may be related to an appreciation of the athletic ability on display. In this way, sports are similar to the unscripted-nature of reality television or the beauty and grace of ballet. For others, watching sports is a social activity, in which individuals of similar cultural or national backgrounds gather to have a community experience. Many ancient sports (e.g., the ancient Olympic Games) started as rituals to honor the gods, a leader, or the deceased and later developed into large public spectacles, with city or country-wide festivities surrounding the games. Interestingly, we see the same sports-cum-cultural-festivals today in the modern Olympic Games, the association football World Cup, and the gridiron football Super Bowl. For some die-hard sports fans ("fanatics"), watching their favorite sport or team is akin to a religious experience. Whatever the reason, for the sports fan "following sport is a worthwhile leisure pursuit that enhances an individual's quality of life" (Smith 1988).

Academic studies have found that violence and aggressive play in sports may serve to enhance the entertainment value of a sporting event. Aggressive and violent play may intensify the entertainment value because it adds drama (Comisky et al. 1977). Bryant et al. (1981) studied the effects of violent play in professional gridiron football on viewer enjoyment. For male participants, the level of enjoyment increased as the roughness and violence increased. Sargent et al. (1998) found similar results for a sample of 25 sport events televised in 1996. Each sport was placed in one of the three categories: combative (e.g., boxing), stylistic (e.g., gymnastics), or mechanized (e.g., bowling). According to the results, male respondents reported the most enjoyment from the violent, combative sports and the least enjoyment from nonrisky, mechanized sports. Female respondents, on the other hand, received the most enjoyment from elegant, stylistic sports. For men, excitement increased when violence was exhibited in athletic forms. These results suggest that spectators of combat sports and contact sports, especially males, are partially drawn to these sports because they provide something that other sports do not: aggressive and violent play.

In addition, anecdotal evidence suggests that spectators enjoy watching violence and aggression. Take the example of the most-popular US sports league: the NFL. During 2010, eight of the top-ten TV programs were NFL games (Nielsonwire 2011a). In February 2011, Super Bowl XLV, which pitted the Pittsburgh Steelers against the Green Bay Packers, brought in the largest US TV audience in history. In addition, five of the top six broadcast audiences of all time were Super Bowls (Nielsonwire 2011b). Although the NFL is clearly popular for many reasons, one could argue that the violence and aggression of the game is an intrinsic part of its lure for the fan. Commentator George Will famously said: "Football combines the two worst things about America: it is violence punctuated by committee meetings." Yes, violence may not be socially acceptable, but it sure makes for an entertaining sports spectacle… and the committee meetings are less than 30 seconds each.

The asserting dominance theory is sometimes used to explain why violence in sports is entertaining (Adler 1927). The hypothesis behind this theory is that spectators live vicariously through athletes, so that when a player slams the quarterback, it is as if the spectator accomplished the play. Betting on their favorite team or player also serves as indirect involvement in sporting events. And, because it is all in the fun of games, spectators believe that their binges (e.g., the taunting of other spectators or the athletes themselves) are harmless. For these spectators, "the excitement of sport spectacles is safely vicarious" (Guttmann 1998).

Catharsis

Some social researchers hypothesize that sporting events provide a way to contain human aggression, for both the athletes and the spectators. The catharsis theory, or the theory of purging of emotions, is based on the work of Austrian ethologist Konrad Lorenz. His theory has several supporting assumptions: "(a) that destructive energy spontaneously builds up in the organism, (b) that the performance of aggressive acts reduces such energy to tolerable levels, a process which is pleasantly experienced, (c) that the performance of competitive actions also serves this pleasing outlet function, and (d) that even merely witnessing competitive actions serves this function, one seems to have accounted for the popularity of sports-doing and viewing" (as quoted in Zillmann et al. 1979). In terms of sport spectatorship, viewing a sporting event serves to both build up and relieve the "destructive energy" (Sipes 1973; Russell 1983; Wann et al. 1999). The theory also suggests that the more violent the sport is, the greater the pleasure received for both the participant and the viewer.

If the catharsis theory holds for sports spectators, we might expect to see less violence outside of the sports arena than would occur in the absence of violent and aggressive sporting contests. However, violent acts committed by fans are a semi-constant feature of sporting events, even those that are undeniably violent in nature. For example, Rees and Schnepel (2009) find that host communities of college football games experience an increase in assaults and other crimes on game day, even when the stadiums ban alcohol. A reinterpretation of the theory of catharsis could be the following: For a certain subset of sports fans, witnessing violent sports is not enough to reduce "such energy to tolerable levels," and only personally experienced "aggressive acts" serve to relieve the tension built up before, during, and after an exciting sports event. Or, maybe some sports fans just enjoy hurting people and breaking stuff.

Discussions of fan violence in modern sports normally surround the issue of violent behavior of the fans of association football (soccer) teams, called "hooliganism." The motivation behind fan violence is researched in depth by sociologists around the globe. Much of the violence appears to be related to socio-economic factors, such as poverty and class, but fan violence related to religion (e.g., Scotland) and regional issues (e.g., Italy and Spain) also occurs (Frosdick and Marsh 2005). Arguably, hooliganism was at its highest point during the 1970s and 1980s in the UK. Two defining events in the history of hooliganism occurred in the latter half of the 1980s and involved English hooligans. In 1985, the Heysel Stadium Disaster led to the death of 39 fans and to English clubs being banned from European competitions until 1990 (BBC News 2000). The Hillsborough Disaster of 1989 led to the Football Spectators Act, since which UK hooliganism has been in decline (Duke 1991). However, hooliganism still exists, as illustrated in Chap. 10 of this book. Recent violence has, unsurprisingly, been reported in locations with a history of hooligan behavior, between fans of Millwall and West Ham United in London (BBC News 2009) and in Argentina (Kelly 2011). However, fan violence has also been reported in some surprising places, such as Viet Nam (Viet Nam News 2010).

Although soccer hooligans are the most infamous violent fans, fan violence is an all-too-normal part of many sporting events. Consider the deaths of two college students in Boston in 2004: a college student was accidentally run over by a vehicle while fans were "celebrating" the New England Patriots' win in the Super Bowl (AP 2004a), and another student died from injuries incurred when she was hit in the face by a nonlethal projectile shot by riot police after the Red Sox of MLB beat the New York Yankees to advance to that year's World Series (AP 2004b). 2004 might have been an exceptional year for bad fan behavior in the USA. In November of that year, a tussle broke out on the court between players of the NBA's Indiana Pacers and Detroit Pistons. As the altercation was broken up, a fan threw his drink at Ron Artest of the Pacers, who leaped into the stands to exact revenge, thereby creating a riot within the confines of the arena. (For readers interested in the minutia of fan violence, the drink in question was a Diet Coke.) Nine players were suspended, with Artest being suspended for the remainder of the season (AP 2004c).

Violence and Aggression in Ancient Sports

Much of the relationship between violence and sports in the ancient world derived from the connection between ancient sports and warfare. Sport had value as a technique for military preparedness, and it also had value as a substitute for direct military conflict. Battlefield tactics required soldiers to be in excellent shape, and fighting skills learned from combat sports were invaluable during times of war. It is believed that Greeks discovered the use of combat sports after the Battle of Marathon as a result of the hand-to-hand fighting that took place (Poliakoff 1987). Violence in modern sports can be traced back to ancient sports where violence was an inevitable outcome. These ancient sports had few restrictions, and even those rules that did exist were not always enforced. Many of these sports only concluded when one opponent succumbed to the superior strength of the winner.

Scholars have debated the relationship between war, violence, and sports. There are two general perspectives. First, some researchers believe that humans have a need to discharge their natural aggression, which can be accomplished in war or in a substitute for war like violent sports. In the drive-discharge theory, war and sports are substitutes in the release of aggression. Similar to the theory of catharsis, spectators use the viewing of aggression and violence to relieve their aggressive tension. Proponents of this theory would suggest that violence in ancient sports developed as a way to redirect the human need to discharge aggression toward a more contained and localized form of violence. Second, some researchers believe that violence in sports merely reflects the aggressive tendencies of society; the cultural-pattern theory suggests that the more warlike a society is the more likely warlike sports will be found in that society. Proponents of this theory would suggest that violent sports in the ancient world were simply a reflection of the violent nature of a given society rather than a relatively safe means to discharge aggression (Sipes 1973).

The Ancient Olympic Games

The most well-known ancient sporting event is the ancient Olympic Games. Begun as a religious festival, the ancient Games consisted of athletic events, such as foot races and discus throwing, combat sports, such as boxing, pankration, and wrestling, and equestrian events, such as chariot racing [information on the ancient Olympic Games is obtained from Poliakoff (1987)]. Many of these sports have modern equivalents: foot racing and discus throwing are still alive in the modern Olympic Games, as are boxing and wrestling. The ancient sport of pankration is the predecessor of modern MMA competitions. Although equestrian events exist in the modern Olympic Games, the true descendent of the chariot race is found in modern-day motor racing. The events with the most potential for violence were the combat sports and chariot racing, and these events appear to have become more violent with time. What is certain is that the ancient Games became much more brutal and barbaric after the Romans conquered the Greeks. Games such as gladiatorial fighting and bullfighting were enjoyed by the Romans not as a way to show strength and bravery of a fighter but rather to show how much one fighter can brutalize his opponent. The Games continued into the time of the Byzantine Empire, until Emperor Theodosius I ended the spectacle in 393 BCE.

The most violent Olympic combat-sport event, at least from the perspective of the Greeks, was boxing. To the modern observer, an ancient Olympic boxing match would look very brutal indeed. Fighters generally wore leather straps over their hands, but this was essentially a bare-knuckle fist fight that only ended when someone was forced to quit. Modern Olympic boxing seems downright genteel in comparison. An ancient Olympic match was not divided into rounds; instead, the match was over when a boxer held up a finger admitting defeat or when one of the combatants was knocked unconscious. One could speculate that more bouts ended in knock out than in capitulation. Lightly padded gloves were used by the Romans and Greeks for practice. In the fourth century BCE, the combatants started using heavier gloves that caused greater, and more dramatic, damage.

In contrast to boxing, the Greeks considered wrestling to be the least violent of the combat sports. A match consisted of a maximum of five rounds, and a wrestler had to score three falls against the opponent to be considered the winner. Similar to its modern cousins, a fall in ancient Olympic wrestling was defined as any part of the back or shoulder touching the ground. Although the Greeks did not think of wrestling as being overly violent, combatants were not hesitant when it came to using rough tactics to win, like strangling, neck-holds, breaking of fingers, or breaking the opponent's back or ribs. Striking an opponent was one of the few tactics that was forbidden. In later competitions, breaking an opponent's fingers was made illegal, but remained commonplace even though the consequences included forfeiture of the match.

Pankration, meaning "complete strength" or "complete victory," was a combination of boxing and wrestling. It was the last sport to be added to the Ancient Olympics in 648 BCE. Pankration was essentially a no-holds-barred brawl. Combatants used the techniques of both boxing and wrestling, and kicking and striking with hands and feet were the sport's main components. Modern observers would no doubt recognize pankration as a forerunner of today's extremely popular mixed-martial-arts competitions, except that MMA would appear less barbaric since rules exist to protect modern athletes from injury or death. Surprisingly, the Greeks did not consider pankration as violent as boxing, possibly due to the inclusion of "less violent" techniques from wrestling. Like boxing, there was only a single round in each pankration match, and the competition ended when a fighter signaled that he was no longer willing or able to continue the fight.

Chariot racing, another sporting event with huge potential for mayhem and violence, was added to the ancient Olympic Games in 680 BCE, extending the games from 1 to 2 days. The races consisted of 12 laps around a track ("circus") with sharp turns around posts at both ends. The turns around the posts were the most exciting and dangerous part of the race; most of the excitement was for the spectators, and all of the danger was for the participants. Deliberately running into another charioteer was illegal, but penalties for doing so were infrequently enforced. In the Roman era, a hard median was placed along the inside of the circus that allowed for even greater danger and excitement. The median allowed a charioteer to try to get in front of his opponent causing the opponent to crash into the barrier. The Greek charioteer generally held the reins in his hands, while the custom for the Roman charioteer was to wrap the reins around his waist. If a Roman charioteer was knocked from his perch, he would be dragged around the circus, an outcome that, no doubt, made the spectacle just that much more exciting to watch.

Although not a part of the ancient Olympic Games, gladiatorial combat was a violent sports spectacle that developed during the Roman Empire. Gladiatorial contests are thought to have started as part of a funeral ritual. The combat consisted of a battle between two gladiators, between a gladiator and an animal, between multiple gladiators and animals, or between groups of gladiators. Unlike ancient Olympic contestants, gladiators were not Roman citizens; instead they were prisoners, slaves, or poor noncitizens. Anyone who was sentenced to the arena or to a gladiatorial school fought in the games until his death, unless he was freed. In the earliest gladiatorial contests, death was considered the proper way to end a match. This life-ending outcome became less likely as the spectacle, and the gladiators themselves, became more popular. Anyone who has seen the 2000 movie "Gladiator" starring Russell Crowe knows that a gladiator could admit defeat to a superior opponent, after which his fate was decided by the crowd.

Blood Sports

A blood sport is defined as any sport that involves the killing or shedding of blood of an animal. Such sports have long been a part of human society. Blood sports that are modern-day spectator sports include dog fighting, cock fighting, and bullfighting. Social acceptance of these sports varies greatly across countries and cultures.

For instance, bull fighting has a special place in the culture of Spain and Mexico, and is practiced in Peru, Colombia, Venezuela, and Ecuador, but the spectacle is banned in many other countries. Bull fighting is also practiced in Portugal where it is not a true blood sport because the bulls generally are not killed, at least not in the arena. No matter what one thinks of the ethics behind such sports, there is no arguing about the inherent violence of the event. Bull fights end in the death of the bull, and dog and cock fights often end with one or both animal-combatants dead or dying… they are not called "blood sports" for nothing. One could argue that the existence of such sports is *de facto* evidence that humans enjoy watching violent spectacles, while the prohibition of these sports in many countries suggests that demand for violent spectacle varies over country and culture.

In the USA, such sports are generally banned and the consequences for being involved with these types of sports can be severe. One such sport is dog fighting, which dates back to the fifth Century BCE as an organized spectacle (Kalof and Taylor 2007). Dog fighting is illegal in all 50 USA states, although the penalties vary by locality. If charged with dog fighting, one could face up to 3 years in prison and up to a $250,000 fine for each offense (CNN 2007). Nonetheless, dog fighting exists in the USA, and the blood sport is accepted and even has a certain amount of social respect in some areas (Mann 2007). A modern dog fighting contest consists of a match between two trained, fighting dogs. These animals are placed in close proximity within a confined space, and the dogs fight until one dog is too injured to continue. Fans of dog fighting enjoy the aggressive fighting and consider dog fighting to be no more brutal than human combat sports. As an anonymous source told ESPN in response to a question about public outrage over the perceived brutality of dog fighting: "They shouldn't be really upset… Because it's only just an animal" (Naqi 2007).

In 2007, the worlds of dog fighting and professional sports converged. In a highly publicized case, Michael Vick of the NFL's Atlanta Falcons was charged for his involvement in dog fighting and was sentenced to 23 months in federal custody. He served the majority of his sentence and was released in the summer of 2009 (AP 2009). Vick was suspended by the NFL due to his legal issues, but he was reinstated in 2009 and currently plays for the Philadelphia Eagles. After the 2009 regular season, his Eagles teammates awarded Vick the Ed Block Courage Award, given to NFL players "who exemplify commitments to the principles of sportsmanship and courage." A player who receives the award symbolizes "professionalism, great strength, and dedication. He is also a community role model" (Chase 2009). One could argue that Vick's reinstatement and subsequent acceptance by NFL players is a testimony to the importance of forgiveness, especially after punishment is served. However, it may also simply be that in a sport as violent and competitive as NFL football, mistreatment of animals is not seen as a big deal.

An equally ancient and brutal blood sport is cock fighting, which has probably existed since the chicken was domesticated around 3000 BCE (McCaghy and Neal 1974). The contest involves gamecocks (roosters specifically bred for fighting) that are fitted with metal spurs or spikes around their ankles and placed in a pit to attack each other while bets on the outcome are made. As is often the case with dog fighting, a cock fight generally ends with the demise of the losing animal, and it is not out of the ordinary for both fighting cocks to fight to the death. Cock fighting is an obsession in some parts of the world. Although cock fighting is illegal in all 50 states, and even being a spectator is a felony in most states, it is a multimillion dollar industry in the USA. Similar to fighting dogs, fighting cocks are revered in some circles for their tenacity and courage. The University of South Carolina even has the gamecock as its mascot. According to their website (http://www.ugba.net), the US-located United Gamefowl Breeder's Association argues that:

> "There are many varieties of gamefowl, all admired for their beauty, strength, health, and longevity... Since early history, gamefowl have been an inspiration to man through their courage, beauty, and spirit... Gamefowl are a significant part of our heritage and culture and have been since the beginning of our country. History records that except for one vote the gamecock would have become our national symbol. The preservation of gamefowl is a must..."

Since cock fighting is illegal in the USA, it is likely that most breeders in the USA raise the birds for export to other countries. Or perhaps they make really good pets.

Bull Fighting

Bull fighting, a "cross between a baseball game, a Roman circus, and a sell-out concert by some X Factor idol" (Richardson 2010), differs from dog and cock fighting in important ways. Foremost, it is a big business practiced openly in major western countries, while dog and cock fighting exist mostly underground. Tour companies and chambers of commerce advertise bull fights as among the attractions in the countries where bull fights take place. Unlike dog and cock fighting, bull fighting has been romanticized in western culture. As an example, consider Ernest Hemingway's novel "Death in the Afternoon." But perhaps most importantly, it is the only one of these three in which a human fights an animal. For these reasons, bull fighting deserves a bit more attention in this chapter than its sister blood sports.

Bull fighting, known in Spanish as "corrida de toros," spread from the Iberian Peninsula to Latin America with the Spanish and Portuguese colonization of the New World, though it was common in ancient Rome. The versions practiced in Spain (and in parts of France) and its former colonies in the Americas differ from that which predominates in Portugal, and not simply because in the former the bull dies in the ring while in the latter it does not. The widely recognized image of the "matador" with a cape and a sword standing close by a charging bull is from the Spanish corrida de toros. Aside from the bull and the common ancestry of the spectacle, the primary similarity between Spanish and Portuguese bull fighting is the great deal of pomp and pageantry of the event, which begin with a parade of all the participants, except the bulls, entering the ring. In both Portuguese and Spanish bull fights, horses and horsemen play a role. In Portugal, these horsemen are the stars and their horses are expensive and highly trained; in the Spanish corrida, the horses are largely mobile platforms for a spearman to spear the bull in the back of the neck weakening his shoulder muscles so his head is lowered, thus providing the matador, who is the star of the show, a better angle for the thrust of the sword to kill the bull in the exhibition's final act.

In the Spanish corrida, matadors are the top of the profession. Below them come "novilleros," matadors-in-training who are generally restricted to fighting young bulls. "Rejoneadores" are horse-mounted bull fighters, similar to those found in Portugal. "Banderilleros" place highly decorated, short lances in the bull's neck, charging at the bull with hands held high, thrusting the lances downward, and dodging as the bull tries to defend itself. "Picadores" are the horse-mounted spearman whose job is to stab the bull with a lance deep into the neck and shoulder muscles. There are also "toreros comicos," individuals dressed in clown costumes or dresses (similar to clowns in North American rodeos) who play with the bull in ways intended to make the audience laugh. Finally, "mozos de espada" are the assistants to the matadors, managing their capes and swords while the matadors are engaged with the bull.

Trends in Demand for Bull Fighting: The Case of Spain

The Spanish Interior Ministry records information on individuals who are registered as one of the types of corrida participants mentioned above. These data are currently available from 2006 to 2009 (MIR, various years). In 2009, there were a total of 7,977 individuals from within the European Community registered as corrida participants, an increase from a total number of registrants of 6,670 reported in 2006. The largest group in 2009 was the mozos de espada (1,945), followed closely by the first class of novilleros (1,861). Matadors numbered only 693 in 2009, an increase from 600 in 2006. The data show that there has been a steady increase in both the total number of participants and in the number of matadors since 2006. Although the sample is small, these data reveal no evidence that the demand for bull fighting in Spain is decreasing; on the contrary, the increase in participants may be indicative of an increase in demand.

The Spanish Interior Ministry also records the number of corrida events each year. This information is available from 2001 to 2009, although the method of reporting has changed somewhat over time and recent data are more detailed. Nonetheless, we can get a feel for the trend in the number of bull fight events over time. In 2001, there were a total of 1,901 "festejos" (translated literally into English as "entertainments") in which bull fighting of one variety or another was a part. Of these, 853 were corridas involving matadors from the top classification of experienced bull fighters. In 2009, the number of events is broken down into festejos and minor festejos, with the former numbering 1,848 and the latter nearly 6,800. There were 778 top-tier corridas in 2009. Examining data for each year, there is no obvious trend in the number of events, but a comparison of 2001 and 2009 does indicate that there was a drop in top-tier bull fights in Spain. However, the total number of bull fighting events in Spain does not appear to have decreased in the first decade of the twenty-first century.

There is a large anticorrida movement that routinely protests outside the "plaza de toros," as the bull fighting arena is known in Spanish, whether it be in Madrid or Mexico City. One of their strategies is to make attendance at bull fights less attractive for tourists, who generally make up a large percentage of spectators. Generally, local fans of the corrida de toros are older, while younger Spaniards have much less interest. There is an interesting dichotomy on the subject of bull fighting in Spain. On the one hand, surveys suggest that more than 60% of Spaniards dislike or have no interest in the corridas (Reuters 2010a, b; Narayana 2010). Nonetheless, bull fighting is an important part of Spain's cultural heritage; in addition, there is still significant demand for the product. Attendance at corridas across Spain was estimated at 30 million for the 2009 season (Ideal Spain 2011). Furthermore, a new subscription TV channel dedicated to bull fighting in Spain and around the world, Canal+Toros, was launched in March 2011 (Amoros 2011). Finally, the limited data on bull fighting as a profession and the number of bull fighting events taken from the Interior Ministry reports discussed above do not convey evidence of an industry on the decline.

Conclusion

Throughout this chapter, we have seen how aggression and violence play, and have always played, a significant part in spectator sports, whether we are talking about modern sports like the extremely popular US-based NFL or ancient spectator sports like gladiatorial contests. Modern spectators take pleasure in, and ancient sports viewers enjoyed, the physical nature of sports, whether it be the grit and determination of the gamecock or fighting dog or the energy and commitment of the NHL defenseman or NFL linebacker. Owners of modern teams and leagues appear to understand that violence and aggression, to a point, appeal to fans. Since the goal of an owner or league is to generate as much interest in their games as possible, there is reason to believe that teams and leagues will encourage violent and aggressive play, as long as the leagues' chief assets (i.e., the players) are protected to some extent. In this way, rules and regulations for on-field behavior can be viewed as an attempt by leagues to encourage aggression and violence within given parameters, while simultaneously limiting the probability of player injury. Given the demand of fans and the encouragement of leagues and teams, it is no wonder that some athletes take violence too far.

From a sociological perspective, demand for violence in spectator sports may be a result of a need for fans to "blow off steam" (i.e., catharsis) or an attempt by fans to vicariously assert dominance over a rival. Whatever the reason, we spectators of modern sports enjoy watching players bring force and energy to the field and thrive off the spectacle the games bring. From an economic perspective, as long as the demand for violence and aggression exists, then sports leagues, teams, and athletes will continue to provide aggressive and violent spectacles. If one accepts the economic perspective, there are still some questions that must be answered. First of all, one would expect that the demand for violence and aggression would vary by sport and by culture. So, for a given sports league, how much violence and aggression do fans demand? Next, given the trade off between aggression and injury and given that there may be an upper bound of violence that is acceptable to fans, what is the appropriate level of restriction on violence and aggression to limit injuries while maximizing spectator demand? The remaining chapters of this book begin to deal with these and other economic and policy questions in professional spectator sports. Hopefully, these chapters will spur further research into the connection between aggressive and violent play and demand in sports.

References

Adler A (1927) Practice and Theory of Individual Psychology. Harcourt, Brace, and World: New York, NY.

Amoros A (2011) Nace Canal Plus Toros. ABC TV España, posted March 8. Accessed online: http://www.abc.es.

Associated Press (AP) (2004a) Violence Mars Celebrations as Fans Cheer Win. Sports Illustrated SI.com, last updated February 2. Accessed online: http://www.sportsillustrated.cnn.com.

Associated Press (AP) (2004b) College Student, 21, Dies from Head Injury. Sports Illustrated SI.com, last updated October 22. Accessed online: http://www.sportsillustrated.cnn.com.

Associated Press (AP) (2004c) NBA Suspends Artest for Rest of Season. NBCSports.com, last updated November 22. Accessed online: http://www.nbcsports.msnbc.com.

Associated Press (AP) (2009) Vick Released from Federal Custody. ESPN.com, last updated July 21. Accessed online: http://www.sports.espn.go.com.

BBC News (2000) The Heysel Disaster. BBC News Online, posted May 29. Accessed online: http://www.news.bbc.co.uk.

BBC News (2009) Violence a Disgrace to Football. BBC News Online, posted August 26. Accessed online: http://www.news.bbc.co.uk.

Bryant J, Comisky P, Zillmann D (1981) The Appeal of Rough-and-Tumble Play in Televised Professional Football. Communication Quarterly 29(4):256–262.

Chase C (2009) Eagles Players Honor Michael Vick with Award for Courage. Yahoo Sports, posted December 23. Accessed online: http://www.sports.yahoo.com.

CNN (2007) Dogfighting a Booming Business, Experts Say. CNN US, posted July 18. Accessed online: http://www.articles.cnn.com.

Comisky P, Bryant J, Zillman D (1977) Commentary as a Substitute for Action. Journal of Communication 27(3):150–153.

Duke V (1991) The Sociology of Football: A Research Agenda for the 1990s. Sociological Review 39:627–645.

Economist (1975) Hockey Sticks and the Law. The Economist, July 26.

Eitzen DS (1985) Violence in Professional Sport and Public Policy. In Government and Sports. The Public Policy Issues, ed. A.T. Johnson AT, Frey JH, pp. 99–114. Rowan and Allanheld: Totowa, NJ.

Frosdick S, Marsh P (2005) Football Hooliganism. Willan Publishing: London, UK.

Gillis C (2004) Bad for Business. Maclean's, March 22.

Guttmann A (1998) The Appeal of Violent Sports. In Why We Watch: The Attractions of Violent Entertainment, ed. Goldstein JH. Oxford University: New York, NY.

Hamlin WA Jr (2007) Deviations from Equity and Parity in the National Football League. Journal of Sports Economics 8(6):596–615.

Ideal Spain (2011) Culture of Spain -- Bullfighting in Spain. Ideal Spain web site, last viewed April 1. Accessed online: http://www.idealspain.com.

Jones JCH, Ferguson DG, Stewart KG (1993) Blood Sports and Cherry Pie: Some Economics of Violence in the National Hockey League. American Journal of Economics and Sociology 52(1):63–78.

Jones, JCH, Stewart KG, Sunderman R (1996) From the Arena into the Streets: Hockey Violence, Economic Incentives, and Public Policy. American Journal of Economics and Sociology 55(2):231–243.

Kalof L, Taylor C (2007) The Discourse of Dog Fighting. Humanity and Society 31(4):319–333.

Kelly S (2011) Another Death Stains Argentine Football. ESPN Soccernet, posted March 25. Accessed online: http://www.soccernet.espn.go.com.

Leahy S (2011) Poll: NFL Beats Baseball Again as America's Most Popular Sport. USA Today, posted January 25. Accessed online: http://www.content.usatoday.com.

Mann B (2007) Illegal Dog Fighting Rings Thrive in US Cities. National Public Radio, posted July 20. Accessed online: http://www.npr.org.

McCaghy CH, Neal AJ (1974) The Fraternity of Cock Fighters: Ethical Embellishments of an Illegal Sport. Journal of Popular Culture 8(3):557–569.

Miller M (2008) Ultimate Cash Machine. Forbes Magazine, posted May 5. Accessed online: http://www.forbes.com.

Ministerio del Interior (MIR) (various years) Estadísticas Correspondientes a la Temporada 2006, 2007, 2008, 2009. Ministerio del Interior (España), Estadísticas Taurinas, last viewed April 2, 2011. Accessed online: http://www.mis.es.

Narayana N (2010) Bullfight to End in Barcelona with Region's Parliament Set to Vote on Its Ban. International Business Times, posted July 28. Accessed online: http://www.ibtimes.com.

Naqi K (2007) Source: Vick 'One of the Heavyweights' in Dog Fighting. ESPN.com, last updated May 31. Accessed online: http://www.sports.espn.go.com.

Nielsonwire (2011a) Football TV Ratings Soar: the NFL's Playbook for Success. Nielsonwire, posted January 28. Accessed online: http://www.blog.nielsen.com/nielsenwire.

Nielsonwire (2011b) Super Bowl XLV Most Viewed Telecast in US Broadcast History. Nielsonwire, posted February 7. Accessed online: http://www.blog.nielsen.com/nielsenwire.

Orwell G (1945) The Sporting Spirit. Tribune, December.

Paul RJ (2003) Variations in NHL Attendance: The Impact of Violence, Scoring, and Regional Rivalries. American Journal of Economics and Sociology 62(2):345–364.

Reuters (2010a) Mayoría de Españoles no está de Acuerdo con Las Corridas de Toros. América Economía, posted August 1. Accessed online: http://www.americaeconomia.com.

Reuters (2010b) Unos 100 Activistas Protestan Desnudos por Corridas de Toros en España. América Economía, posted August 21. Accessed online: http://www.americaeconomia.com.

Plunkett Research (2010) Sports Industry Overview. Plunkett Research, Ltd, last viewed March 23, 2011. Accessed online: http://www.plunkettresearch.com.

Poliakoff MB (1987) Combat Sports in the Ancient World. Yale University Press: New Haven, CT.

Rees DI, Schnepel KT (2009) College Football Games and Crime. Journal of Sports Economics 10(1):68–87.

Richardson P (2010) How Spain Took the Bull by the Horns. The Observer, June 6.

Russell GW (1983) Psychological Issues in Sports Aggression. In Sports Violence, ed. Goldstein JH, pp. 157–181. Springer-Verlag: New York, NY.

Sargent SL, Zillmann D, Weaver JB III (1998) The Gender Gap in the Development of Televised Sports. Journal of Sport and Social Issues 22(1):46–64.

Sipes RG (1973) War, Sports, and Aggression: An Empirical Test of Two Rival Theories. American Anthropologist, New Series 75(1):64–86.

Smith GJ (1988) The Noble Sports Fan. Journal of Sports and Social Issues 12(1):54–65.

Stewart KG, Ferguson DG, Jones JCH (1992) On Violence in Professional Team Sport as the Endogenous Result of Profit Maximization. Atlantic Economic Journal 20(4):55–64.

Viet Nam News (2010) Crackdown on Hooligan Violence. Viet Nam News Online, posted August 7. Accessed online: http://www.vietnamnews.vnagency.com.vn.

Wann DL, Carlson JD, Holland LC, Jacob BE, Owens DA, Wells DD (1999) Beliefs in Symbolic Catharsis: The Importance of Involvement with Aggressive Sports. Social Behavior and Personality 27(3):155–164.

Zillmann D, Bryant J, Sapolsky BS (1979) The Enjoyment of Watching Sports Contests. In Sports, Games, and Play: Social and Psychological Viewpoints, ed. Goldstein JH, pp. 297–335. Lawrence Eribaum: Hillsdale, NJ.

Part II
North American Team Sports

Chapter 3
Incentive for Aggression in American Football

Janice A. Hauge

Abstract This chapter focuses on the United States' National Football League (NFL) and the continuing attempt to control the level of violence inherent in the game. The study uses data from 1995 to 2009 to analyze the effect of violence and aggression on the success of a team and on fan attendance. Results show that penalties are negatively associated with wins from 1995 through 2005; after 2005, this relationship is statistically insignificant, although trends apparent in the data make it essential to watch the progression of this relationship. In addition, data suggest a correlation between attendance and more egregious rule infractions over the past five seasons; however, such correlation is not found to be statistically significant.

> *"Physical, tough football is what people are attracted to. Violent, unnecessary hits that put people at risk, not just for the careers but lives ... we're not subscribing to the notion fans want that."*
>
> – Ray Anderson, the NFL's executive vice president of football operations (AP 2010)

> *"If I get a chance to knock somebody out, I'm going to knock them out and take what they give me. They give me a helmet, I'm going to use it."*
>
> – Channing Crowder, *Miami Dolphins linebacker* (Sabia 2010)

Introduction

The National Football League (NFL) began in its most basic form in 1876, when the first rules of the game were written. The sport developed from the English sport of rugby, which, although a physical game, has been referred to as "elegant." American football, however, typically is far from elegant. American football developed with a more violent tact that continues to predominate today. The tendency toward violence, both intentional and unintentional, seems to have progressed more quickly than

J.A. Hauge (✉)
University of North Texas, Denton, TX, USA
e-mail: jhauge@unt.edu

R.T. Jewell (ed.), *Violence and Aggression in Sporting Contests: Economics, History and Policy*, Sports Economics, Management and Policy 4,
DOI 10.1007/978-1-4419-6630-8_3, © Springer Science+Business Media, LLC 2011

official rules and the ability to enforce codes of safety have. For example, from its inception, while the sport quickly established teams, organized schedules, designed a college player draft, and negotiated television contracts, it took until 1943 for the league to mandate that players must wear helmets, and until 1948 to mandate that such helmets could not be simple plastic.

This chapter considers the relationship between violence in the NFL and the success of teams during the regular and postseason, and addresses the unique characteristics of the sport that cause fans' demand for violence to be difficult to measure. The chapter begins by highlighting rules and rule changes designed to protect players from egregious acts of violence, and by recording fines and penalties associated with various on-field infractions. After this cursory look at violence and safety, data from 1995 to 2009 are used to examine the potential relationship between egregious infractions and fan attendance and to empirically estimate effects of penalties on teams' winning percentages and postseason success. Finally, results are provided and the implications of the findings are discussed.

NFL Rules Related to Safety and Aggression

The NFL experienced a number of trends beginning in the mid-1950s with respect to an emphasis on rules designed to protect players and to limit unnecessary violence within the game. The first such rules were rather basic, focusing on ensuring players stopped play simultaneously and limiting obviously dangerous actions such as grabbing an opponent's facemask. Rules were added sparingly until 1974 when extensive rule changes were implemented. These changes were designed to increase the tempo of games and to intensify the action in games; their primary intent was not to address safety. By 1979, the changes to the game had effectively increased the level of intensity with which games were played, and unsurprisingly also had increased the likelihood of player injury. To address this increased likelihood of injury, in 1979 and 1980 a variety of regulations were passed that were designed solely to protect players from injury. Changes prohibited dangerous forms of blocking and restricted contact to the head, neck, and face, for example. The personal foul was introduced to prohibit players from directly striking an opponent. There were few rule changes in the subsequent decades. Then in the mid-2000s, numerous rule changes were implemented. Such changes followed an apparent awareness by the NFL of the use of steroids and other performance enhancing supplements that were contributing to players growing increasingly stronger, faster, and more violent.

While little empirical evidence exists to support the notion that fans, owners, and players might have reached the threshold of their tolerance for egregious acts of violence, anecdotal evidence of this notion does exist. By 2010, the NFL had not only begun to put forward press releases on their intent to focus on safety, but the number of safety-related rule changes had roughly quadrupled from the number of safety-related rule changes made in the two decades prior. NFL Executive Vice President of Football Operations Ray Anderson introduced stricter standards by stating: "We want to make the game safer both for the player getting hit and the player doing the hitting," (Valentine 2010). During the 2010 season, the NFL also released to the media information regarding safety-related factors in the game that would be emphasized during the season. In addition, they stated that good sportsmanship would continue to be emphasized, and that abusive, threatening, or insulting language or gestures would result in an unsportsmanlike conduct penalty of 15 yards. The NFL also expressly noted that all rules that encourage player safety would continue to be strictly enforced.

Interestingly, despite the early emphasis on player safety, the 2010 season saw some of the most violent play to date. By the 6th week of play, there had been 46 head injuries, 11 of which occurred in that week (Romanowski 2010). The league responded to this increase in violent play by instituting suspensions and fines of unprecedented amounts: New England Patriots safety Brandon Meriweather and Atlanta Falcons cornerback Dunta Robinson were each fined $50,000, and Pittsburgh Steelers outside linebacker James Harrison was fined $75,000. Meriweather's 2010 salary of $550,000 means the fine is 9.09% of his total yearly salary, which is much higher than for Robinson (2010 base salary of $5 million plus $7 million signing bonus, fine=0.0042%) and Harrison (2010 base salary of $755,000 plus $2.8 million reporting bonus, fine=0.0210%).

Following this spate of fines, NFL Commissioner Roger Goodell notified teams that more significant discipline, including suspensions even for first-time offenders, would continue to be imposed on aggressive acts. The Appendix provides a summary of safety-related rule changes from 1955 through 2010. Table 3.1 summarizes safety-related rules as of the 2010–2011 NFL season. As is clear, nonsafety-related penalties typically are assessed less-severe penalties of 5 and 10 yards: of those infractions warranting the maximum penalties of 15 yards and above, 72.4% are safety related; only 12.8% of infractions warranting penalties of 10 yards and below are safety related.

Demand for Aggressive Play

There are two possibilities for changes in the level of aggression and violence in the NFL: aggressive actions either are inadvertent or they are intentional. In the first case, it is reasonable to assume that as players have progressively become stronger and faster, more violent plays can be expected to occur. Such a possibility coincides with league rule changes designed to open up the game to make it more entertaining to fans. In the second case, it is possible that fan demand for aggressive play has provided an incentive for the league to incorporate rule changes that permit more egregiously violent play to occur. Along with this possibility is the likelihood that players, realizing fans' demand for aggressive play, respond to that demand accordingly.

There is scant literature to date on fan demand for violence in the NFL. Part of this is due to the competitive structure of the league and the difficulty in measuring

Table 3.1 Safety and aggression-related penalties in the NFL, 2010

Penalty assessed	Safety-related infraction
5 Yards	
32 Infractions receive this penalty; 3 of these (about 9%) are safety related	Encroachment Running into kicker Grasping facemask of the ball carrier or quarterback
10 Yards	
7 Infractions receive this penalty; 2 of these (about 29%) are safety related	Tripping by a member of either team Illegal block above the waist
15 Yards	
19 Infractions receive this penalty; 13 of these (about 68%) are safety related	Chop block Clipping below the waist Fair catch interference Illegal crackback block by offense Piling on Roughing the kicker Roughing the passer Twisting, turning, or pulling an opponent by the facemask Unnecessary roughness Unsportsmanlike conduct Illegal low block A tackler using his helmet to butt, spear, or ram an opponent
15 Yards (and disqualification if flagrant)	
8 Infractions receive this penalty; 7 of these (about 88%) are safety related	Striking opponent with fist Kicking or kneeing opponent Striking opponent on head or neck with forearm, elbow, or hands whether or not the initial contact is made below the neck area Roughing kicker Roughing passer Malicious unnecessary roughness Unsportsmanlike conduct
15 Yards and automatic disqualification	
2 Infractions receive this penalty; 1 of these (50%) is safety related	Using a helmet (not worn) as a weapon

Source: NFL History Web site (http://www.nflteamhistory.com)

demand for games. Coates and Humphreys (2007) attempt to estimate the demand elasticity for tickets to NFL games. They use a fan-cost index and empirical demand model, but because NFL games sell out frequently (despite a high fan-cost index), the authors are unable to find empirical support for demand estimates. They conclude that demand for tickets to NFL games is unlike demand for professional baseball or basketball game tickets, and find that only winning percentage and lagged attendance drive fan demand.

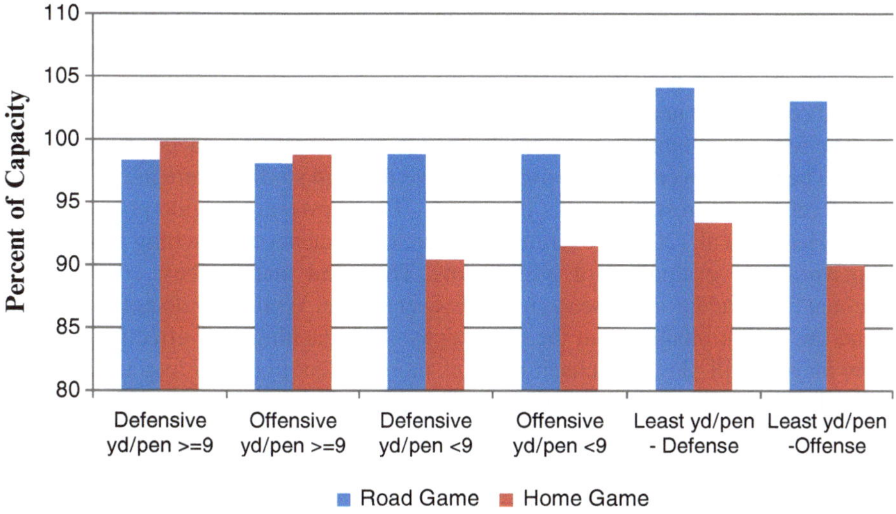

Fig. 3.1 Average percent of capacity by degree of penalty, 2006–2009

Brunkhorst and Fenn (2010) similarly find that NFL demand is difficult to measure due to the binding attendance capacity constraint. They design a model to test whether NFL teams maximize profit (rather than maximizing winning percentage as a goal) and find that over 80% of NFL teams do set ticket prices consistent with profit maximization, despite frequent sell-outs. Frequent sell-outs are the greatest hindrance to determining elasticity of demand for tickets. For example, in 2006, every game for every team sold out through the first 11 (of 16) weeks of the season. Clearly, this makes it impossible to determine if fans demand violent or aggressive play as there is no measurable difference in attendance regardless of the existence of such play. Demand for NFL games typically is high enough that the capacity constraint binds. From 2006 through 2010, only eight teams had home capacity for any season less than 90%; the Oakland Raiders in 2009 had the lowest home game capacity at 70.3% (ESPN, various years). Even fantasy football has been shown to impact demand for attending games. Nesbit and King (2010) show that fans engaged in fantasy football are not only more likely to attend a game, they also attend more games. In sum, it is difficult with the data currently available to correlate demand for tickets with violence or aggression during games.

Despite the statistical difficulties in finding an empirically significant correlation between attendance and violent play, data suggest that a relationship may exist. Figure 3.1 illustrates the percent of capacity of a stadium for both home games and away games (road games), qualified by the average yards per penalty for the years 2006 through 2009. As noted above, penalties that are assessed 15 yards typically are for more violent infractions. Figure 3.1 indicates that while generally stadiums are filled to capacity, in cases in which the home team has fewer egregious infractions, capacity is slightly lower (though never lower than 90%). This relationship is not statistically significant and causation cannot be determined (i.e., if stadiums do not sell out, players may not play as aggressively; or, if players do not play as aggressively, stadiums do not sell out). The relationship is something that ongoing research should continue to analyze.

The second possibility mentioned above is that players or coaches believe there to be a benefit to overly aggressive play. Like demand studies, there are few studies to reference with respect to this possibility. Two, however, provide possible guidance. Hadley et al. (2000) generate a measure of efficiency in coaching and conduct a performance evaluation of NFL teams. They find that the best coaching can account for an additional three to four wins per season. While they do not use penalty data, one might imagine that the philosophy of a coaching staff effectively guides how players will play. If a coach believes more violent play will lead to additional wins, he may suggest this type of play. This possibility seems reasonable: consider the reputation of the Oakland Raiders, who still are perceived by many fans and opponents' fans to be notoriously violent on the field, or conversely, the reputation of the 1972 Miami Dolphins.

Tangentially related, Priks (2010) considers the link between frustration and aggression, analyzing the hypothesis that thwarted expectations lead to aggressiveness. While his study uses data from Swedish soccer leagues and focuses on hooliganism, the link remains: poor results are a source of frustration, and frustration leads to aggression (Edmans et al. 2007). Interestingly, Priks also finds that home supporters are more easily frustrated than away supporters, a factor that may carry over to home versus away players in NFL games.

Figure 3.2 shows the ten most penalized teams from 1995 through 2009. Some seasons appear to have more serious infractions (e.g., 2001 with three of the most penalized teams over the years), and some teams appear to have more serious infractions (e.g., Green Bay and Indianapolis each appear four times among the top 20 penalized teams overall). It is possible that referees, umpires, and rule changes contribute to the former, and team culture contributes to the latter.

Finally, Stair et al. (2008) analyze factors that contribute to winning percentage among NFL teams from 2003 to 2007. Their study is most closely linked with the analyses in this chapter. They include the quarterback rating and offensive and defensive performance statistics. Also, they use team penalties per season and the number of arrests per team. This latter variable is not found to be significant, although Edmans et al. (2007) find that athletes who incur a greater number of penalties have a tendency to be unruly elsewhere. Daily news reports lead many fans to believe this to be true. Consider, for example, the Patriots' Meriweather, who was present at a recent shooting of two men in his hometown (Farley 2011), or Adam "Pac-Man" Jones, who was a force on the field since being picked sixth in the first round of the 2005 draft, but was suspended all of 2007 and part of the 2008 season for his off-field conduct (Farmer 2008).

In short, there is little empirical work to date examining the effect of penalties on teams' winning percentage and considering possible benefits of intentional violence. This chapter provides evidence that generally penalties have not contributed to winning, but that the last five seasons may reflect a change in that tendency. Penalties do have a statistically significant effect on points scored by a team and

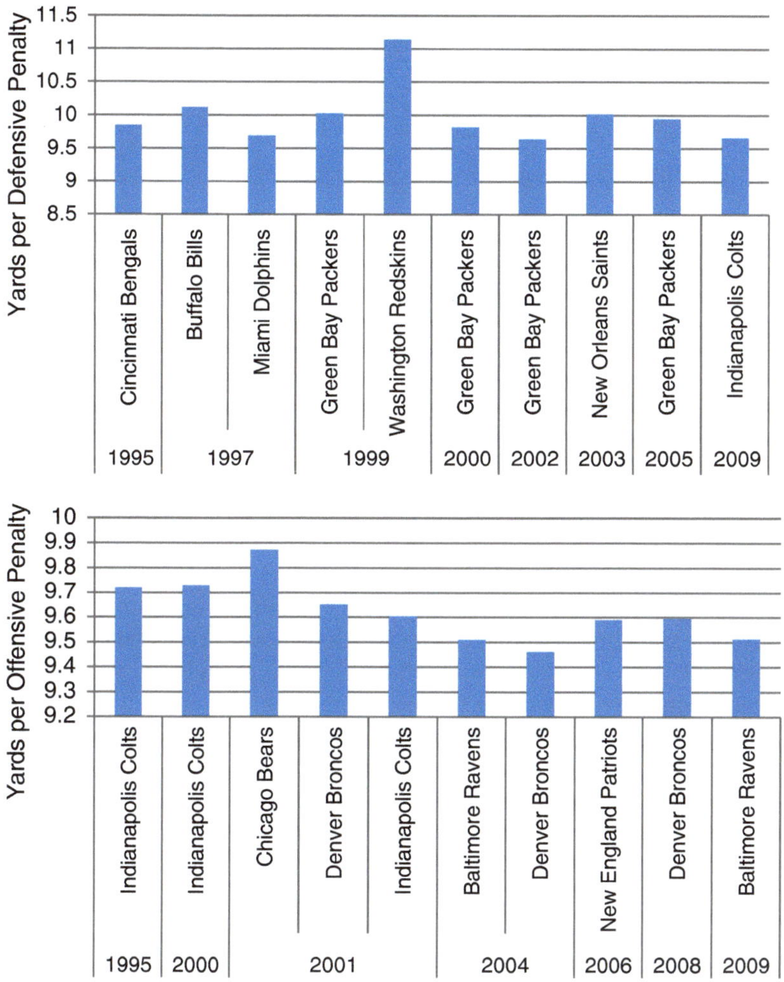

Fig. 3.2 Average yards per penalty of top ten penalized teams, 1995–2009

against a team, which are directly correlated with winning percentage. Furthermore, offensive yards per penalty and egregious offensive penalties are correlated with a lower winning percentage.

Data and Empirical Models

The data used in this study contain observations on all regular and postseason games played in the NFL from September 1995 through January 2010. The data are from the NFL directly, and include by season and team the total number of offensive and defensive penalties and the total number of yards assessed for such penalties.

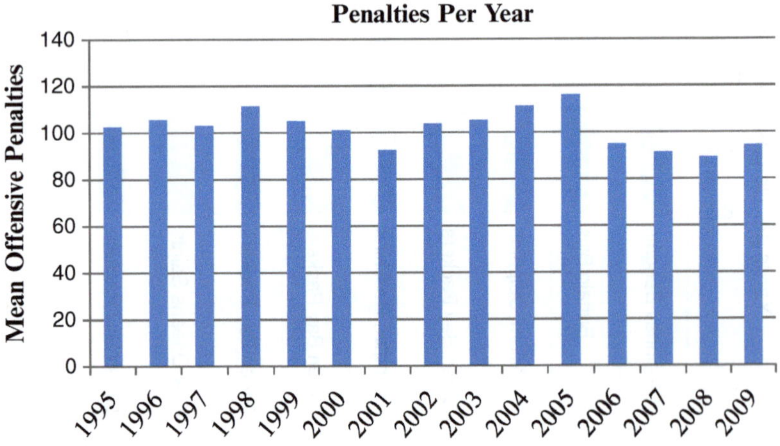

Fig. 3.3 Average number of offensive penalties per year, 1995–2009

While penalties are aggregated by team and year, the level of violence for any given team is reflected in the team's average yards per penalty as infractions deemed to be more severe incur a higher yardage penalty. All data were accessed online from the NFL's official Web site (http://www.nfl.com). Also included are the division in which each team played, whether the team competed in divisional playoffs, championship playoffs, or the Super Bowl, and whether the team won the Super Bowl upon playing, and finally, various success statistics such as the team's winning percentage, points scored, and points scored against. Finally, the data include attendance figures for games played from the 2006 season through the 2009 season. In total, the dataset includes 470 observations composed of 32 teams over 15 years. This total accounts for the Baltimore Ravens organization starting in 1996, the Houston Texans beginning in 2002, and 2 years of missing data from the Cleveland Browns organization. The movement of the Houston Oilers to become the Tennessee Oilers in 1997 and, subsequently, the Tennessee Titans in 1999, maintains a full 15 seasons for this franchise that both moved and changed names.

Overview of the Data

Frequent review and revision of rules by the NFL suggests that trends in penalties may be found from a cursory examination of the data. Figure 3.3 illustrates the progression of penalties from 1995 through 2009. Interestingly, years in which a greater number of major rule revisions were implemented do appear to have affected play. For example, in 2001, the prohibition of anabolic steroids was strengthened to include supplements containing ephedrine and other high-risk supplements, and there is evidence of a slight decrease in penalties, although the severity of those infractions that did occur was higher than average (refer again to Fig. 3.2).

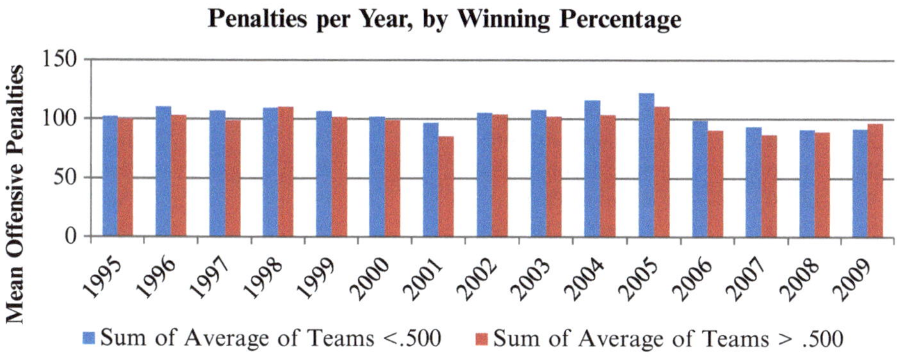

Fig. 3.4 Average number of offensive penalties per year by winning percentage, 1995–2009

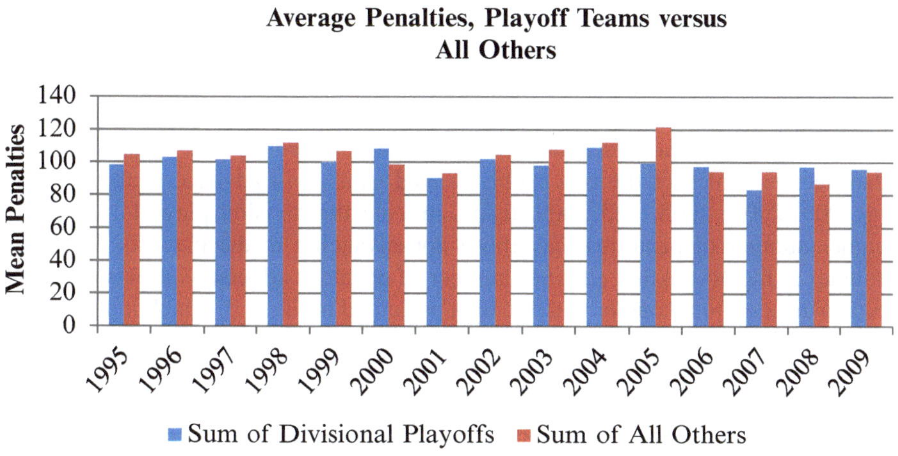

Fig. 3.5 Average number of penalties per year for playoff teams versus all others, 1995–2009

This decrease in total penalties is followed by an upward trend until 2006. The halt in the upward trend may be due in part to the adoption of the Olympic testosterone testing standard in 2005, which tripled the number of times a player can be randomly tested during the off-season from two to six, and which added substances to the list of banned substances. Also in 2005, additional rules regarding the manner in which a player could tackle another were implemented, and unnecessary roughness was more clearly specified. See the Appendix for a complete listing of NFL rule changes.

To further consider the variation in penalties over the years of the study, teams with a winning season are compared to those finishing the season with a winning percentage under 0.500. Figure 3.4 shows that in every year except 1998 and 2009, teams with a winning percentage greater than 0.500 had fewer penalties than those with a winning percentage less than 0.500.

If a team's winning percentage is related to its penalties, that relationship might be expected to hold across the playoffs. Figure 3.5 illustrates the average number of

Table 3.2 Highest penalty differential by team and season, 1995–2009

	Greatest difference in penalties (committed against > committed)		Greatest difference in penalties (committed > committed against)	
1	1998	Cincinnati Bengals	2005	Oakland Raiders
2	1999	Indianapolis Colts	1996	Oakland Raiders
3	1996	Indianapolis Colts	2005	Arizona Cardinals
4	2000	Carolina Panthers	1995	Oakland Raiders
5	2003	Cleveland Browns	2002	Minnesota Vikings
6	2005	Dallas Cowboys	2003	Minnesota Vikings
7	1996	New England Patriots	2008	Oakland Raiders
8	1999	Arizona Cardinals	2002	Houston Texans
9	2005	Denver Broncos	2007	Cleveland Browns
10	2007	New York Giants	1998	Tennessee Oilers

penalties for those teams advancing to the divisional playoffs in a given year. Eight teams each season advance to the divisional round of the playoffs. Those eight teams are determined by season records and, when necessary, a "wild card" game that decides which of the two evenly ranked teams will advance to the playoffs. In 2000, 2006, 2008, and 2009, teams making the division playoffs incurred a higher number of penalties than those not advancing to the playoffs. This runs counter to the notion that a higher number of penalties adversely affects a team. It is also difficult to reconcile with the data presented in Fig. 3.3, which indicates that generally teams with winning seasons have fewer penalties than teams with losing seasons.

Fans of the NFL hold beliefs not only about their teams' style of play, but also about opponents' style of play with respect to their propensity to commit penalties. During the period of this study, the five least-penalized teams overall were (with least penalized listed first), New York Jets, Indianapolis Colts, Pittsburgh Steelers, Seattle Seahawks, and Houston Oilers. The five most penalized teams were (with most penalized listed first) Oakland Raiders, Tennessee Oilers, St. Louis Rams, Minnesota Vikings, and Detroit Lions. It is also interesting to note those teams with the greatest difference in penalties committed versus penalties committed against in any given season. Table 3.2 provides this information.

Empirical Model and Analysis

In order to determine whether penalties are correlated with either winning percentage or fan attendance, two models are utilized; the first model is structured to determine whether offensive and defensive field penalties levied on teams affect such teams' winning percentages. Because the dependent variable, *winning percentage*, by definition is between 0 and 1, the most appropriate model to use for analysis is a fractional response panel data model using a quasi-maximum likelihood estimator, or QMLE model, as proposed by Papke and Wooldridge (2008). A MLE model assumes a normal distribution with unknown mean and variance, which are estimated based on a sample of the overall population. The MLE estimate is the population that is most likely to have generated the observed data. The model must be amended slightly, however, to account for the dependent variable that is censored, since winning percentage is measured as a rate that is bounded between 0 and 1. With the quasi-maximum likelihood estimation, the model is able to account for unobserved year and team effects that capture differences across years and teams, so that penalties can be related to winning percentage as the average effect of penalties on winning percentage. Papke and Wooldridge applied this method of quasi-maximum likelihood estimation to obtain robust estimators of conditional mean parameters. Similar models have been applied in other empirical studies (e.g., Hausman and Leonard 1997).

The independent variables of greatest interest for the primary model include the total number of penalties incurred by a given team in a given year (*penalties*), the total number of yards penalized by team by year (*penalty yards*), offensive and defensive penalties incurred by team by year (*offensive penalties* and *defensive penalties*), and offensive and defensive yards penalized by team by year (*offensive yards* and *defensive yards*). Additional explanatory variables include total points scored by a team and against a team (*points for* and *points against*), and the penalty differential between penalties incurred by a given team and those incurred by the team's opponent during a given season (*penalty difference*). For a subset of the specifications, the model also includes a binary variable that reflects information on the most severe offensive and defensive penalties (*egregious offensive* and *egregious defensive*). These variables take a value of 1 if the team's average penalized yards is 9 or greater, and 0 otherwise. Finally, dummy variables indicating the team and division are included in all appropriate specifications. Summary statistics are provided in Table 3.3.

Results of the model's various specifications are presented in Table 3.4. *Winning percentage* is negatively correlated with both the number of offensive penalties and the total number of yards in offensive penalties. This relationship holds regardless of whether the model estimates defensive penalties (in number or yards) or total penalties. These results are in accordance with data presented in Fig. 3.4 that indicates teams with a greater number of penalties generally have a winning percentage below 0.500. Also, offensive penalties attributed to severe infractions has a negative and statistically significant effect on *winning percentage*, although the same is not true of defensive penalties.

The second model considers whether the number of offensive, defensive, and total penalties or the magnitude of such penalties (in terms of yards) levied during a game is correlated with in-season and postseason success. The model is a binomial probit in which the dependent variable is whether a given team competed in a given level of playoffs (*divisional playoffs*, *NFC-AFC championship*, *Super Bowl*, and *Super Bowl champion*). Specifications also consider the relationship between penalties and points scored by a team and points allowed by a team.

Table 3.3 Summary statistics, 1995–2009

Summary statistics (470 observations)				
	Mean	SD	Minimum	Maximum
Winning percentage	0.500	0.190	0	1
Penalties	204.07	25.86	134	296
Penalty yards	1,669.52	227.43	1,040	2,596
Points for	336.87	68.49	161	589
Points against	335.46	60.50	42	517
Penalty difference	0	18.03	–46	58
Egregious offensive	0.14	0.35	0	1
Egregious defensive	0.16	0.37	0	1
Divisional playoffs	0.255	0.437	0	1
NFC-AFC championship	0.128	0.334	0	1
Super Bowl	0.064	0.245	0	1
Super Bowl champion	0.032	0.176	0	1
Year	2002.11	4.31	1995	2009

Table 3.4 QMLE model results

Dependent Variable:	Winning Percentage	Winning Percentage	Winning Percentage	Winning Percentage
Penalties	–0.0059***		–0.0019	–0.0001
	(0.0019)		(0.0016)	(0.0004)
Penalty yards		–0.0006**		–0.0006**
		(0.0002)		(0.0002)
Penalty difference			0.0004	
			(0.0014)	
Points for			0.0089***	0.0016***
			(0.0004)	(0.0001)
Points against			–0.0068***	–0.0017***
			(0.0008)	(0.0001)
Egregious offensive				–0.0735***
				(0.0278)
Egregious defensive				0.0172
				(0.0241)

Robust standard errors are given in parentheses
*Significant at 10% level; **significant at 5% level; ***significant at 1% level

The primary hypothesis is that because penalties are shown to adversely affect winning percentage, aggressive play that results in penalties will be reflected in a lower likelihood of advancing to postseason play and through additional rounds of such play. The secondary hypothesis is that there exists a negative relationship between penalties a team incurs and points scored, and a positive relationship between penalties a team incurs and points allowed. Table 3.5 provides the results, reported as marginal effects, of the probit model with relevant dependent variable. Results indicate that *penalties* and *penalty yards* are negatively correlated with

Table 3.5 Probit regression results

Dependent variable	*Divisional playoffs*	*NFC-AFC championship*	*Super Bowl*
Penalties		–0.0002	0.00005
		(0.0004)	(0.0002)
Penalty yards	–0.0003**	–0.0001	–7.36E–06
	(0.0001)	(0.0001)	(0.0000)
Points for	0.0021***	0.0009***	0.0004*
	(0.0012)	(0.0002)	(0.0003)
Points against	–0.0017***	–0.0009***	–0.0003***
	(0.0008)	(0.0002)	(0.0001)
Penalties if year < 2006	–0.0036**		
	(0.0015)		
Penalties if year <= 2006	0.0009		
	(0.0025)		

Robust standard errors are given in parentheses
*Significant at 10% level; **significant at 5% level; ***significant at 1% level

advancing to the *divisional playoffs*; however, no other round of playoffs appears to be similarly affected in any way by penalties incurred by participating teams. It is possible that there is not enough variance in penalties across teams given the limited number of playoff games played for there to be a statistically significant correlation. The *divisional playoffs* specification separates the model by considering seasons before and after 2005. This division reflects the drop in penalties following the 2005 season, as shown in Figs. 3.3–3.5. *Divisional playoffs* is negatively correlated with the number of penalties incurred (*penalties*) for years prior to 2006. After 2006, there is no statistically significant relationship among the dependent variable and any of the independent variables other than *points for* and *points against* (as reflected in all columns of Table 3.5).

The final model considers the effect of penalties on points scored and points allowed. The model used is a cross-sectional, fixed-effects, generalized least squares model with *points for* and *points against* as dependent variables in the two specifications. The correlation between these variables and the remainder of those in the dataset limit the scope of the model to simply the total effect of penalties (offensive and defensive combined, as individual results were insignificant), and a team's average difference in penalties by year. Results are shown in Table 3.6.

The results indicate that teams on the "plus" side of the penalty differential, meaning teams that incurred fewer penalties than their opponents, had on average more points scored than their opponents. This result is reflected equally in the specification that considers points allowed by a given team. Teams that committed more infractions than their opponents had on average more points scored against them than they scored. Clearly, *points for* and *points against* are highly correlated with *winning percentage* (0.749 and –0.636, respectively), although the correlation between *points for* and *points against* is –0.022. This result mirrors the result obtained using the QMLE model.

Table 3.6 FGLS results

Dependent variable	*Points for*	*Points against*
Penalties	0.1222	0.0634
	(0.1274)	(0.1124)
Penalty difference	0.4509*	–0.4681**
	(0.1767)	(0.1559)
Year	0.9627	0.8610
	(0.7520)	(0.6636)

Robust standard errors are given in parentheses
*Significant at 5% level; **significant at 1% level

Implications for the Game

Analysis of the effect of aggressive play as measured by the total number of penalties incurred by a given team is subject to dispute. Other factors must certainly come into play, for example referees' and umpires' predispositions to watch for infractions differently across teams. Still, data on team, division, and even playing surface are found to be insignificant regardless of the model used and therefore these variables are not even included in the analyses discussed in the section on "Data and Empirical Models." This suggests that the results of the models discussed in the chapter are reasonably strong enough to draw some meaningful conclusions about the effect of penalties on winning percentage. Any attempt to draw a more general conclusion or a conclusion about fans' demand for aggressive play is inappropriate.

The violence of the 2010 season has continued to be a primary factor in the NFL's off-season work. The NFL has stated that they will be more aggressive in suspending players for illegal hits, they will look for repeat offenders, and they have re-defined the definition of "defenseless player" in an attempt to curb flagrant infractions (AP 2011). Still, the question of whether more aggressive play is in demand by fans, or is an unwanted by-product of rules that increase the intensity of the game remains difficult to answer given data limitations.

Results indicate that offensive penalties and, in particular, serious offensive penalties have a negative and significant effect on teams' winning percentage. Also, total penalty yards have a small, significant effect on reaching the divisional playoffs. This suggests that the hypothesis that coachers, owners, or players may prefer more aggressive play that results in a greater number of penalties is false. If fans accept the notion that coaches and owners effectively manage games and the league more generally, such fans must also believe that such coaches are aware of the negative effects of penalties: penalties are not proven to be beneficial to a team on average.

These findings are in accordance with the NFL's stated policy during the 2010 season that violent acts of aggression will be more heavily monitored and will not be tolerated. One possibility is that owners have a strong incentive to protect the value of their investment. As players have become stronger and faster and the game has changed to allow more open field contact, the likelihood of injury has risen. While fans may demand more aggressive play, having a top-rated player injured is likely to decrease fan support quickly. Owners may not be willing to risk this, and therefore are working to scale back the level of aggression through increased fines, suspensions, and additional monitoring.

The years following 2005 saw a slight shift in penalties incurred, although no break in attendance figures is evident around this time. It is possible that rule changes and changes in the way owners and coaches manage the teams have affected the style of play; however, given no concurrent change in attendance figures it is impossible to link fan attendance to fan demand for a change in the level of violence in the sport. Currently, the NFL is exceptionally popular as well as profitable. If games continue to sell out, it will be difficult to determine those aspects of the game that are most attractive to fans. This leaves team owners and league officials to do no more than protect the assets they have in an effort to continue to provide the product fans so eagerly demand. If owners continue to focus on this aspect of the game, future research is likely to reveal more about the level of violence that fans find optimal.

Appendix

History of NFL rules since 1955	
1955	The ball is dead immediately if the ball carrier touched the ground with any part of his body except his hands or feet while in the grasp of an opponent
1956	Grabbing an opponent's facemask (other than the ball carrier) is illegal
1962	Grabbing any player's facemask is illegal
1974	Roll-blocking and cutting of wide receivers was eliminated; the extent of downfield contact a defender could have with an eligible receiver was restricted; the penalties for offensive holding, illegal use of the hands, and tripping were reduced from 15 to 10 yards; wide receivers blocking back toward the ball within 3 yards of the line of scrimmage were prevented from blocking below the waist
1977	Defenders permitted to make contact with eligible receivers only once; the head slap was outlawed; offensive linemen were prohibited from thrusting their hands to an opponent's neck, face, or head; and wide receivers were prohibited from clipping, even in the legal clipping zone
1978	Rules changes permitted a defender to maintain contact with a receiver within 5 yards of the line of scrimmage, but restricted contact beyond that point
1979	Changes prohibited players on the receiving team from blocking below the waist during kickoffs, punts, and field-goal attempts; prohibited the wearing of torn or altered equipment and exposed pads that could be hazardous; extended the zone in which there could be no crack back blocks; and instructed officials to quickly whistle a play dead when a quarterback was clearly in the grasp of a tackler
1980	Under the heading of "personal foul," players were prohibited from directly striking, swinging, or clubbing on the head, neck, or face. A penalty could be called for such contact whether or not the initial contact was made below the neck area
1996	Hits with the helmet or to the head by the defender will be flagged as personal fouls and subject to fines
1997	No player may remove his helmet while on the playing field (except during timeouts and between quarters)
1999	Clipping illegal around the line of scrimmage just as it is on the rest of the field

(continued)

Appendix (continued)

History of NFL rules since 1955	
2001	Prohibition of anabolic steroids and related substances was strengthened to include supplements containing ephedrine and other high-risk supplements
2002	The chop-block technique is illegal on kicking plays. It is illegal to hit a quarterback helmet-to-helmet anytime after a change of possession
2005	Adoption of the Olympic testosterone testing standard, tripling the number of times a player can be randomly tested during the off-season from two to six, adding substances to the list of banned substances, and putting new language in the policy to allow for testing of designer drugs and other substances that may have evaded detection
	Players prohibited from grabbing the inside collar of the back or side of the shoulder pads and immediately pulling down the runner
	The "peel back" block is illegal. Previously, a player aligned in the tackle box could hit an opponent on the side and below the waist from any direction
	No unnecessary roughness, including unnecessarily running, diving into, cutting, or throwing the body against or on a player who is out of the play before or after the ball is dead
	A kicker or punter standing still after the ball has been kicked is out of the play and must not be unnecessarily contacted by the receiving team until he assumes a distinctly defensive position. An opponent may not unnecessarily initiate helmet-to-helmet contact to the kicker/punter at anytime during the kick or during the return
2006	Rushing defenders must make a conscious effort to avoid low hits on the quarterback
	Prohibits blocking in the back above the waist applies to a player of the kicking team while the ball is in flight during a scrimmage kick
	Increased the scope of the "horse-collar" tackle rule
	During a field-goal attempt or a PAT, any defensive player within 1 yard of the line of scrimmage at the snap must have his helmet outside the snapper's shoulder pad
	No more than six players can line up on the same side of a formation on a kickoff
2007	Players will be subject to a fine from the league for playing with an unbuckled chin strap
	15-Yard penalty (rather than 5 yards) for a player blocking below the waist against an eligible receiver while the quarterback is in the pocket
2008	No incidental face mask rule; 15-yard penalty for any other face mask call remains
2009	New and expanded guidelines on return-to-play for any player who sustains a concussion. Protection for defenseless players standardized and expanded, protection of a player who has just completed a catch from blows to the head or neck by an opponent who launches. Additional protection also given to long snappers. Play will now stop if a ball carrier's helmet is removed
	Initial contact to the head of a defenseless receiver will draw a 15-yard penalty
	The initial force of a blindside block cannot be delivered by a helmet, forearm, or shoulder to an opponent's head or neck
	On kickoffs, no blocking wedge of more than two players will be allowed
	On onside kicks, the kicking team cannot have more than five players bunched together in pursuit
	A defensive player on the ground may no longer lunge or dive at the quarterback's lower legs

(continued)

Appendix (continued)

History of NFL rules since 1955	
2010	A play will now be whistled dead if a ball carrier loses his helmet while still in possession of the football
	During field goals and punts, opposing defensive players cannot line up directly over the center. They must have their entire body outside the snapper's shoulder pads
	Officials will call more penalties for spearing or launching at a defenseless player.
	Defenseless players are players who: just threw a pass, attempt to catch a pass, are in the grasp, attempting a kick, on the ground at the end of the play. Also, the centers (snappers) for field goal and extra points are considered defenseless

Sources:
http://www.steelersfever.com/nfl_history_of_rules.html, last accessed September 20, 2010.
http://www.nfl.com/rulebook/penaltysummaries, last accessed April 2, 2011.
http://nwe.scout.com/2/425806.html, last accessed April 2, 2011.
http://profootball.scout.com/2/556118.html, last accessed April 2, 2011.
http://www.giants.com/news/press_releases/story.asp?story_id=25050, last accessed April 2, 2011.
http://www.nfl.com/news/story?id=09000d5d809f6279, last accessed April 2, 2011.
http://bleacherreport.com/articles/144605-nfl-rule-changes-for-2009-a-study-guide, last accessed April 2, 2011
http://blogs.palmbeachpost.com/thedailydolphin/2010/08/06/explaining-the-nfl-rules-changes-for-2010/, last accessed April 2, 2011
http://www.bleedinggreennation.com/2010/8/10/1615365/2010-nfl-rule-changes-hitting, last accessed April 2, 2011

References

Associated Press (AP) (2010) Players Fear Crackdown on Hits Will Change Essence of Football. NFL.com, last updated October 20. Accessed online: http://www.nfl.com.

Associated Press (AP) (2011) NFL Plans Harsher Penalties for Hits. FoxSports.com, last updated March 16. Accessed online: http://www.msn.foxsports.com.

Brunkhorst J, Fenn AJ (2010) Profit Maximization in the NFL. Journal of Applied Business Research 26(1):45–59.

Coates D, Humphreys BR (2007) Ticket Prices, Concessions, and Attendance at Professional Sporting Events. International Journal of Sport Finance 2:161–170.

Edmans A, Garcia D, Norli O (2007) Sports Sentiments and Stock Returns. Journal of Finance 62:1967–1998.

Farley G (2011) Sheriff's Office: Pats' Meriweather Present at Shooting. EnterpriseNews.com, last updated March 10. Accessed online: http://www.enterprisenews.com.

ESPN (various years).NFL Attendance, 2006, 2007, 2008, 2009, 2010. ESPN.com, last viewed April 2, 2011. Accessed online: http://www.espn.go.com.

Farmer S (2008) 'Pacman' Jones Gets Indefinite Suspension. Los Angeles Times, posted October 15. Accessed online: http://www.articles.latimes.com.

Hadley L, Poitras M, Ruggiero J, Knowles S (2000). Performance Evaluation of National Football League Teams. Managerial and Decision Economics 21:63–70.

Hausman, JA, Leonard GK (1997)Superstars in the National Basketball Association: Economic Value and Policy. Journal of Labor Economics 15:586–624.

Nesbit TM, King KA (2010) The Impact of Fantasy Football Participation on NFL Attendance. Atlantic Economic Journal 38:95–108.

Papke LE, Wooldridge JM (2008) Panel Data Methods for Fractional Response Variables with an Application to Test Pass Rates. Journal of Econometrics 145:121–133.

Priks M (2010) Does Frustration Lead to Violence? Evidence from the Swedish Hooligan Scene. Kyklos 63(3):450–460.

Romanowski B (2010) New Rules in an Old Game; Evaluating the Appropriateness of the New NFL Hitting Regulations. Yahoo! Sports, posted October 22. Accessed online: http://www.sports.yahoo.com.

Sabia D (2010) Channing Crowder: "They Give Me a Helmet, I'm Going to Use It." Football News Now, posted October 21. Accessed online: http://www.footballnewsnow.

Stair A, Mizak D, Day A, Neral J (2008) The Factors Affecting Team Performance in the NFL: Does Off-Field Conduct Matter? Economics Bulletin 26(2):1–9.

Valentine E (2010) NFL Rules Changes. Big Blue View, posted July 25. Accessed online: http://www.bigblueview.com.

Chapter 4
Does Violence in Professional Ice Hockey Pay? Cross Country Evidence from Three Leagues

Dennis Coates, Marcel Battré, and Christian Deutscher

Abstract Hockey is inherently a rough, physical game. We analyze the impact of physical violence on the success of professional hockey clubs from the highest leagues in North America, Finland, and Germany. Using penalty min as an indicator of violence, the evidence is that incurring penalties will not improve the team's points and may even reduce them. Actual fights between players are linked to reductions in team points in the National Hockey League (North America). Nor is attendance clearly greater at the home games of highly penalized clubs, though weak evidence of such a relationship is found for the German Ice Hockey League. Team revenues are available only for the North American league, and there is also weak evidence that more penalized teams earn greater revenues.

Introduction

The National Hockey League (NHL) experienced substantial financial distress in the late 1990s and early 2000s resulting in the 2004/2005 season being lost due to the league locking out the players. Players ultimately accepted a salary cap under a new Collective Bargaining Agreement, and teams returned to the ice for the 2005/2006 season. Believing that fan interest in ice hockey was declining because the game was insufficiently exciting because the style of play and the rules limited scoring, reducing demand for attendance and broadcasts, the CBA introduced a Competition Committee composed of five active players and five executives with the purpose of "examining and making recommendations associated with issues affecting the game and the way the game is played." Interestingly, this was not the first time concerns about the style of play in the NHL were an issue. Macintosh and Greenhorn (1993) argued that Canadian hockey teams playing an overly physical

D. Coates (✉)
University of Maryland, Baltimore County, Baltimore, MD, USA
e-mail: coates@umbc.edu

R.T. Jewell (ed.), *Violence and Aggression in Sporting Contests: Economics, History and Policy*, Sports Economics, Management and Policy 4,
DOI 10.1007/978-1-4419-6630-8_4,

style, combined with bad behavior toward referees and the opposing teams, had created bad perceptions of Canada among the international community. Moreover, the Board of Governors of the NHL

> "approved a series of rule changes that will emphasize entertainment, skill, and competition on the ice."
>
> "One primary objective of the new rules will be to reduce the scope of defensive 'tools' a team may effectively employ, and to create a corresponding benefit to the offensive part of the game – thus allowing skill players to use their skills and increasing the number and quality of scoring chances in the game" (NHL.com 2005).

The rule changes included limits on goalie pads to open more of the net for shooters, adjustments to the rule on "two line" passes and to offsides. Stricter enforcement of rules on holding and hooking also were included in the plan to enable speed and skating ability to become more prominent aspects of the game. Physical play and violence came under scrutiny and the NHL added new rules to punish owners, coaches, and players for such acts, attempting to deter them from engaging in these behaviors. The fight instigator rule subjects coaches to a fine of 10,000 dollars if their actions are determined to cause a fight in the last 5 minutes of a game. The players involved in such an act are also subject to a game misconduct penalty and automatic one game suspension if it is determined that they instigated a fight during the final 5 minutes of a game (Burnside 2005). An action that could be judged as an infraction of this new rule is a coach sending a player with an affinity for fighting on the ice in the last 5 minutes of the game if the opposing team has an insurmountable lead. The rule was in response to how frequently levels of physical play increased toward the end of games.

Interestingly, players are critical of the fight instigator rule. In *The Code: The Unwritten Rules of Fighting and Retaliation in the NHL*, Ross Bernstein (2006) suggests players, at least, thought that violence in hockey was limited and under control by "the code." Teams employ enforcers or fighters to punish opposing players who "take liberties" by grabbing, hitting, and otherwise impeding the abilities of the goal scorers and skill players. These enforcers fight so other players do not have to do it. The instigator rule means that the enforcers are not allowed to do their jobs keeping the rough play under control and protecting the scorers from the other team.

The rule changes for the 2005/2006 season outline a "zero tolerance policy" for physical play that slows the game. Penalties in the NHL are assessed for many different reasons; most commonly they are awarded for impeding play by means deemed unsportsmanlike and in some cases dangerous. Common examples are: slashing, "any forceful or powerful chop with the stick on an opponent's body, the opponent's stick, or on or near the opponent's hands" (NHL 2007, Rule 61); cross checking, "the action of using the shaft of the stick between the two hands to forcefully check an opponent" (NHL 2007, Rule 59); and boarding, when a player "checks an opponent in such a manner that causes the opponent to be thrown violently in the boards" (NHL 2007, Rule 42). Defensive schemes relying on clutching and grabbing are no longer useful; hooking, holding, and cross checking penalties are to be called more consistently and with much more frequency. In other words, according to the NHL, it is "time to put an end to the grappling, wrestling, and bear-hugging that sucks the speed and skill from the game" (Fitzpatrick 2004).

The NHL believes the way to increase the fan base of the sport and thus league revenue is to increase the scoring and speed of the game. The NHL views the physical side of the game as detrimental to this effort and wishes to minimize it by discouraging that type of play.

It may be that team management, owners, and coaches have a different opinion regarding the effects of physical play and violence on team revenues. Previous work on the impact of violence has shown that there is a positive relationship between physical play, attendance, revenue, and profit maximization (Stewart et al. 1992; Jones et al. 1993, 1996; Paul 2003). This paper examines the relationship between physical play and outcomes of interest to hockey clubs and their fans. Specifically, we examine the impact of physical play on a team's success on the ice, on attendance, and, for NHL clubs, on revenue.

We examine data from the Finnish and German professional ice hockey leagues as well as from the NHL. Research in sport and exercise psychology and medicine has examined the question of violent behavior in hockey asking whether there are differences between North American and European-born players in the NHL (Gee and Leith 2007) and whether violent play is instrumental in, or detrimental to, winning (Widmeyer and Birch 1984; McGuire et al. 1992; McCaw and Walker 1999). The purpose is to assess whether violence is the result of the context of the game or is cultural. European games are played on a larger rink than North American games, putting different emphasis on speed, passing, checking, and physical contact for the games. Analyzing leagues from different countries also enables a test of the cultural sources of violence in hockey. Specifically, we assess whether violence, represented by penalty min, is related to sporting and economic success in the different leagues. If the answers differ by league, then there is support for the cultural explanation for violence in hockey.

International comparisons are limited to the effects of penalties on season success and attendance as revenue data is not available for either of the European leagues. However, not all hockey revenue is generated by attendance, so it is also useful to examine the impact of physical play on revenue in the NHL.

The paper proceeds by first discussing literature on the role of violence in professional ice hockey, which heretofore has concentrated on the NHL. We then turn to a brief discussion of the three leagues in our analysis followed by a description of the models, the data used in this analysis, and the results of our regressions. The results section first compares the three leagues relating violence to playing success and attendance, then focuses on the NHL to evaluate the connection of violence to revenues. A summary concludes the paper.

Economic Analysis of Professional Ice Hockey

We have found no published research on professional ice hockey outside the National Hockey League. Economic analysis of the NHL parallels economic analysis of North American professional sports in many respects. One aspect of hockey that is markedly different than studies of the other major sports in the USA concerns the role of violence. A number of studies in the psychology of sport literature have examined the relationship between violence in hockey and success or failure on the ice (McCarthy and Kelly 1978; Widmeyer and Birch 1984; Gee and Leith 2007). A key issue in these studies is what types of behaviors are violence/aggression and what are not. These studies have put focus on acts intended to cause harm and have used game reports to identify incidents that meet this standard. Gee and Leith (2007) finds that more aggressive activity does not translate into either more goals, more shots, more assists, or more points for the individual player. This finding contradicts the evidence from McCarthy and Kelly (1978) but is consistent with the results in Widmeyer and Birch (1984). They do find evidence that North American born players commit more aggressive acts. The difference narrows over time as European-born players gain more experience in the NHL. This sort of evidence suggests and motivates analysis of European leagues side by side with the NHL.

Stewart et al. (1992) hypothesize that violence in hockey is a profit-maximizing choice of the clubs. In their model, violence affects demand for attendance in two ways. First, fans are interested in hockey precisely because of the violent hits, players crashing into the boards, and the fights that break out. Consider the website http://www.hockey-fights.com which chronicles fights from hockey games including videos, descriptions, and even a chance for fans to vote on the winner. The site also lists fights by team and season, even identifying the home and visiting teams and the players involved. These activities directly enhance the experience of the game for many fans. Second, teams that play a more physical style may be less successful, winning fewer games, and fewer wins translates into lower fan demand. Stewart et al. (1992) hypothesize that clubs balance the demand-enhancing aspect of violence against the demand-reducing aspect of violence on wins.

Several studies, support the contention that violence enhances demand and revenues of clubs. Jones and Ferguson (1988), Jones et al. (1993), Jones et al. (1996), and Paul (2003) all provide evidence that violence increases demand for attendance at NHL games. Stewart et al. (1992) also find that winning in the NHL is quite elastic with respect to violence, measured as the total number of penalties against the home team in its own arena during the season. Their estimate of the elasticity is –2.58, indicating that 1% more penalties of any kind against the home team would reduce the percentage of the total points possible for the team over the season by 2.58 or about one and a quarter fewer wins.

Other work has focused on the impact of violence on player compensation. Jones and Walsh (1988) find a positive impact of penalty min per game on the salary of forwards but find no such effect for defensemen. Jones et al. (1997) find that there are two types of players, Grunts and non-Grunts. The two types of players are rewarded differently for the skills they bring to the game. Among forwards, scoring is rewarded about the same for Grunts and non-Grunts. For defensemen, however, non-Grunts are rewarded for scoring but Grunts are not. Grunt forwards are compensated for penalty min, but non-Grunt forwards and both Grunt and non-Grunt defensemen are not. The estimates indicate that the compensation that exists is fairly small. Given an estimated coefficient of 0.0696 on penalty min per game in a log salary regression, the implication is that an additional penalty min per game raises log salary by about 0.07. The average penalty min per game of a Grunt forward is 3.14. In other words, an additional penalty min per game is about a 30% increase in penalty min, and produces a salary increase of about 7.25%. Said differently, Jones, Nadeau, and Walsh find that for forwards who specialize in physical play, perhaps as "enforcers," 30% more penalty min raise pay by 7%. For these players, salary is quite inelastic with respect to penalty min. Moreover, salary is unresponsive, in the statistical sense, to penalty min for all other types of players.

League Histories and Characteristics

The National Hockey League is the most prominent professional hockey league in the world, attracting players from a variety of countries from northern and eastern Europe as well as from Canada and the USA. The NHL was founded in 1917, replacing its failing predecessor the National Hockey Association, with clubs from Montreal, Quebec, Ottawa, and Toronto, and expanded into the USA in 1924 with the introduction of the Boston Bruins. The league now is composed of 30 teams, 6 from Canada and 24 from the USA. The NHL has expanded west and south, like the other major North American professional sports leagues, away from its cold weather roots. It now boasts teams in Florida, Texas, Arizona, and California.

The German Hockey League, called DEL (Deutsche Eishockey Liga), had its inaugural season in 1995 as the replacement for the Hockey Bundesliga. It has alternated between an open and closed league system, as the number of league members and the rules concerning promotion and relegation were changed many times. The number of teams never remained constant for more than five consecutive seasons ranging between 14 and 18 from the league's foundation until today. This variation in the size of the league is explained by the fact that the number of teams who got relegated ranged between zero and three. Teams were relegated either for reasons of bad sporting performance or financial problems. The number of teams participating in the playoffs also varied between 8 and 16 teams. For the analysis, we included data for the seasons 2004/2005 to 2009/2010, the only seasons for which the data was available. During this time period, the number of teams and games per team remained constant at 14 and 52, respectively. For the 2006/2007 season, the league changed the playoff format, as it previously incorporated the best eight teams of the regular season. This number was reduced to the six best teams being directly qualified and four teams playing a playoff qualification round.

The SM-liiga is the top professional hockey league in Finland and was constituted in 1975. It started with 10 teams and 36 games, only to increase these numbers to 14 teams and 58 games per season today. Over the seasons from 2001/2002 to 2009/2010, there have been many changes comparable to those in the German DEL. The SM-liiga was a closed league system up until the most recent 2009/2010 season, as the last placed team now faces the champion of the second division, which is called Mestis, in a best of seven playoff series. The Finnish league had a constant number of playoff contenders at eight and introduced a playoff qualification round for the 2003/2004 season. Like in the German DEL, six teams are directly qualified for the playoffs while four teams participate in a playoff qualification round to determine two additional playoff teams.

Germany and Finland are both members of the International Ice Hockey Federation (IIHF) and follow that organization's regulations concerning the dimensions of the ice. The rinks are 200 ft by 98 ft with a distance of 56 ft from each blue line to the nearest goal line. This varies from the rinks in the National Hockey League, especially with respect to width and the distance from the goals to the blue lines. NHL rinks are 200 ft by 85 ft and the distance between the goals and the blue lines is 64 ft making the attacking zone bigger and the neutral zone smaller than in Germany and Finland. The narrower rinks and larger attacking areas lead to a faster and more aggressive style of play in North America compared to European leagues. Despite this difference in style of play, a considerable number of European players succeed in getting contracts in the NHL. During the time period under observation, 7 players born in Germany and 33 players born in Finland played in the NHL.

Data

The data for this analysis was collected from a variety of sources. Unfortunately, data covering the same time period is not available for all the years. Data for the DEL is the most limiting, covering only six seasons from 2004/2005 through 2009/2010. The Finnish sample covers the seasons from 2001/2002 through 2009/2010. Each team is in the Finnish data in every year, but the German data is unbalanced as some teams are not in the data for all six seasons. The NHL data is also an unbalanced panel. Two clubs, Columbus and Minnesota, joined the league for the 2000/2001 season. The NHL data covers seasons before and after the lockout that cost the entire 2004/2005 NHL season.

For each team from each league the data includes team points, goals for, goals allowed, total penalty min, and attendance for each of the seasons. The data also includes population of the city or metropolitan area for each year for the DEL and NHL clubs. Population data for the Finnish cities was limited to only the first year. The age of the arena in which each club plays is also in the data. For the NHL, our data includes the number of fights a team was involved in during each season.

It is necessary to say a bit about the use of penalty min and types of penalties as proxies for the physicality of play and the degree of violence on the ice. Penalty min are likely a reasonable measure of how physical a player is and summed across all players on a given team it is also likely to be a reasonable proxy for that team's aggregate physicality. There has been some dissention on this issue in the literature, however. Some researchers have used fights (Paul 2003); one paper used a first stage regression to determine whether a player is a fighter or not and penalties have been broken down into different categories such as minor, major, and misconduct (Jones et al. 1996), or the focus has been on actions that are "hostile aggression" (McCarthy and Kelly 1978). The research commonly makes use of penalty min, but McCarthy and Kelly (1978) uses the type of infraction.

Table 4.1 NHL descriptive statistics

Variable	Observations	Mean	SD	Minimum	Maximum
Goals for	298	226.185	26.939	164	313
Goals against	298	226.185	29.939	164	313
Penalty min	298	1,168.326	188.263	698	1,968
Points	298	88.893	15.244	39	124
Log of population	250	14.952	0.868	12.44	16.76
Log of arena age	288	2.18	0.881	0	3.74
Log of penalty min	298	7.05	0.161	6.55	7.58
Log of attendance	298	13.437	0.133	12.9	13.72
Attendance	298	691,098	88,967	399,671	912,155
Population	250	4,666,781	4,670,414	804,508	1.90E+07
Arena age	298	12.091	10.419	0	42
Fights	298	44.393	15.736	6	118

However, it is possible that neither penalty min nor the more specific infractions adequately capture the style of physical play the fans want to see. For example, minor penalties such as hooking and high sticking may affect the outcome of the game by giving the opposing team power-play opportunities, but these are not the jarring hits, and fights, that make television highlight shows and were immortalized in the movie *Slap Shot*. Hostile aggressive acts, like slashing and butt-ending, may also not be the action that fans want. In addition, it is possible that the minor penalties lead to hostile aggressive acts, retaliation, escalation, and ultimately to fights, so that including them will not bias the sample (Jones et al. 1993). Jones states it much more eloquently and light heartedly:

> The simplest measure would be total penalty min, but not all penalties indicate physical violence or even physical contact. There are eight broad categories of penalties, some of which do not necessarily indicate physical violence. In addition, within these categories, some of the most severe penalties are for what could be called "non-physical" contact offenses; using obscene gestures ("we're always number 1," misconduct), profane or abusive language (a misconduct), spitting (on officials, other players, coaches or fans, a match penalty), unsportsmanlike conduct (a catch-all for a raft of non-physical offenses, various penalties), and a bench penalty (for example, for "the coach who is standing on the bench voicing oddities about the official's sex life that are not listed in the souvenir program," (Nicol and More (1978), various penalties). All these offenses involve abuse, but they do not represent physical violence per se. However, to the extent that they are frequently the result of, or lead to, physical violence (it is often true that expectoration or profanity are the prologue and/or the epilogue to violence), including them does not unduly bias the measure.

Penalty min increase in step with violence, the more violent the action the more penalty min assigned; this being the case, penalty min seems like a fair measure. Penalties by type are readily available, so we can break penalty min into categories of penalties as well. The difficulty with this is that there is not a perfect correspondence between penalty types in the European leagues and penalty types in the NHL, nor does the severity of punishment correspond perfectly. Nonetheless, we estimate the models with penalties split by types. Tables 4.1–4.3 show the descriptive statistics for the basic data used in the analysis for each league separately.

Table 4.2 Descriptive statistics for Germany

Variable	Observations	Mean	SD	Minimum	Maximum
Goals for	88	163.636	23.478	118	231
Goals against	88	163.636	23.938	120	225
Penalty min	88	1,076.011	152.077	728	1,488
Points	88	80.045	17.634	35	123
Log of population	88	12.841	1.028	10.7	15.04
Log of arena age	88	2.568	1.148	0	4.26
Log of penalty min	88	6.971	0.139	6.59	7.31
Attendance	88	155,467	84,346	45,572	393,700
Population	88	625,740	712,734	44,380	3,404,037
Arena age	88	21.784	18.458	1	71

Table 4.3 Descriptive statistics for Finland

Variable	Observations	Mean	SD	Minimum	Maximum
Goals for	122	152.35	22.99	100	221
Goals against	122	152.35	27.84	96	237
Penalty min	122	954.94	184.93	636	1,698
Points	122	4.28	0.32	3.3	4.8
Log of population	122	11.89	0.77	10.59	13.28
Log of arena age	122	3.23	0.59	1.1	3.81
Log of penalty min	122	6.84	0.19	6.46	7.44
Attendance	122	5,004	1,651	2,858	9,662
Population	122	198,089	171,885	39,793	583,484
Arena age	122	28.84	11.3	3	45

Analyzing the Data

The question this analysis addresses is the extent to which physical and aggressive actions translate into success, or lack of success, on the ice or at the turnstiles, for teams in the DEL, SM-liiga, and the NHL. The methodological approach is regression analysis, with the panel data structure allowing the use of fixed effects techniques. Success on the ice means season-long playing effectiveness measured by the number of points earned by a team; success at the turnstiles is measured by attendance. In our analysis, points for team i in season t are a function of goals for, goals allowed, and penalty min recorded by that team during that season as well as season and team-specific effects. We chose logs for variables which do not show a normal distribution.

We estimate the following model,

$$\text{success}_{it} = \beta_0 + \beta_1 \text{goals for}_{it} + \beta_2 \text{goals against}_{it} + \beta_3 \text{penalty minutes}_{it} + \sum_k^K \gamma_k \text{season}_{itk} + \varepsilon_{it} \quad \varepsilon_{it} = \mu_i + \omega_{it},$$

where βs and γs are parameters to be estimated, μ are city/club-specific effects, and ω is a random error term that is not correlated with the explanatory variables. Success is measured as: (1) points per team per season; (2) attendance per team per season; and (3) revenue per team per season for the NHL. The model is estimated separately for each league. For the NHL, the model is also estimated replacing penalty min with the number of fights. The null hypothesis is that as penalty min (fights) increase, the team tends to attain fewer points.

When estimating the model with attendance, additional explanatory variables are included, and the model is interpreted as a reduced form of demand for attendance. Lack of consistent availability of income and ticket price data make estimation of structural demands problematic. To account for persistence or habit of attendance (Buraimo and Simmons 2008), we include lagged attendance as a regressor. We also include previous season points to account for persistence in club quality. In addition, age of the stadium and, where possible, population of the city where the club plays its home games are also included in the attendance equations. The expectation is that population and goals for a team are associated with greater attendance and that stadium age and goals allowed are negatively related to attendance.

The connection of penalties or violent play to attendance and revenues is ambiguous. Teams that perform better will draw more fans, and penalties are expected to reduce the number of games won; hence, penalties may have a harmful indirect effect on attendance. At the same time, fans are thought to be interested in and to derive enjoyment from the violent aspects of the game. If this is the case, a violent team may have a direct effect of attracting fans to games. Consequently, penalties and violent play reduce attendance by making the team less successful, but they raise attendance because fans enjoy those aspects of the game. Whether one of these effects dominates or if they cancel each other out is an empirical question. A finding that penalty min or violence has no effect may be evidence of equal but opposite influences or simply that violence and physical play has no effect on attendance.

Points Regressions

Table 4.4 shows for each league the regression results explaining season point totals using goals for and against as well as the natural logarithm of penalty min per game. The evidence is fairly clear from these results that scoring and preventing the other team from scoring are significant determinants of season success. It is, perhaps, interesting that scoring has a larger effect on points than does keeping the other team from scoring in the NHL and the SM-liiga.

Of more interest for our purposes is the effect of penalty min on points. More penalty min per game, and more fights, clearly reduce the points earned by a team in the NHL. This result is intuitive, as penalties generally alter the relative playing strength of the teams, making it both harder to score and to defend for the penalized team. In neither the German nor the Finnish league do penalty min affect season point totals. One possible reason for penalties being less important or even unimportant to

Table 4.4 Points regression

Variables	(1) NHL	(2) NHL	(3) DEL	(4) SM-liiga
Goals for	0.3826***	0.3773***	0.3982***	0.4285***
	(0.0000)	(0.0000)	(0.0000)	(0.0000)
Goals against	–0.2598***	–0.2646***	–0.4664***	–0.3697***
	(0.0000)	(0.0000)	(0.0000)	(0.0000)
Log of penalty min	–10.7849***		5.6687	–6.5676
	(0.0007)		(0.3807)	(0.2196)
Log of fights per game		–3.4996**		
		(0.0173)		
Constant	86.6907***	58.0372***	71.2026***	67.0937***
	(0.0000)	(0.0000)	(0.0015)	(0.0001)
Observations	298	298	88	122
R^2	0.7663	0.7609	0.7863	0.9086
Number of teams	30	30	16	14

p-Values are given in parentheses
$^{***}p<0.01$; $^{**}p<0.05$; $^{*}p<0.1$

Table 4.5 Goals against regression

Variables	(1) NHL	(2) NHL	(3) DEL	(4) SM-liiga
Log of penalty min	32.1545***		11.1462	32.3994
	(0.0045)		(0.4655)	(0.1036)
Log of fights per game		12.7893**		
		(0.0151)		
Constant	140.8313***	234.8012***	118.3921**	64.5077
	(0.0000)	(0.0000)	(0.0129)	(0.2445)
Observations	298	298	88	122
R^2	0.1683	0.1613	0.45	0.0659
Number of teams	30	30	16	14

p-Values are given in parentheses
$^{***}p<0.01$; $^{**}p<0.05$; $^{*}p<0.1$

game outcomes in the DEL and SM-liiga is the difference in rink size. As noted above, the Europeans play on a wider rink making for more spacing for the players, even when teams are at full strength, compared to the NHL; removing a defensive player from the ice has a smaller marginal impact on the ability to "get open," and hence to score, on the larger ice of the DEL and SM-liiga than on the smaller rinks of the NHL. Support for this explanation comes from evidence on goals allowed as a function of penalty min per game reported in Table 4.5. In the NHL, goals allowed rises with penalty min per game and is statistically significant with a *p*-value of 0.005. For neither the DEL nor the SM-liiga is there a significant relationship between penalty min per game and goals allowed.

The evidence here is that violence, in the form of penalty min, has no beneficial effect on a team's season-long success, whether in the DEL, the SM-liiga, or the NHL. Moreover, the most blatant form of violence, actual fights between players,

Table 4.6 Points regression with penalty types

	(1)	(2)	(3)
Variables	NHL	DEL	SM-liiga
Goals for	0.3835***	0.3432***	0.4217***
	(0.0000)	(0.0001)	(0.0000)
Goals against	−0.2552***	−0.5244***	−0.3662***
	(0.0000)	(0.0000)	(0.0000)
Log of minor	−11.6780**	30.9783	−5.6848
	(0.0177)	(0.161)	(0.6063)
Log of major	−2.5519	1.5236	−4.4069
	(0.1358)	(0.8895)	(0.1586)
Log of misc	0.1417	−8.1322	−0.4074
	(0.8424)	(0.1877)	(0.7895)
Constant	74.0428***	36.5027	54.1439***
	(0.0000)	(0.4876)	(0.0091)
Observations	291	42	117
R^2	0.7667	0.8065	0.9119
Number of teams	30	16	14

p-Values are given in parentheses
***$p<0.01$; **$p<0.05$; *$p<0.1$

exerts statistically significant negative pressure on team success on the ice. Of course, it may be that fans are drawn to the violent contests, with attendance increasing with the more violent play.

Table 4.6 reports results of regressions explaining points earned during the season when the log of penalty min is replaced by the log of minor penalties, log of major penalties, and log of misconduct penalties for the NHL, and by log of 2, 5, 10, and 20 min penalties in the DEL and SM-liiga. We have labeled the 2, 5, and 10 as minor, major, and misconduct penalties, respectively, though there are differences between the NHL and international infractions. We note that the regressions for the DEL and the SM-liiga include the 20 minutes penalties, but the NHL regressions do not include game misconduct or match penalties. Inclusion of the later costs a large number of observations in the log penalty specifications because there are so many zeros in the variables.

The evidence is clear that minor penalties matter for points earned in the NHL but that is the only type of penalty that affects points in any league. The estimates for goals for and goals against are very similar to those from Table 4.4 when penalty min are aggregated across the types of penalties. One possible explanation for the lack of significance of major and misconduct penalties is that they are both relatively rare and often assessed on players from both teams at the same time.

Attendance Regressions

Table 4.7 reports results of attendance regressions for each of the three leagues. Each model includes controls for arena age, goals for and allowed, and, when possible,

Table 4.7 Log attendance regression

Variables	(1) NHL	(2) DEL	(3) SM-liiga
Goals for	0.0017***	0.0013	0.0015***
	(0.0000)	(0.3010)	(0.0000)
Goals against	–0.0002	–0.0034**	–0.0018***
	(0.4380)	(0.0250)	(0.0000)
Log of penalty min	–0.0853**	0.2107	0.0347
	(0.0310)	(0.2610)	(0.5130)
Log of arena age	–0.0260**	–0.0778***	–0.1309**
	(0.0190)	(0.0080)	(0.0240)
Log of population	0.0076	–0.9920***	
	(0.6500)	(0.0000)	
Constant	13.2354***	24.4313***	12.1470***
	(0.0000)	(0.0000)	(0.0000)
Observations	243	88	122
R^2	0.298	0.459	0.568
Number of teams	30	16	14

p-Values are given in parentheses
***p<0.01; **p<0.05; *p<0.1

population. In every regression, the arena age variable is negative statistically significant at conventional levels. In other words, whether in the USA and Canada or in Germany and Finland, clubs with newer facilities draw more fans than clubs in old facilities. NHL and SM-liiga teams that score more goals draw better than teams that score fewer goals, but scoring seems less important in the DEL. Giving up goals always has a negative coefficient, and is statistically significant in the DEL and SM-liiga regressions but it is not significant in the NHL regression. Population is not significant for the NHL clubs, though the coefficient is positive, while population is significant and, unexpectedly, negative in the German DEL model. Population is not available on an annual basis for the Finnish sample.

Penalty min have no significant effect on attendance in either the DEL or the SM-liiga, though the coefficients are positive. Penalty min are significant and negative for the NHL sample. The attendance elasticity with respect to penalty min is about –0.09 meaning a 1% increase in penalty min reduces attendance by about 0.09%. The estimate of the elasticity of attendance with respect to fights is not different from zero. The actual estimates imply reductions of less than 0.03% from 1% more fights. There is, therefore, only weak evidence of a link between violent play and attendance.

Table 4.8 shows results of the attendance equation when lagged attendance and lagged team points are included as regressors. These variables are intended to control for fan loyalty, or "habit" of attendance, and long-term team quality effects on current season attendance. In each case, lagged attendance has a positive and statistically significant impact on current attendance, with a 1% higher attendance in the last season translating into between a quarter of a percent and four tenths of a percent higher attendance this season. The largest effect is for Finland, the smallest

Table 4.8 Log attendance regression with lagged variables

	(1)	(2)	(3)
Variables	NHL	DEL	SM-liiga
Goals for	0.0013***	0.0026**	0.0016***
	(0.0000)	(0.038)	(0.0000)
Goals against	0.0000	−0.0021	−0.0014***
	(0.795)	(0.175)	(0.0000)
Log of penalty min	−0.0157	0.3531*	−0.0078
	(0.666)	(0.064)	(0.890)
Log of arena age	−0.0226**	−0.0431	−0.0538
	(0.030)	(0.267)	(0.444)
Log of population	−0.0041	−0.7749***	
	(0.779)	(0.0000)	
Lagged log of attendance	0.2546***	0.3165***	0.4365***
	(0.0000)	(0.009)	(0.0000)
Lagged season point total	0.0018***	0.0015	−0.0012**
	(0.0000)	(0.399)	(0.016)
Constant	9.7083***	16.9523***	6.9170***
	(0.0000)	(0.0000)	(0.0000)
Observations	227	72	108
R^2	0.486	0.591	0.648
Number of teams	30	16	14

p-Values are given in parentheses
***$p<0.01$; **$p<0.05$; *$p<0.1$

for the NHL. Previous season success, measured by points, is positive and significant in the NHL, positive but not significant in the DEL and negative and significant in the SM-liiga. Goals scored by the team is positive and statistically significant in each league while goals allowed is negative in all three but only significantly so in Finland. Note that the addition of lagged attendance and lagged points made goals for statistically significant in the DEL equation. Similarly, arena age is negative in all three equations but only significant for the NHL. Population is significant and negative in Germany, as in Table 4.7, and negative but insignificant in the NHL.

The addition of the previous season attendance and points has changed the estimates of the effect of penalty min for the DEL and NHL but not for the Finnish league. In the DEL equation, penalty min are now positive and significant, whereas in Table 4.7 the coefficients were negative but insignificant. The coefficient on NHL penalty min is negative but insignificant in Table 4.8, while it was negative and significant in Table 4.7.

The evidence from attendance regressions is mixed and not what one would expect given the literature on violent play in hockey. The results in Tables 4.7 and 4.8 do not focus specifically on violent play, as the explanatory variable of interest is penalty min. The literature has clearly argued that not all penalties in hockey are for violent play, where violent play is aggressive behavior with an intent to injure. This suggests a focus on penalties of specific types, especially those that carry heavier

Table 4.9 Log attendance regression with penalty types

	(1)	(2)	(3)
Variables	NHL	DEL	SM-liiga
Goals for	0.0013***	–0.0005	0.0017***
	(0.0000)	(0.3598)	(0.0001)
Goals against	0.0000	–0.0014	–0.0012***
	(0.9536)	(0.227)	(0.0015)
Log of minor	–0.0086	1.4478*	–0.0912
	(0.8753)	(0.0673)	(0.4299)
Log of major	–0.0327*	0.9223*	0.0064
	(0.0747)	(0.0899)	(0.8321)
Log of misc	0.0102	–0.1458	0.0091
	(0.1778)	(0.1384)	(0.5334)
Log of arena age	–0.0269**	–0.0691*	–0.0517
	(0.012)	(0.0523)	(0.4797)
Log of population	–0.0088	–31.3739	
	(0.5576)	(0.1031)	
Lagged log of attendance	0.2460***	–0.5855	0.4479***
	(0.0001)	(0.1286)	(0.0000)
Lagged season point total	0.0018***	0.0016	–0.0013**
	(0.0000)	(0.136)	(0.0194)
Constant	9.8582***	425.7528	6.8466***
	(0.0000)	(0.1009)	(0.0000)
Observations	220	26	103
R^2	0.4974	0.9993	0.655
Number of teams	30	14	14

p-Values are given in parentheses
***$p<0.01$; **$p<0.05$; *$p<0.1$

punishments. Table 4.9 reports results from a log attendance regression similar to that reported in Table 4.8, replacing penalty min with penalty types.

The evidence from Table 4.9 is consistent with that from the aggregated penalty log attendance equations in Table 4.8. Specifically, the coefficients on goals for and goals against are similar for both the NHL and the SM-liiga as are the role of arena age and lagged attendance and previous season points. Aggregate penalty min per game was not significant, though the coefficient was negative, in the NHL equation in Table 4.8. In Table 4.9, both minor and major penalties carry negative signs, and major penalties are significant at the 10% level. Consequently, for both the NHL and the SM-liiga, putting the focus on the different types of penalties shows no evidence of fans wanting to see more violent actions. Indeed, the only significant coefficient from these leagues carries a negative sign, indicating lower attendance at games played by teams that make more penalties.

For the DEL, the results are the opposite. Both minor and major penalties are associated with increased attendance, and significantly so at the 10% level. Aggregate penalty min per game had been positive and significant for the DEL regression in Table 4.8. However, for the German Ice Hockey League, results are suspect. Goals scored is no longer significant and even has a negative sign; lagged attendance is no

Table 4.10 Log real revenue regression in the NHL

	(1)	(2)
Variables	NHL	NHL
Goals for	0.0017***	0.0018***
	(0.0000)	(0.0000)
Goals against	–0.0004	–0.0003
	(0.2268)	(0.365)
Log of minor		–0.0098
		(0.9245)
Log of major		0.0238
		(0.4521)
Log of misc		0.014
		(0.3052)
Log of penalty min	0.1119*	
	(0.0921)	
Log of arena age	–0.0947***	–0.0897***
	(0.0000)	(0.0001)
Log of population	–0.0123	–0.0146
	(0.6506)	(0.5956)
Lagged log of attendance	0.4785***	0.4978***
	(0.0000)	(0.0000)
Lagged season point total	0.0008	0.0006
	(0.2298)	(0.3313)
Constant	–2.1648	–2.0752
	(0.1304)	(0.1543)
Observations	203	198
R^2	0.6782	0.6926
Number of teams	30	30

p-Values are given in parentheses
$^{***}p<0.01$; $^{**}p<0.05$; $^{*}p<0.1$

longer significant, and log of population has an impossibly large negative effect. Consequently, while it is true that the positive and significant coefficients on log of minor and log of major penalties are consistent with the positive and significant coefficient on log of penalty min per game reported in Table 4.8, we conclude that these results for the DEL are unreliable. This outcome may simply be a small sample-size problem, as the sample drops to 26 observations, because disaggregated penalties are not available for the last three seasons.

NHL Revenue Regression

One last test of the relationship between violence and success can only be conducted for the NHL. In this regression, we explain team revenues as a function of population, goals for, goals allowed, and so on, as well as with penalty min per game. Table 4.10 shows the results for aggregate penalty min and for penalties disaggregated by minor, major, and misconduct. Across the two equations, the nonpenalty variables are quite consistent both in terms of size and statistical significance. The log of penalty min per game is positive and significant at the 10% level, suggesting team revenues rise with the level of aggressive play. On the other hand, none of the individual penalty types carries a significant coefficient, though both major and misconduct penalties do have positive signs. Interestingly, log of fights (regression available from the authors) carries a positive sign with a p-value of about 0.18 when it is used instead of a penalty-min variable.

Conclusion

This study has looked for links between aggressive or violent play in hockey and success either on the ice or at the gate. The evidence is clear that incurring penalties does not increase team points and, as in the NHL, will even reduce them. Fights between players in the NHL are also linked to reduced performance in terms of team points earned. Considering attendance, the evidence is also clear that fans do not seem to turn out in larger numbers to see highly penalized teams in either the NHL or the Finnish SM-liiga. There is some evidence, however, that attendance is enhanced by more physical play in the German Ice Hockey League.

The availability of revenue data for the NHL clubs allows for a test of the relationship between physical play and team revenues. Here, there is weak evidence that more penalized teams earn greater revenues. This is somewhat at odds with the attendance results that indicate either no relationship or a negative relationship between attendance and penalties. However, disaggregating the penalties, none of the individual penalty variables is found significant.

Stewart et al. (1992) suggest that hockey clubs choose the level of violence to maximize profits. In their model, added violence reduces the team success on the ice, as we found here, but compensates by attracting more fans and greater revenues, something we found only meager evidence to support. It may be that pooling the data from the NHL from before and after the lockout season of 2005 masks the effects. After the lockout, it was clearly a goal of the NHL to open up the game and reduce the physical defense that hindered scoring. Coates and Grillo (2009) found some evidence that at least temporarily there were fewer penalties and more scoring. But that explanation does not work for either the DEL or SM-liiga. Moreover, we have the unexpected result that more penalties may produce greater attendance in Germany. This may in fact be support for the Stewart et al. (1992) hypothesis as we found no harm from penalties on either team points earned nor on goals allowed in either Germany or Finland.

References

Bernstein R (2006) The Code: The Unwritten Rules of Fighting and Retaliation in the NHL. Triumph Books: Chicago, IL.

Buraimo B, Simmons R (2008) Competitive Balance and Attendance in Major League Baseball: An Empirical Test of the Uncertainty of Outcome Hypothesis. International Journal of Sport Finance 8:146–155.

Burnside S (2005) Rule Changes Geared Toward Entertainment. ESPN.com, updated July 25. Accessed online: http://www.sports.espn.go.com.

Coates D, Grillo A (2009) Does Crime Pay? Evidence from the NHL. Unpublished manuscript.

Fitzpatrick J (2004) League and Players Spar Over the NHL Financial Mess. About.com, posted February 13. Accessed online: http://www.proicehockey.about.com.

Gee CJ, Leith LM (2007) Aggressive Behavior in Professional Ice Hockey: A Cross-Cultural Comparison of North American and European-Born NHL Players. Psychology of Sport and Exercise 8(4):567–583.

Jones JCH, Ferguson DG (1988) Location and Survival in the National Hockey League. Journal of Industrial Economics 36(4):443–457.

Jones JCH, Ferguson DG, Stewart KG (1993) Blood Sports and Cherry Pie: Some Economics of Violence in the National Hockey League. American Journal of Economics and Sociology 52(1):63–78.

Jones JCH, Nadeau S, Walsh WD (1997) The Wages of Sin: Employment and Salary Effects of Violence. Atlantic Economic Journal 25(2):191–206.

Jones, JCH, Stewart KG, Sunderman R (1996) From the Arena Into the Streets: Hockey Violence, Economic Incentives, and Public Policy. American Journal of Economics and Sociology 55(2):231–243.

Jones JCH, Walsh WD (1988) Salary Determination in the National Hockey League: The Effects of Skills, Franchise Characteristics, and Discrimination. Industrial and Labor Relations Review 41(4):592–604.

Macintosh D, Greenhorn D (1993) Hockey Diplomacy and Canadian Foreign Policy. Journal of Canadian Studies 28(2):6–112.

McCarthy JF, Kelly BR (1978) Aggressive Behavior and its Effect on Performance over Time in Ice Hockey Athletes: An Archival Study. International Journal of Sport Psychology 9:90–96.

McCaw ST, Walker JD (1999). Winning the Stanley Cup Final Series is Related to Incurring Fewer Penalties for Violent Behavior. Texas Medicine 95(4):66–69.

McGuire EJ, Courneya KS, Widmeyer WN, Carron AV (1992) Aggression as a Potential Mediator of the Home Advantage in Professional Ice Hockey. Journal of Sport and Exercise Psychology 14:148–158.

NHL (2005) NHL Enacts Rule Changes, Creates Competition Committee. NHL.com, posted July 22. Accessed online: http://www.nhl.com.

NHL (2007) National Hockey League Official Rules 2007–2008. Triumph Books: Chicago, IL.

Nicol E, More D (1978). The Joy of Hockey. Hurtig Publishers: Edmonton, AB.

Paul RJ (2003) Variations in NHL Attendance: The Impact of Violence, Scoring, and Regional Rivalries. American Journal of Economics and Sociology 62(2):345–364.

Stewart KG, Ferguson DG, Jones JCH (1992) On Violence in Professional Team Sport as the Endogenous Result of Profit Maximization. Atlantic Economic Journal 20(4):55–64.

Widmeyer WN, Birch JS (1984) Aggression in Professional Ice Hockey: A Strategy for Success or a Reaction to Failure? Journal of Psychology 117(1):77–84.

Chapter 5
Crime and Punishment in the National Basketball Association

David J. Berri and Ryan M. Rodenberg

Abstract This chapter investigates the overlap between National Basketball Association (NBA) referees, the league's on-court rule enforcers, and the impact of player violence and aggression on individual salary, team wins, and team revenue. The authors' meta-analysis highlights emerging research on the role of referees in regulating the sport and describes systematic referee bias in connection with race, league profits, and social pressure in the literature. More narrowly, and in contrast to several high-profile media reports, the authors unearth little to no evidence of NBA referees being biased against specific players, coaches, or team owners. With personal fouls as a proxy for player-level aggression, the analysis finds that players who commit more fouls earn lower salaries and hurt their respective team's chances of winning. Using the high-profile example of Shaquille O'Neal, the authors also demonstrate how O'Neal's inability to make free throws had a detrimental impact on how many wins he helped produce for his team and a negative effect on his team's revenue. Such results reveal the overlapping tension between the NBA's player discipline protocol, efforts toward referee consistency, and certain marketing and public relation goals the league may have.

Introduction

My major concern about it is that it's wrong.

David Stern (AP 2007a)

"It" was an academic paper by Joe Price and Justin Wolfers that investigated racial bias among NBA referees and was featured in a front page *New York Times* story (Schwarz 2007). The reaction to the Price–Wolfers research was neither fleeting

D.J. Berri (✉)
Southern Utah University, Cedar City, UT, USA
e-mail: berri@suu.edu

R.T. Jewell (ed.), *Violence and Aggression in Sporting Contests: Economics, History and Policy*, Sports Economics, Management and Policy 4,
DOI 10.1007/978-1-4419-6630-8_5, © Springer Science+Business Media, LLC 2011

nor muted. Commissioner Stern elaborated: "We think our cut at the data is more powerful, more robust, and demonstrates that there is no bias" (Schwarz 2007). NBA President Joel Litvin said the *New York Times* article "is based upon a paper that is flat-out wrong in its conclusions" (Sheridan 2007). Hollinger (2007) summed up the NBA's response to the Price–Wolfers research:

> Predictably, the NBA has launched a PR offensive defending its officials' work and saying its own study, which looked at individual refs who made a call rather than the results of a three-man crew, showed no bias by the officials.

In addition to the NBA's response and internal counter-study, criticism of the Price–Wolfers research similarly rained down from others. NBA player Chris Duhon said "I don't think there's any prejudice or racial stereotype" (AP 2007b). LeBron James simply said "It's stupid" (AP 2007b). Noted journalists wrote in similar tones. Bob Ryan of the *Boston Globe* described the study as "offline" and a "needless distraction" (Ryan 2007). *Houston Chronicle* columnist Jonathan Feigen posited that "it is easy to see that the study was full of holes and so lacking in perspective that it seemed as if the analysis was done by two accountants who had no idea what they were talking about" (Feigen 2007). David Aldridge of the *Philadelphia Inquirer* opined that the study "has many gray areas" (Aldridge 2007). The NBA's own statistical consultant and an academic economist also interjected. Fluhr (2007) stated: "The conclusions drawn in the Price/Wolfers paper…are based on flawed statistics and logic." Zimbalist (2007) concurred: "Wolfers/Price not only use an incomplete database, but they provide insufficient justification for the modeling they present."

Price and Wolfers were not without defenders, however. Over a year after the *New York Times* story featuring the Price–Wolfers research ran, while the NBA was dealing with the gambling scandal involving ex-referee Tim Donaghy, Henry Abbott of ESPN summarized the fallout:

> Much like during this referee scandal, the NBA conducted an internal investigation, and then pronounced the matter settled in their favor without taking the step of letting the public see what the people in the league office know. The only problem was that the NBA was evidently not working with the best facts available, and in the final analysis was almost certainly wrong all along. That notion is supported by countless economists who have vouched for Wolfers' work, and even, apparently, the NBA's own secretive internal study, which was eventually handed over to Wolfers and media outlets" (Abbott 2008).

One such economist was the University of Chicago's Thomas Miles. Miles analyzed the Price–Wolfers research vis-à-vis the NBA's own study and concluded:

> I believe [Price and Wolfers have] the better points. [Their] study focused on the interactions of the race of the referee and the race of the player. The NBA was more concerned with the number of fouls called on black players and comparisons with the number of fouls called on white players. It is remarkable how [Price and Wolfers were] able to use the NBA's own data set and show that it supported what [they] said at the beginning (Munson 2007).

There was also some early treatment of the NBA's counter-study. Bialik (2007b) questioned the NBA's research on the basis that it: (1) confirmed Price and Wolfers in the context of one narrow subset of players and (2) omitted players who were not called for any fouls. Regarding the former point, Bialik (2007a) quoted University of California-Irvine professor Hal Stern as saying that the NBA's study "can't be said to disprove the Price–Wolfers analysis." Pertaining to the latter issue, Columbia University professor Andrew Gelman described the NBA's study as "suspect" given its omission of players with no fouls (Bialik 2007a).

After being vetted at a number of academic conferences and undergoing peer review, the paper was published in the *Quarterly Journal of Economics* (Price and Wolfers 2010). Following publication, Abbott (2010), in relevant part, reflected:

> When the *New York Times* published the preliminary results of research about referees and race…the top brass at the NBA were livid. Stern and others at the NBA lashed out in spectacular fashion. Three years later, emotions have mellowed. The NBA's position, meanwhile, is looking weaker than ever. The NBA created a credibility contest, and lost.

The visceral response to the Price–Wolfers research, more so than any other in recent memory, highlighted the sometimes tenuous relationship between independent academic research and league policy/public relations objectives. The same tension is revealed in the competing, and occasionally mutually exclusive, goals of the NBA front office. The league looks to maximize profit while also maintaining a socially acceptable level of on-court violence and aggression. More specifically, the entire episode provides an insightful look into how the league's referees regulate the game and an anecdotal example of how rules are enforced and punishment is meted out. Detecting referee-specific bias, like the analysis of the optimal levels of violence and aggression in sporting contests, is an empirical challenge (Persico 2009). In the remainder of this chapter, we address both topics, answering the following questions: (1) If NBA referees are biased, how is such bias manifested? (2) Does aggressive play and on-court violence, as measured by personal fouls, contribute to player salary, team wins, and league revenue?

Are NBA Referees Biased?

NBA referees are regulators. Basketball officials are responsible for enforcing the game's rules. On-court crime and punishment is specifically within the referees' jurisdiction. Alker et al. (1973) posit that consistent referees are superior referees. Bias, whether overt or subliminal, would almost certainly cause inconsistent officiating. All current NBA referees are employed by the league and are members of the National Basketball Referees Association (NBRA), a government-recognized labor union. The NBA–NBRA collective bargaining agreement grants the commissioner broad powers to direct the action of his employee referees. More generally, the commissioner has near-plenary power in connection with player discipline for both on-court and off-court conduct that is detrimental or prejudicial to the league (Kim and Parlow 2009; Showalter 2007; Bard and Kurlantzick 2002).

The NBA has, at times, outwardly directed or subtly nudged its referees. In 2006, the NBA enacted a "Respect for the Game" rule aimed at reducing excessive levels of complaining by players through the imposition of more technical fouls by the referees. Enforcement of the rule was relaxed from 2007 to 2010 likely due to the lingering referee gambling scandal. However, the rule was renewed for the 2010–2011 season (Zillgitt 2010). Such league-generated directives toward its referees are consistent with broader mandates unrelated to on-court officials. Examples include the NBA's rookie wage scale, player dress code, age eligibility rule, and attempted genetic testing of players, all examples that have, according to McCann (2006), "usurped player autonomy" (p. 821).

Given that egregious violent behavior during sporting contests has occasionally resulted in criminal prosecutions (Standen 2009), the NBA certainly has a vested interest in using its referees in such a way to maintain order and prevent injury. The credibility of the league's product is also at stake. For example, Russia's top-tier basketball league disbanded in 2010 after governing body representatives were recorded instructing referees to fix the outcome of the country's championships (Schwirtz 2010). Outright game-fixing by referees, whether ordered by the league or not, would, undoubtedly, adversely impact the game's competitive purity, uncertainty of outcome, and fairness of on-court punishment. Less certain is the impact of referee bias, or even the perception of any such bias, on the integrity of the sporting contest. In the subsections that follow, we provide an overview of rapidly emerging research analyzing referee-level bias and explain how such findings may impact aggressive play.

A number of papers have investigated across-the-board bias by basketball referees. The primary finding of Price and Wolfers (2010) is easily summarized: "[M]ore personal fouls are awarded against players when they are officiated by an opposite-race officiating crew than when they are officiated by an own-race refereeing crew" (p. 1859). The authors conclude that such biases are large enough to affect game outcomes. The Price–Wolfers NBA referee research line spawned two spin-off papers. In the first, the authors determine that a profitable gambling strategy could have been employed by exploiting own-race referee bias (Larson et al. 2008). In the other sequel, the authors, in the course of reconciling their own results with those in the NBA's counter-study, explain that the NBA's own data, albeit in a limited way, support their original findings (Price and Wolfers 2011).

Other researchers with their analytical lens pointed toward basketball referees have made similar findings consistent with bias on the part of officials. Thu et al. (2002) found evidence that college basketball referees call more fouls on teams that are leading, but such "close bias" disappears when games are not televised nationally. Anderson and Pierce (2009) pinpointed the same "close bias" in the college ranks, which the authors find incentivizes teams to play more aggressively, causing the level of physicality to increase. Moskowitz and Wertheim (2011) found basketball officials, as well as referees in other sports, to suffer from omission bias (so-called "whistle swallowing") in noncalls. Lehman and Reifman (1987) determined NBA referees to be influenced by crowd reactions when calling fouls on star players but not nonstars.

Price et al. (2011) focused on "profitable biases" among NBA referees that could help boost league ticket sales, television-related revenue, and consumer demand. By measuring "discretionary" turnovers such as traveling and offensive fouls with "nondiscretionary" turnovers such as steals or out-of-bounds calls, the authors found that referees favor teams: (1) playing at home; (2) behind in a game; and (3) trailing in a playoff series. Price et al.'s evidence of lengthier playoff series is consistent with the analogous results of Zimmer and Kuethe (2009) and Hassett (2008).

As a result of the NBA referee gambling scandal (Donaghy 2009; Griffin 2011), the NBA commissioned an investigation of its own officials (Pedowitz 2008). The resulting Pedowitz Report made three bias-related findings. First, it acknowledged that the integrity of the game is threatened by referee bias (p. 57). Second, the report revealed that a non-*de minimis* number of team representatives believe bias sometimes influences referee calls (p. 56). Third, it confirmed that the NBA is taking action to "help identify patterns consistent with referee bias for/against certain players or teams" (p. 114). Nevertheless, even after the Pedowitz Report's release, the perception of referee bias remained (Aldridge 2009; Adande 2008; Stein 2008).

Macrolevel referee bias has also been identified outside of basketball. In soccer (or football as it is generally know outside of North America), both crowd noise (Nevill et al. 2002) and social pressure (Garicano et al. 2005; Dohmen 2008) have been found to impact referee decision-making. Like Price and Wolfers (2010), Parsons et al. (2011) found evidence of racial bias by baseball umpires, although such bias dissipated in games featuring a technologically advanced monitoring system. A home-ice advantage was pinpointed in hockey (Brimberg and Hurley 2009). Judges in Olympic diving (Emerson et al. 2009) and gymnastics (Morgan and Rotthoff 2010) were also found to be biased. Finally, nationalistic bias has been found in rugby (Page and Page 2010) and figure skating (Zitzewitz 2006; Fenwick and Chatterjee 1981).

A number of papers have looked at the issue of referee bias with a narrower focus. Shmanske (2008) analyzed over 1,000 NBA games during the 2007–2008 season and found no evidence of referee-related corruption with regard to game outcomes or point spread gambling. However, he did isolate one referee (Dick Bavetta) who significantly favored the home team on the basis of scoring, free throws awarded, foul calling, and game ejections (p. 133). Rodenberg and Lim (2009) did not find any systematic bias by specific referees against Dallas Mavericks owner Mark Cuban when looking at 654 regular season and playoff games over the course of seven seasons, although trace evidence was pinpointed in a smaller sub-sample of the team's playoff games. Similarly, Rodenberg (2011) did not find any bias on the part of two officials (Derrick Stafford and Steve Javie) involved in high-profile altercations with Miami Heat coach and general manager Pat Riley. Finally, Winston (2009) analyzed the interaction between long-time NBA referee Joey Crawford and Tim Duncan of the San Antonio Spurs and found Crawford to have no significant adverse effect on the performance of the Spurs. Such an inquiry was ripe following an on-court dispute between the two that resulted in Crawford's multimonth suspension by Commissioner Stern.

Are NBA referees biased? It depends on how one defines "biased." Specifically, it depends on the type and scope of bias being investigated. A number of research papers have pinpointed various macrolevel biases that are subconscious or unconscious in nature. Such findings, rooted in implicit associations and social cognition

(Bertrand et al. 2005), seem to be at odds with NBA President Joel Litvin, who opined: "I do believe, and I think it is the case, that [NBA referees] are, in fact, immune to the things that you and I would say are just human nature" (Bachman 2009). In contrast, research investigating referee bias at the narrower owner/coach/player level has not revealed any bias of a systematic nature that coincides with several high-profile anecdotal examples of alleged nefarious conduct by referees.

How Does Aggressive Play Contribute to Outcomes?

The discussion of referee bias suggests that personal fouls are "important." Such a suggestion leads us to ask how personal fouls impact player salary, as well as team revenue and team wins. The factors that determine an NBA player's salary have been investigated for more than two decades. See Berri (2006) for a review of the literature. A recent investigation was offered by Berri et al. (2007), a model later updated by Berri and Schmidt (2010). Their results reveal that an NBA's free agent salary is driven by points scored, points-per-shot (i.e., shooting efficiency from the field), rebounds, blocked shots, assists, and personal fouls. As Berri and Schmidt (2010) report, free agent salaries are most responsive to total points scored. In addition to scoring, we see players are paid for increases in shooting efficiency from the field, rebounds, blocked shots, and assists. Free throw percentage, steals, and turnovers were not found to impact a player's salary. Beyond these factors, personal fouls also matter. Players who commit more fouls will see their salaries fall. Part of this is due to the nature of the game. Once a player commits six fouls in a game, he is removed from the contest. So, additional fouls can impact how much time a player can see on the court.

The issue of playing time, though, is not the only concern. Personal fouls also impact the efficiency of a team's scoring. To understand this point, we need to consider the impact of shooting efficiency on wins. Berri (2008) details how the statistics tracked for NBA players' impact on team wins. This work reveals the following marginal impact for the statistics tracked specifically for scoring: a point scored = 0.033 wins; a field goal attempt = –0.034 wins; and a free throw attempt = –0.015 wins. Given these marginal impacts, a player must achieve the following shooting efficiency marks to break-even: for two-point field goal attempts, 51.5%; for three-point field goal attempts, 34.4%; and for free throw attempts, 46.5%. During the 2009–2010 NBA season, players posted the following averages with respect to shooting efficiency from each place on the floor: two-point field goal attempts, 49.2%; three-point field goal attempts, 35.5%; and free throw attempts, 75.9%. These results indicate that players can generate significant returns at the free throw line in terms of points and ultimately wins. So, players who commit fouls impede their team's ability to produce wins, and correspondingly, the ability to draw fouls and connect at the free throw line is quite valuable in producing wins.

Table 5.1 A sample of the most productive players in NBA history

Player	Career WP48	Best WP48	Career free throw percentage (%)
Magic Johnson	0.429	0.512	84.8
Michael Jordan	0.332	0.486	83.5
Larry Bird	0.366	0.434	88.6
Charles Barkley	0.383	0.458	73.5
David Robinson	0.350	0.444	73.6

Table 5.2 Two views of Shaquille O'Neal

Player	Career WP48	Best WP48	Career free throw percentage (%)
O'Neal (actual FT%)	0.293	0.411	52.7
O'Neal (average FT%)	0.386	0.502	74.9

The Case of Shaquille O'Neal

Shaquille O'Neal ("Shaq") was selected by the Orlando Magic with the first pick in the 1992 NBA draft. Standing 7′1″ and weighing 325 pounds, Shaq is an imposing physical presence. Not only is he big, Shaq is athletically gifted and a player whom less-agile big men clearly had trouble guarding. NBA coaches and players, though, learned there was one aspect of the game where Shaq came up short. Shaq was not very good at hitting free throws. In his first season, he only converted 59.4% of these shots. And rather than improving, Shaq actually became less efficient in each of his first five seasons. In 1996–1997, Shaq only hit on 48.4% of his free throws. Shaq's inability to hit free throws led opponents to adopt a strategy that became known as "Hack-a-Shaq," the use of continued intentional fouling of the player in order to minimize his ability to score. Over his career, Shaq hit 58.2% of his shots from two-point range and only 52.7% of his free throws. Given these percentages, it made sense to force Shaq to score from the charity stripe. And that meant that teams frequently intentionally fouled Shaq.

To illustrate how Shaq's inability to convert free throws impacted his value, consider a sample of the most productive players in the NBA since 1977 based on the "Wins Produced" metric of Berri (2008). An average NBA player will post a Wins Produced per 48 minutes (WP48) mark of 0.100. The five players listed in Table 5.1 posted marks far in excess of the level for an average player across their respective careers, and their career-best marks were obviously even better. Given his ability to impact a game, one might think that Shaquille O'Neal would produce at the same level as these all-time great players. But as the results in Table 5.2 indicate, Shaq's inability to connect at the free throw line left him a bit short in the area of producing wins for his team.

As a player vulnerable to the Hack-a-Shaq strategy, O'Neal offered a career WP48 mark that is not quite as good as the marks offered by our sample of all-time greats.

Table 5.3 Value of Shaquille O'Neal hitting free throws at an average rate

Team	Year	Value of wins	Change in wins	Impact of wins
Orlando	1992–1993	$140,597	3.7	$516,424
Orlando	1993–1994	$130,494	5.4	$702,862
Orlando	1994–1995	$130,420	6.0	$783,198
Orlando	1995–1996	$139,134	4.4	$605,392
LA Lakers	1996–1997	$146,447	4.1	$604,026
LA Lakers	1997–1998	$173,678	4.9	$853,359
LA Lakers	1999–2000	$272,088	6.0	$1,638,760
LA Lakers	2000–2001	$339,407	7.4	$2,528,553
LA Lakers	2001–2002	$326,314	4.5	$1,475,152
LA Lakers	2002–2003	$295,450	3.0	$882,949
LA Lakers	2003–2004	$273,622	5.7	$1,560,746
Miami	2004–2005	$162,631	7.2	$1,164,154
Miami	2005–2006	$197,029	4.3	$844,834
Miami	2006–2007	$247,819	3.1	$775,948
Miami-Phoenix	2007–2008	$478,054	2.7	$1,293,301
		Totals	72.4	$16,229,659

The same story is told for Shaq's career-best mark. However, if we imagine Shaq as an average free throw shooter, his career marks are only surpassed by Magic Johnson. Across Shaq's entire career, he produced 251.1 wins. But had he hit his free throws at an average rate (74.9%), he would have produced 331.3 wins or 80.3 additional victories. If Shaq had converted free throws at the average rate, one would suspect that his ability to draw fouls would decline. Therefore, the estimate of wins offered is likely too high, but it does give an indication of the losses incurred by his below-average free throwing. Although Shaq was clearly a very productive player, his inability to hit free throws consistently was costly to his team in terms of wins.

Further, consider the cost of Shaq's free throw inconsistency on gate revenues. Using data from NBA seasons 1992–1993 to 2007–2008, Price et al. (2010) estimate the effect of wins on gate revenues for each team and each year. Based on these estimates, Table 5.3 predicts the increase in gate revenues for the team that employed Shaquille O'Neal from 1992–2003 to 2007–2008 had he shot the league average free throw percentage. Overall, O'Neal would have generated over $16 million for his employers. The story of Shaquille O'Neal's woes at the free throw line illustrates how personal fouls can substantially impact a team's performance on the court and at the gate.

Why Do Celebrities Misbehave and How Should Coaches Respond?

Shaquille O'Neal's inability to shoot free throws prevented him from producing as many wins for his team as other star players, such as Michael Jordan and Magic Johnson. But, he was still an incredibly productive player, especially in his prime.

In fact, from 1992–1993 to 2005–2006, Shaq's teams won 754 regular season games. Of these wins, 234.3 could be traced to the statistical production of Shaq. In other words, Shaq produced 31.1% of his team's regular season wins during his most productive years.

The dominance of Shaq is not entirely unusual in the NBA. As noted in Berri and Schmidt (2010), most wins in the NBA are produced by a minority of players. In fact, the Pareto Principle – initially observed by Vilfredo Pareto in a discussion of wealth in Italy – appears to apply to the NBA. Pareto argued that 80% of observed outcomes come from 20% of the people involved. Although it is not clear that the Pareto Principle has many applications [see Fox (2009) for details], Berri and Schmidt (2010) report that from 1977–1978 to 2007–2008, 80% of all wins were produced from 22.6% of player season observations. An average NBA team employs about 16 players, so for an average NBA team, about 80% of wins are produced by the team's three most productive players.

The relative scarcity of productive players creates a problem for NBA coaches. Imagine if one of these players does not follow the rules? Can an NBA team afford to discipline these players? Kendall (2008) investigated this issue and found that, after controlling for a variety of factors, the highest paid player on a team was charged with a technical foul about 7% more often than the second highest paid player. Kendall considered a variety of explanations for this increase in misbehavior but ultimately argued that the evidence "suggests a significant role for the lack of substitutability in the production process" (p. 245). Essentially, highly paid players know teams cannot easily replace their talents. Consequently, misbehavior is harder to punish.

Although teams cannot easily punish a player who engages in behavior that earns technical fouls, teams do routinely sit players who get in foul trouble. And this is even true for "star" players. Does this practice make sense? To answer this question, Maymin et al. (2011) utilize play-by-play data from four NBA seasons (2006–2007 to 2009–2010). Via a model designed to explain the probability that a team will win a given game, the authors looked at the impact of removing a player in foul trouble from the game. The results indicate that unless a player is substantially better than his replacement, it makes sense for a coach to remove a player in foul trouble. As the authors argue, foul trouble may lead a player to play tentatively. Consequently, although a player might normally be quite productive, foul trouble reduces his effectiveness.

Concluding Observations

The study of crime and punishment in the NBA encompasses a variety of issues. As we note, crime and punishment in the NBA mirrors that in other sports (Bard and Kurlantzick 2002) and society in general. Greenberg et al. (1985), citing Brickman (1977), concluded that penalties in sports have the aim of restoring equity or serving as a deterrent. Referee bias, even that of the nonvolitional variety, has the potential to disrupt equitable rule enforcement. More so, as Anderson and Pierce (2009) make clear, such uneven rule enforcement may incentivize aggressiveness, causing increased physicality. Similarly, given the NBA's move to proactively reign in excessive violence and aggression on the court, our findings regarding the efficacy of fouling on team wins and the impact of aggressive play on revenue tell a similar story of how the teams' objective of winning games may sometimes be at odds with the league's policy and public relation goals.

When we move from league issues to the level of a team, we see that personal fouls do have a negative impact on player salaries. Similarly, the failure to hit free throws can have a substantial negative impact on team success. Nevertheless, because star players are difficult to replace, disciplining players in the NBA is difficult.

References

Abbott H (2008) Justin Wolfers and the Quality of an NBA Denial. ESPN.com, posted June 12. Accessed online: http://www.espn.go.com.

Abbott H (2010) Study on Referees and Race Still Dogs NBA. ESPN.com, posted December 8. Accessed online: http://www.espn.go.com.

Adande JA (2008) In Official Conduct, Personal Bias Still the Great Unanswered Question. ESPN.com, posted October 3. Accessed online: http://www.espn.go.com.

Aldridge D (2007) NBA Referee Bias Story Has Many Gray Areas. Pantagraph.com, posted May 5. Accessed online: http://www.pantagraph.com/sports.

Aldridge D (2009) The State of Officiating: What's Wrong and How to Fix It. NBA.com, posted June 16. Accessed online: http://www.nba.com.

Alker HA, Straub WF, Leary J (1973) Achieving Consistency: A Study of Basketball Officiating. Journal of Vocational Behavior 3:335–343.

Anderson KJ, Pierce DA (2009) Officiating Bias: The Effect of Foul Differential on Foul Calls in NCAA Basketball. Journal of Sports Sciences 27(7):687–694.

Associated Press (AP) (2007a) Stern Criticizes Study on Refs, Rips New York Times. ESPN.com, posted May 4. Accessed online: http://www.espn.go.com.

Associated Press (AP) (2007b) Players, NBA Dismiss Racial Bias in Officiating. ESPN.com, posted May 4. Accessed online: http://www.espn.go.com.

Bachman R (2009) Researchers' NBA Officiating Study Detects Biases, but Not Necessarily the Ones Fans Suspect. The Oregonian, posted June 3. Accessed online: http://www.people.oregonstate.edu/~stonedan/oregonian.htm.

Bard RL, Kurlantzick L (2002) Knicks-Heat and the Appropriateness of Sanctions in Sport. Cardozo Arts and Entertainment Law Journal 20:507–524.

Berri DJ (2006) Economics and the National Basketball Association: Surveying the Literature at the Tip-off. In Handbook of Sports Economic Research, ed. Fizel J, pp. 21–48. ME Sharpe: Armonk, NY.

Berri DJ (2008) A Simple Measure of Worker Productivity in the National Basketball Association. In The Business of Sport, eds. Humphreys B, Howard D, pp. 1–40. Praeger: Westport, CT.

Berri DJ, Schmidt MB (2010) Stumbling on Wins: Two Economists Explore the Pitfalls on the Road to Victory in Professional Sports. Financial Times Press: Princeton, NJ.

Berri DJ, Brook SL, Schmidt MB (2007) Does One Simply Need to Score to Score? International Journal of Sport Finance 2(4):190–205.

Bertrand M, Chugh D, Mullainathan S (2005) Implicit Discrimination. American Economic Review 95(2):94–98.

Bialik C (2007a) Parsing the NBA's Study on Refs and Race. Wall Street Journal, posted May 14. Accessed online: http://www.blogs.wsj.com.

Bialik, C (2007b). Follow-up on NBA's Study of Race and Refs. Wall Street Journal, posted May 22. Accessed online: http://www.blogs.wsj.com.
Brickman, P (1977) Crime and Punishment in Sports and Society. Journal of Social Issues 33(1):140–164.
Brimberg J, Hurley WJ (2009) Are National Hockey League Referees Markov? Operations Research Insight 22(4):234–243.
Dohmen TJ (2008) The Influence of Social Forces: Evidence from the Behavior of Football Referees. Economic Inquiry 46:411–424.
Donaghy T (2009) Personal Foul. Four Daughters LLC: Sarasota, FL.
Emerson JW, Seltzer M, Lin D (2009) Assessing Judging Bias: An Example from the 2000 Olympic Games. American Statistician 63(2):124–131.
Fenwick I, Chatterjee S (1981) Perception, Preference, and Patriotism: An Exploratory Analysis of the 1980 Winter Olympics. American Statistician 35(3):170–173.
Feigen D (2007) Study Detailing Refs' Racial Bias Goes Way Off Course. Houston Chronicle, posted May 5. Accessed online: http://www.chron.com.
Fluhr H (2007) Superior Data, Analysis Shows No Race Bias among NBA Referees. Sports Business Journal, July 23, p. 44.
Fox J (2009) The Myth of the Rational Market: A History of Risk, Reward, and Delusion on Wall Street. Harper Collins: New York, NY.
Garicano L, Palacios-Huerta I, Prendergast C (2005) Favoritism under Social Pressure. Review of Economics and Statistics 87:208–216.
Greenberg J, Mark MM, Lehman DR (1985) Justice in Sports and Games. Journal of Sport Behavior 8(1):18–33.
Griffin SP (2011) Gaming the Game. Barricade Books: Fort Lee, NJ.
Hassett KA (2008) NBA Home Bias Suggests Referees Committing Fouls. American Enterprise Institute, posted June 23. Accessed online: http://www.aei.org.
Hollinger J (2007) Closer Look at Ref Study. ESPN.com, posted May 9. Accessed online: http://www.espn.go.com.
Kendall TK (2008) Celebrity Misbehavior in the NBA. Journal of Sports Economics 9(3): 231–249.
Kim JY, Parlow MJ (2009) Off-Court Misbehavior: Sports Leagues and Private Punishment. Journal of Criminal Law and Criminology 99(3):573–597.
Larson T, Price J, Wolfers J (2008). Racial Bias in the NBA: Implications in Betting Markets. Journal of Quantitative Analysis in Sports 4(2):Article 7.
Lehman DR, Reifman A (1987) Spectator Influence on Basketball Officiating. Journal of Social Psychology 127:673–675.
Maymin A, Maymin P, Shen E (2011) How Much Trouble is Early Foul Trouble? Strategically Idling Resources in the NBA. Unpublished manuscript.
McCann MA (2006) The Reckless Pursuit of Dominion: A Situational Analysis of the NBA and Diminishing Player Autonomy. Pennsylvania Journal of Labor and Employment Law 8(4): 819–860.
Morgan H, Rotthoff K (2010) Bias in Sequential Order Judging: Primacy, Recency, Sequential bias, and Difficulty bias. Unpublished manuscript.
Moskowitz T, Wertheim LJ (2011) Scorecasting. Crown Books: New York, NY.
Munson L (2007) Even NBA Study Might Confirm Racial Bias in Officiating. ESPN.com, posted May 15. Accessed online: http://www.espn.go.com.
Nevill AM, Balmer NJ, Williams AM (2002) The Influence of Crowd Noise and Experience upon Refereeing Decisions in Football. Psychology of Sport and Exercise 3:261–272.
Page L, Page K (2010) Evidence of Referees' National Favoritism in Rugby. Unpublished manuscript.
Parsons CA, Sulaeman J, Yates MC, Hamermesh DC (2011) Strike Three: Umpires' Demand for Discrimination. American Economic Review, forthcoming.
Pedowitz LB (2008) Report to the Board of Governors of the National Basketball Association. NBA, posted October 1. Accessed online: http://www.nba.com.

Persico N (2009) Racial Profiling? Detecting Bias Using Statistical Evidence. Annual Review of Economics 1:229–253.

Price J, Soebbing B, Berri DJ, Humphreys B (2010) Tournament Incentives, League Policy, and NBA Team Performance Revisited. Journal of Sports Economics 11(2):117–135.

Price J, Remer M, Stone DF (2011) Sub-Perfect Game: Profitable Biases of NBA Referees. Journal of Economics and Management Strategy, forthcoming.

Price J, Wolfers J (2010) Racial Discrimination among NBA Referees. Quarterly Journal of Economics 125(4):1859–1887.

Price J, Wolfers J (2011) Biased Referees? Reconciling Results with the NBA's Analysis. Contemporary Economic Policy, forthcoming.

Rodenberg RM (2011). Perception ≠ Reality: Analyzing Specific Allegations of NBA Referee Bias. Journal of Quantitative Analysis of Sports, forthcoming.

Rodenberg RM, Lim CH (2009) Payback Calls: A Starting Point for Measuring Basketball Referee Bias and Impact on Team Performance. European Sport Management Quarterly 9(4):375–387.

Ryan B (2007) Position on Foul Calls is Offline. Boston Globe, posted May 3. Accessed online: http://www.boston.com.

Sheridan C (2007) NBA: Claims of Racial Officiating Bias 'Flat-Out Wrong.' ESPN.com, posted May 4. Accessed online: http://www.espn.go.com.

Schwarz A (2007) Study of NBA Sees Racial Bias in Calling Fouls. New York Times, posted May 2. Accessed online: http://www.nytimes.com.

Schwirtz M (2010) Hoping to Stir a Revival of Basketball in Russia. New York Times, posted October 10. Accessed online: http://www.nytimes.com.

Shmanske S (2008) Point Spreads and Referee Bias in the NBA. In Threats to Sports and Sports Participation, ed. Rodriguez P, Kesenne S, Garcia J, pp. 115–136. Ediciones de la Universidad de Oviedo: Oviedo, Spain.

Standen J (2009) The Manly Sports: The Problematic Use of Criminal Law to Regulate Sports Violence. Journal of Criminal Law and Criminology 99(3): 619–642.

Stein M (2008) Heft Alone Unlikely to Change Perceptions of Officiating. ESPN.com, posted October 5. Accessed online: http://www.espen.go.com.

Showalter BD (2007) Technical Foul: David Stern's Excessive Use of Rule-Making Authority. Marquette Sports Law Review 18(1):205–223.

Thu KM, Hattman K, Hutchinson V, Lueken S, Davis N, Linboom E (2002) Keeping the Game Close: 'Fair Play' among Men's College Basketball Referees. Human Organization 61(1):1–8.

Winston WL (2009) Mathletics. Princeton University Press: Princeton, NJ.

Zillgitt J (2010) 'Respect for the Game': NBA Wants Players on Best Behavior. USA Today, posted September 24. Accessed online: http://www.usatoday.com.

Zimbalist A (2007) Study's Credibility Suffers in Race to Report NBA Referees' Race Bias. Sports Business Journal, May 21, p. 37.

Zimmer T, Kuethe TH (2009) Testing for Bias and Manipulation in the NBA Playoffs. Journal of Quantitative Analysis of Sports 5(3):Article 4.

Zitzewitz E (2006) Nationalism in Winter Sports Judging and Its Lessons for Organizational Decision Making. Journal of Economics and Management Strategy 15:67–99.

Part III
North American Individual Sports

Chapter 6
The Demand for Aggressive Behavior in American Stock Car Racing

Peter von Allmen and John Solow

Abstract Aggressive driving is an inherent feature of auto racing, and nowhere more so than in NASCAR's Sprint Cup Series. This chapter explores the role that aggressive driving plays in the demand for NASCAR racing in the USA. We examine a set of models that estimate the impact of aggressive driving, including the accidents that often are its result, on the size of the Sprint Cup television audience. Our results indicate that aggressive driving is a very important determinant of fan demand. After controlling for the availability of substitutes, the anticipated speed and closeness of competition, a variety of institutional parameters, and other variables that are likely to affect viewers' choices, we find evidence that the degree of aggressive driving is positively related to the number of people watching Sprint Cup broadcasts in the pre-chase era, and that the effects are both quantitatively large and statistically significant.

Introduction

In his book *Sunday Money*, Jeff MacGregor describes a race at a short track in Bristol, TN. "The race is carnage: yellow flags every few laps, a demolition derby, every car on the track looks like a total-loss salvage from the NYPD impound lot. In other words, best race of the season so far" (pp. 169–170). It is often asserted in popular press that fans like to watch NASCAR (National Association of Stock Car Auto Racing) racing to see the crashes. Yet, to the best of our knowledge, there has been no empirical research published with the specific goal of confirming or dispelling this assertion. The lone exception is Scribbins (2006), who investigated the demand for crashes in NASCAR in an unpublished manuscript.

P. von Allmen (✉)
Skidmore College, Saratoga Springs, NY, USA
e-mail: pvonallm@skidmore.edu

R.T. Jewell (ed.), *Violence and Aggression in Sporting Contests: Economics, History and Policy*, Sports Economics, Management and Policy 4,
DOI 10.1007/978-1-4419-6630-8_6, © Springer Science+Business Media, LLC 2011

This chapter explores the nature of demand for stock car racing in the USA in the premier NASCAR racing series known as the Sprint Cup (previously known as the Winston Cup and Nextel Cup and in its earliest iterations before widespread corporate sponsorship, "Grand National"). Specifically, our goal is to explore the role of aggressive driving in the determination of fan demand as measured by television ratings produced by The Nielsen Company. We control for a variety of institutional parameters of NASCAR (i.e., the rules governing drivers and cars), the characteristics of the tracks on which races are held, the closeness of competition, and the availability of substitutes such as other televised sporting events that conflict with the NASCAR season. Our results indicate that aggressive driving is a very important determinant of fan demand.

Part of the pleasure that fans derive from professional sports is the vicarious pleasure they experience from not only watching, but at the same time thinking "that could be me." If you give a group of young kids who watch the NFL a football and send them out in the yard to play, it won't be long until they have assumed the persona of their favorite player, throwing and catching long passes for game winning touchdowns. Among adults, this phenomenon persists, and for evidence one need look no further than the thousands of fans at a typical game, wearing the jersey of the home team with the name of their favorite player – or perhaps even their own name – sewn across the back. Clearly then, when considering the demand for aggression and violence in any particular sport, we must consider both the nature of the sport itself, the characteristics of the fans that follow it, and the relationship between those fans and the game.

The relationship between the fan and the professional sport is unique in automobile racing for one simple reason: virtually all fans drive cars on a regular basis. While many fans of other sports such as professional football, ice hockey, or boxing may have participated in the sport at some level at one time in their lives, many ardent fans of professional team sports have never played the game at any level. For this reason, the nature of the vicarious pleasure derived from watching a favorite driver execute a daring and highly aggressive maneuver to pass another is very different from fan demand for watching a fight in an ice hockey game. The intrinsic appeal of watching a race is not only the excitement of who wins or loses but may also be the demand for aggressive behavior derived from watching participants drive cars in a way that is at the same time enabled by manufacturers (as evidenced by the ever increasing horsepower and performance of sports car offerings) and frowned upon by authorities (speeding and other driving laws designed to increase safety).

This vicarious link between driver and fan is particularly true in stock car racing in the USA, wherein the cars are (loosely) derived from cars that are available to consumers. Historically, this link was much stronger. Pierce (2010) notes that in the earliest days of racing in the Piedmont region during the 1940s, part of the attraction of this type of racing is that the cars used were ones that anyone could buy at relatively low cost. While over time the need to alter the cars for speed and safety reasons has created an increasing disparity between race cars and stock cars, the association with "stock" cars continues today as the cars used by current teams carry the name of vehicles available at dealerships (e.g., teams that race Fords drive cars that are loosely based on the Ford Fusion).

While the relationship between crashes and fan demand remains largely unexplored, there are a number of authors who have considered the impact of institutional structure on the incentive to drive aggressively, beginning with an empirical paper by Becker and Huselid (1992). Von Allmen (2001) proposed a theoretical model based on the work of Lazear (1989) and Lazear and Rosen (1981) that offered several hypotheses regarding the efficiency of the payoff scheme employed by NASCAR at the time. Subsequent tests of his theoretical predictions found mixed support for hypotheses related to aggressive behavior (Depken and Wilson 2004a; Schwartz et al. 2007). Another branch of the literature on racing explores the impact of changes to institutional regulations such as the use of restrictor plates and other safety regulations on accident rates. O'Roark and Wood (2004) found that the use of restrictor plates at tracks known for very high speeds do increase crash rates but not driver injuries.

Sobel and Nesbit (2007) investigated changes in driver incentives – the incentive to drive more recklessly as cars become safer. To the best of our knowledge, only Berkowitz et al. (2010) have attempted to measure the determinants of fan demand using Nielsen television ratings data. Their focus was primarily on the role of competitiveness in determining demand and the macroeconomic environment and its possible role in the downturn in attendance in the late 2000s. While they did control for the number of caution flags (temporary cessation of racing due to accidents or other track-related problems), the impact of crashes on television ratings in their model is ambiguous.

In addition to prior research specific to automobile racing, Peltzman's famous 1975 paper on "The Effects of Automobile Safety Regulation" provides important context for our work. In this paper, Peltzman argued that the mandatory installation of safety devices in passenger vehicles that resulted from the passage of the National Traffic and Motor Vehicle Safety Act of 1966 did not reduce the highway death rate. He suggests that drivers offset greater vehicle safety with increased risk taking. In support of his claim, he finds that while death rates did not decrease, property damage (and pedestrian injuries) increased. This is relevant for our research because if, as Sobel and Nesbit (2007) find, efforts by NASCAR to increase the safety of cars has allowed drivers to feel more insulated from the fear of fatality, it may cause them to drive more aggressively than they would otherwise. This increased safety may also leave fans feeling less ambivalent about regarding a crash as thrilling.

Table 6.1 shows the number of vehicles exiting NASCAR races due to accident over the course of the season for every year from 2001 to 2009. The data in column two represent the maximum potential miles raced (43 cars times the stated length of the race). The total number of potential miles raced across all cars exceeds six million. The actual miles raced is less, as cars exit the race or fall substantially off the pace such that they do not complete the prescribed number of laps due to accident and mechanical failure. As indicated by the wide variation between the minimum and maximum cars out of a single race in a given year, the number of crashes in any single race varies substantially. In every year at least one race featured no cars lost to accident and at least one race featured double digit car losses. The average number

Table 6.1 Overview of NASCAR accident data 2001–2009

Year	Miles raced	Cars out of race due to accident[a]	Average cars out	Cars out per 1,000 miles	Maximum	Minimum
2001	678,200	142	3.94	0.209	17	0
2002	678,100	129	3.51	0.19	11	0
2003	678,100	163	4.53	0.24	9	0
2004	682,400	137	3.81	0.201	10	0
2005	686,700	154	4.28	0.224	12	0
2006	691,000	118	3.28	0.171	11	0
2007	691,000	128	3.56	0.185	13	0
2008	691,000	101	2.81	0.146	11	0
2009	692,000	93	2.58	0.134	11	0

[a]The actual number of miles raced is lower as not all cars complete the full number of laps
Source: Nascar.com Race schedule pages and authors' calculations based on data therein, at http://www.NASCAR.com

of cars lost per 1,000 miles is just under 0.20. Thus, about one car is damaged beyond being able to continue for every 5,000 miles raced. Note that because the actual miles raced is less than the potential shown in the table, these figures understate the accident rate during races. It is important to note also that the actual number of "accidents" as we might think of such an event in normal highway driving (i.e., including "fender benders") far exceeds that shown in the table. Drivers are routinely involved in relatively minor bumps and scrapes that do not render the car undrivable, and they continue without pause.

In all of these miles and crashes, only a single fatality occurred – Dale Earnhardt in 2001. Dubner and Levitt (2006) make this point while noting that interstate travel averages substantially more fatalities than NASCAR racing. In the years that they considered (the 5 years immediately following Earnhardt's death), there were 5.2 crashes per 1,000 highway miles driven, compared to near zero in NASCAR. Thus, while fans may well expect to see crashes or "violence" at the races, they may also feel that these crashes have little to do with human violence and instead feature only the destruction of the machines. It is routine for drivers to climb out of cars and walk away from even the most horrific of NASCAR crashes. We have no way to know – or to test – how fans would respond to auto racing if serious or fatal injury were more commonplace. We argue only that there may well be a sort of "spectator Peltzman effect" in that fans may enjoy crashes based on the expectation that the violence of a crash is limited to the vehicles.

Racing as Aggressive Behavior

Aggressive driving is the essence of racing. While one could argue that fans watch to see who wins, races in which the outcomes are just as close, and even much closer, could be staged with cars traveling at a maximum speed of 20 miles per hour rather than 200. Such a contest would surely be a television ratings disaster. What makes racing exciting is that drivers push their cars to the absolute limit of control and sometimes beyond in an effort to best their opponents. In our daily commute, we consider a driver who speeds past a slower driver and then cuts in front of him to make a quick turn to be driving aggressively. While such behavior is not uncommon, it is considered undesirable because it is dangerous on public roads. On some roads, authorities even have signs posted on roads with phone number to call to report such behavior. On the race course, we expect drivers to behave in this way as a matter of course.

MacGregor (2005) describes a technique known as "bump 'n' run" "wherein the trailing car gets the right side of its nose up under the left rear quarter panel of the leading car, gives it a little push coming out of the turn, thereby causing it to swerve and slow, at which point the trailing car speeds on by" (pp. 170–171). Later, MacGregor cites as a potential explanation for the sport's appeal, the drivers' willingness to participate in a sport that is extremely dangerous, making them hero figures (p. 227). Interestingly, Pierce (2010) finds both similar behavior and response from fans in early (pre-NASCAR) stock car racing, as "wrecks were common, with drivers using their bumpers to get by slower cars by getting underneath them and pushing them up the track…" (p. 54).

Fan expectations regarding competition at the limits of safety and beyond are inherent in nearly all forms of racing and so are not limited to automobile racing. Consider the tragedy of the fatal luge crash at the 2010 Winter Olympics in Vancouver. The track was made to run so fast that lugers' open questions regarding its safety turned out to be prophetic (Botchford 2010). In a report on the incident and related safety concerns at the games, *Philadelphia Inquirer* columnist Phil Sheridan wrote

> It was inevitable. The other day, Canadian snowboard slalom racer Jasey-Jay Anderson lamented the relative lack of buzz around his sport. 'I guess we're just not there,' he said. 'We want people to kill themselves and break themselves apart to entertain us.' Chilling words, but how can you argue with him now? Risk has always been a vital element in some of these sports of course…Alpine ski racers have the same death-defying cachet about them as stock car racers. Take away the danger, and the sliding sports – luge, bobsledding and skeleton – are just so much sledding. (Sheridan 2010, pp. E1, E6).

Thus, there is no need to establish that fans watch races "just to see the crashes" to support the idea that fan demand for aggressive behavior exists in auto racing. All motor racing is by definition aggressive driving and NASCAR is an extremely popular form of racing. According to Hagstrom (1998), American football is the only sport to surpass the popularity of NASCAR on ESPN. He notes that popularity was particularly strong in the 1990s, as average ratings over the period 1992–1996 were higher than both regular season basketball and baseball (p. 82). Howell (1997) also comments on the growth in popularity of NASCAR during this same period as it moved from the occasional appearance on *Wide World of Sports* to a steady stream of television broadcasts with 120 million viewers in 1995.

That NASCAR has become one of America's top spectator sports is *prima facie* evidence that fans find highly aggressive driving entertaining to watch.

A more compelling question then, is *how much* aggressive behavior will maximize fan interest; that is, do fans prefer races in which behavior is so aggressive that it would be more accurate to say that there is substantive demand for violent behavior? The distinction is important because NASCAR, through rules and regulations, can heavily influence the amount of aggressiveness and violence fans are likely to see during a race and must balance it against the primary need to keep the participants and spectators safe.

There are a number of challenges to modeling the demand for aggression and violence in racing. One problem is subjective nature of the terminology. At the margin, it is a matter of semantics. For example, is there some meaningful difference between "bumping," "nudging," "clipping," and "hitting" another driver during a race? Second, unlike boxing or football wherein the type of aggressiveness and violence that are fundamental to the appeal of the sport are guaranteed to occur in every contest, crashes are probabilistic, unscheduled events. As such, fans do not know how many (if any) crashes they may see during a given race. In our attempt to learn about the forces that drive fan demand, the latter problem is frustrating as it prevents direct testing of alternative hypotheses regarding why races are appealing. We discuss this further in the following section. The former problem is more complex and merits further discussion.

Aggression vs. Violence in Racing

Is racing aggressive or violent if one car intentionally bumps another as they go around the track? One could argue that it depends why one car bumps another (e.g., retribution for a previous incident), or instead that it depends on what happens after the bump. Clear cut cases in which driver behavior that has intent to crash other cars out of the race as its motive are extremely rare, yet not unheard of in racing. In March of 2010, Carl Edwards, who was 156 laps behind the leader at the time, hit the car of Brad Keselowski in an apparent payback for Keselowski hitting him earlier in the race (Spencer 2010). Keselowski's car was sent airborne as a result, crashing into a wall with grandstands immediately behind it. Edwards was not suspended for the incident, though he was placed on probation for three races. In this case, aggression appears to have directly led to a violent outcome and a sanction from NASCAR. Yet still, there is no clear answer here. Do such events increase fan demand, or would fans have been happier to see no crash and a simple pass of Keselowski by Edwards instead?

Consider the following two incidents in which the intent and outcome are completely different. First, suppose Driver A deliberately bumps Driver B as they exit a corner as payback for a previous similar maneuver by Driver B, but the bump does not result in a serious crash. Second, late in a race, the second place car deliberately bumps the first place car from behind as they move down the straightaway in a technique known as "bump drafting" (allowed under the rules) in an effort to move both cars farther ahead of the pack. In the process, the second place driver accidentally bumps the first place driver too hard, causing a violent crash of both cars. In the one case, fans see highly aggressive behavior and no crash. In the other, they see less aggressive behavior and a violent crash.

To provide some clarity for the purposes of this chapter, we define aggression as a behavior exhibited by drivers. Because there is no way to know with certainty the intent of the driver, we do not distinguish between what psychologists call "hostile aggression" which has inflicting pain as a primary goal and "instrumental aggression" in which aggression is a means to another goal (Aronson et al. 2007). We define violence in reference to outcomes. Although aggression may lead to violent outcomes, such outcomes may also occur due to unintended outcomes of mechanical failure or driver error.

Unfortunately, we cannot observe aggressive driving directly. We can, however, observe several outcomes that are likely to result from aggressive driving. One, which we have already discussed, is the number or frequency of crashes. Another is the number of lead changes that occur during a race. Passing another car on the race track typically requires an aggressive move, and this is likely to be more so at the front of the race, where what is at stake is not merely one position but the difference between winning and not winning, and the leader can be expected to act to protect their position. Passing can also occur in the pits, which likely represents a strategic move rather than aggression. Both of these measures, as with the degree of aggressive driving that underlies them, are likely to be endogenously determined, depending on both the costs and benefits of acting aggressively.

Television Demand for Racing

In modeling the demand for racing, we have two choices regarding the type of dependent variable we might employ. We could either base the model on data on live attendance at races or on the size of the television audience. There are significant problems with modeling attendance. Unlike baseball or any other team sport in which cities host teams, there is no such thing as a home or away event. The Sprint Cup consists of 36 races per year with no overlapping dates. Thus, each race attracts all of the top racing teams and so by extension, all fans of Sprint Cup racing. So while it is reasonable to analyze demand for MLB teams by tracking changes in attendance over the course of a season, doing so in the Sprint Cup introduces too many sources of variation that are unique to each location. Transportation, parking, and related nonticket expenditures likely vary substantially from location to location.

More problematic, races are held at over 30 venues, all with different seating capacities, and until recently sellouts were the norm in Sprint Cup racing. For example, Bristol Motor Speedway in Bristol, TN had a run of 55 consecutive sellouts end in 2010, and Richmond International Raceway in Richmond, VA sold out 33 consecutive NASCAR events from 1991 to 2008 (AP 2010). Thus, to say that there were 100,000 fans at one race, and 125,000 fans at the next race is likely to represent a simple announcement of the track's capacity constraint than a measure of demand. While econometric techniques are available to deal with censored observations (e.g., tobit models), they require sufficient numbers of noncensored observations in order to be effective.

As an alternative, we chose to model demand using Nielsen television ratings data. The Nielsen Company employs an electronic monitoring system to measure the number of household members viewing a particular broadcast. Measuring the television audience removes any capacity constraint (though of course one must be able to receive the broadcast to watch games). As Berkowitz et al. (2010) point out, the use of TV viewing data also changes the nature of substitutability. If we were to model attendance, once a fan is physically at a race, s/he has made a choice to consume that good which effectively eliminates all other consumption possibilities for entertainment during the same time period. In the case of television demand, however, fans have zero switching costs to either change to a different channel or turning off the set entirely. The Nielsen Company measures the number of viewers on a minute-by-minute basis, and the reported audience size is the average of those measurements over the length of the broadcast, so that if viewers turn off the television or switch to other programming in the middle of the broadcast, that is reflected in a reduced audience size.

Following other studies of the demand for television audiences in sports (e.g., Buraimo 2008; Buraimo and Simmons 2009; and Forrest et al. 2005, for European football games; Depken and Wilson 2004b, for National Hockey League games), we assume that the aggregate demand is given by a semilogarithmic demand function:

$$\ln(\text{TVAUD}) = f(S, U, O, M, A), \tag{6.1}$$

where TVAUD represents the number of viewers watching a given race, based on Nielsen estimates. The specific audience estimate is the Live Average Audience, Persons 2 years and older, from the National People Meter Panel, which covers approximately 50,000 people in 20,000 homes. These are proprietary data, and we are not at liberty to share them with other researchers. Interested parties can contact The Nielsen Company to inquire about licensing arrangements. S is a measure of the speed that cars are likely to attain; presumably, one of the main reasons to watch auto racing is to see cars going fast. Since the average speed actually achieved over the course of the race depends on the events that take place during the race and is therefore endogenously determined, we measure the anticipated speed of the race by the top speed attained in the qualifying laps that are used to determine the starting order for the actual race (POLE). These laps are run one car at a time, thus removing the influence of other cars, and drivers have a strong incentive to achieve the highest speed possible, since a better position at the start of the race is an important advantage.

U is a measure of the uncertainty of outcome. While it could be argued that every race is equally uncertain in terms of who will win, it is often the case that one driver has established his superiority over the course of the season by establishing a large lead in the series standings. In addition, to the extent that viewers care not only about the uncertainty of outcome of the individual race but also about the uncertainty of outcome of the overall championship, large leads in the season point standings make the latter result less uncertain. We measure closeness of competition at each point in the season by the difference between the point totals for the leader and the fifth place driver in the standings, divided by the number of races remaining until the end of the season (CLOSE5) – and also experiment with similar differences between the leader and the third place driver (CLOSE3), and between the leader and the second place drive (CLOSE2). A smaller value for these variables indicates closer standings and greater uncertainty of outcome.

Another source of outcome uncertainty is the Chase for the Championship, which was introduced in 2004 (and modified in 2007) as a way to ensure uncertainty near the end of the season. For the last ten races of each season, point totals are reset and a new competition is created to determine a champion. As originally implemented in 2004, the ten drivers with the highest point totals plus any other driver within 400 points of the lead after 26 races had their point totals reset, beginning with 5,050 for the top driver and decreasing by 5 point increments to 5,000 for the tenth place driver (NASCAR.com 2004). Under the modification adopted in 2007, the championship field was increased to the top 12 drivers. Each driver is awarded 5,000 points, plus 10 points for each race they won over the course of the first 26 races. Only the drivers with the 12 highest point totals are eligible for the championship (NASCAR.com 2010).

During the Chase period, points are awarded as in the previous 26 races, but given the closeness of the total points for each driver once reset, a high degree of uncertainty about the ultimate champion is created. The Chase system changes incentives to drive aggressively in several ways. First, the institution of this new scoring system places a greater premium on winning races in the period leading up to the Chase. Second, it gives drivers who are near the 12th position (or 10th from 2004 to 2006) leading into the last weeks before the Chase field is set an additional incentive to pass other drivers in order to increase their point totals. Finally, once the Chase group is set, each race essentially has two groups of cars participating: those that are in the Chase and so could win the championship, and those that have already been eliminated from the championship.

Drivers not in the Chase compete for a one million dollar consolation prize for finishing 13th. Drivers in the top 12 have a clear incentive to win or place as high as possible. To the extent that driving aggressively increases one's chances of winning, we expect to see more aggressive driving. In addition, drivers near the 13th position who are not in the Chase have the same type of incentive as they try to win the consolation prize. To capture these effects, we consider the difference in points between the 8th and 12th place cars divided by the number of races remaining until the Chase field is determined (adjusting to 10th and 14th place cars when the Chase field was expanded to 12) to capture the excitement of seeing who becomes eligible for the championship as the season ends (CLOSECH2) and a dummy variable for Chase races (CHASE).

O represents a vector of other viewing alternatives that might serve as substitutes for watching televised NASCAR racing. In principle, practically anything on television could fit into this category, but we focus on other sporting events that might compete for the viewer's attention. Most important among these are National Football League games; since Sprint Cup races are typically held on Sundays, the beginning of the NFL season provides an important substitute for viewers. We use a dummy variable that takes on the value of one if NFL games are being televised on the day of the race, and zero otherwise (NFL). We also consider similar dummy variables for Major League Baseball playoff games (MLB), Professional Golf Association major tournaments (GOLF), horse racing's Triple Crown events (HORSE), the Indianapolis 500 race (INDY), and World Wrestling Entertainment major events (WWE).

M represents a vector of miscellaneous variables that might impact viewer demand. Chief among these is a dummy variable that indicates whether the race is run on a weekday (WEEKDAY). As noted above, NASCAR races are typically run on Sundays, but on some occasions, primarily due to bad weather, races are postponed to the following Monday or even Tuesday. Since races are broadcast during working hours, we would expect that to see a reduction in viewing on these occasions. We also consider a dummy variable that indicates whether the race is being run on a road course rather than the traditional oval racetrack (ROAD), the size of the prize payout (PURSE) because the viewers may prefer to watch when the stakes are higher, and year dummies to capture changes in audience viewing preferences over time. The omitted year is 2001, the first year of our sample, except in models that examine the effect of the Chase, in which case the sample is limited to 2004 through 2009 and the omitted year is 2004.

Finally, of primary importance for this study is *A*, which measures aggressiveness or violence that fans might expect or encounter as they watch the broadcast. As discussed above, there are several potential measures of aggression, including the number of crashes that occur during the race (CRASHES), and the number of lead changes that take place during the race (LEADCHNG). However, we cannot assume that any of these variables is exogenous. Aggressive driving is a choice, and the decision to drive more or less aggressively is likely to depend on the potential costs and benefits of doing so. These, in turn, are likely to depend on such things as what is at stake in a given race in terms of prize money and points standings, how close the racing is in a given race, and a variety of other variables. The existence of such confounding variables that are correlated with both the error term and the aggression variable makes that variable endogenous.

Endogeneity of an explanatory variable calls for the use of a two-stage least squares instrumental variables method to estimate the regression; otherwise the coefficients measuring the estimated effects of the explanatory variables will be biased and inconsistent. Good instruments are correlated with the endogenous explanatory variable but uncorrelated with the error term. While we were able to determine a valid set of instruments for CRASHES, described below, we were not able to do so for LEADCHNG. Thus, we were only able to measure aggressiveness using CRASHES.

Data and Results

Our overall sample consists of 304 of the 324 NASCAR races from 2001 through 2009 in what is currently called the Sprint Cup Series; Nielsen audience data were not available for the remaining 20 races, some of which may not have been televised.

Table 6.2 Summary statistics

Variable	Mean	SD	Minimum	Maximum
TVAUD (thousands)	7,436	2,637	1,711	19,267
CRASHES	3.592	2.815	0	17
LEADCHNG	19.68	9.53	4	64
AVGCRASH	3.673	1.625	0.33	9
CLOSE5	29.38	57.00	0	506
CLOSE3	19.83	41.09	0	402
CLOSE2	13.61	32.10	0	371
CLOSECH2	17.82	37.07	0	287
POLE (mph)	162.05	30.94	92.15	194.69
PURSE (thousand $)	4,630	1,927	2,523	16,378
WEEKDAY	0.039	0.195	0	1
NFL	0.250	0.434	0	1
HORSE	0.020	0.139	0	1
GOLF	0.089	0.285	0	1
MLB	0.089	0.285	0	1
INDY	0.023	0.150	0	1
WWE	0.230	0.422	0	1
ROAD	0.056	0.230	0	1
RESTRICT	0.115	0.320	0	1
COT	0.289	0.454	0	1
LEN (miles)	1.57	0.665	0.526	2.66

Our sample is reduced to 267 observations due to the fact that not all races use qualifying laps to determine starting position; hence the POLE speed variable is not available for some races. Regressions using the point differential between the last cars trying to make the chase field are further limited to 135 observations, since that variable has no values for the actual Chase for the Championship races or for the years before the Chase was instituted. The television audience estimates were obtained from The Nielsen Company, and the remaining data were obtained primarily from the NASCAR Web site (http://www.NASCAR.com) and http://www.racing-reference.info. Summary statistics for the data are shown in Table 6.2.

Table 6.3 presents our results when the number of crashes is used as a measure of aggressive driving. Each column uses a different measure for uncertainty of outcome; each of the first three columns uses a different measure of closeness in the overall standings, while the last column uses both a measure of the closeness of the overall standings and also a measure of the closeness of the competition for the last positions in the Chase for the Championship. In the last column, the sample is thus restricted to races during the Chase era, and also to races leading up to the Chase races themselves. As a result, the year dummies in the first three columns and those in the last column are not comparable. In the first three columns, they represent changes in the audience from 2001 which is reflected in the constant term, while in the last column the constant term reflects 2004 and the year dummies give variations from that base year. We focus first on the results from the overall sample; as discussed

Table 6.3 Regression results using CRASHES

Variable	Model 1	Model 2	Model 3	Model 4
Constant	8.335**	8.332**	8.334**	8.622**
	(0.107)	(0.107)	(0.107)	(0.097)
POLE	0.001	0.001	0.001	0.002**
	(0.001)	(0.001)	(0.001)	(0.001)
CLOSE5	0.0004	–	–	–0.016**
	(0.0004)			(0.002)
CLOSE3	–	0.0005	–	–
		(0.0005)		
CLOSE2	–	–	0.0004	–
			(0.0007)	
CLOSECH2	–	–	–	–0.0014**
				(0.0005)
NFL	–0.213**	–0.213**	–0.204**	–0.116
	(0.045)	(0.045)	(0.044)	(0.170)
WEEKDAY	–0.930**	–0.931**	–0.932**	–0.874**
	(0.087)	(0.087)	(0.087)	(0.071)
ROAD	0.115	0.116	0.117	0.081
	(0.082)	(0.082)	(0.081)	(0.075)
PURSE	0.065**	0.065**	0.065**	0.063**
	(0.010)	(0.010)	(0.010)	(0.007)
CRASHES	0.058**	0.057**	0.057**	0.003
	(0.016)	(0.016)	(0.016)	(0.006)
Y2002	0.089	0.089	0.089	–
	(0.069)	(0.069)	(0.069)	
Y2003	0.011	0.010	0.010	–
	(0.064)	(0.064)	(0.064)	
Y2004	0.030	0.032	0.030	–
	(0.067)	(0.067)	(0.067)	
Y2005	0.023	0.025	0.023	0.060
	(0.067)	(0.067)	(0.067)	(0.049)
Y2006	–0.008	–0.007	–0.008	–0.074
	(0.079)	(0.079)	(0.079)	(0.050)
Y2007	–0.168**	–0.165*	–0.164*	–0.115
	(0.068)	(0.069)	(0.069)	(0.050)
Y2008	–0.120	–0.118	–0.120	–0.160**
	(0.077)	(0.077)	(0.077)	(0.051)
Y2009	–0.192**	–0.189*	–0.192**	–0.196**
	(0.078)	(0.078)	(0.078)	(0.052)
No. of observations	267	267	267	135
R^2	0.462	0.463	0.467	0.819
Durbin test	18.36**	18.25**	17.93**	–
Wu–Hausman test	18.46**	18.34**	17.99**	–
Sargan test	0.749	0.762	0.770	–

Notes:
Models 1–3: two-stage least squares, instruments = LEN and RESTRICT
Model 4: ordinary least squares
Standard errors are given in parentheses; * and ** denote statistical significance at 5% and 1% levels, respectively

below, it appears that the introduction of the Chase for the Championship changed the NASCAR "product" in fundamental ways with important consequences for viewer demand.

Of primary interest are the results on aggressive behavior. CRASHES is endogenous in Models 1–3, as indicated by both the Durbin and Wu–Hausman tests which strongly reject the null hypothesis of exogeneity. Thus, the use of an instrumental variables approach is appropriate. Valid instruments must be both relevant (i.e., correlated with the endogenous variable) and exogenous (i.e., has no direct effect on the dependent variable, but affects the dependent variable only indirectly through its impact on the endogenous variable). Possible instruments include several variables expected to be correlated with the level of aggressive driving: the length of the track (LEN), because shorter tracks are believed to encourage aggressive driving tactics; whether the race is run using restrictor plates that reduce the variance in top speeds (RESTRICT); and whether the race utilizes the Car of Tomorrow (COT). Restrictor plates are utilized at "superspeedways" (Daytona and Talladega). They reduce airflow to the carburetor, slowing the cars to increase safety. As noted earlier, O'Roark and Wood (2004) found that the use of restrictor plates increases crash rates by keeping cars closer together on the track. The Car of Tomorrow design, introduced for part of the 2007 racing season and adopted for the 2008 season and beyond, is intended to be safer and make for closer competition. We tested various combinations of LEN, RESTRICT, and COT to find a set of instruments that meet these criteria using the Sargan test of the null hypothesis that the instruments are exogenous. Using the combination of LEN and RESTRICT as instruments, we could not reject the null hypothesis of exogeneity, but with any combination that included COT we could reject that hypothesis at the 1% significance level. Hence, we use LEN and RESTRICT as our instruments in the 2SLS regressions.

The results indicate that aggressive driving is an important determinant of viewer interest in Sprint Cup racing. In the semilogarithmic specification, the coefficients represent percentage changes in the dependent variable given a change in the level of the independent variable. Thus, each additional crash per race increases the viewing audience by about 6% regardless of specification in the pre-chase era, and all coefficients in the first three specifications are statistically significant. When looking at the overall sample, we were unable to find any evidence that our measures of the uncertainty of outcome increase viewer demand for Sprint Cup racing. We report results using CLOSE5, CLOSE3, and CLOSE2; in each case the effect is small and statistically insignificant, and the coefficients are very similar regardless of which measure of aggressive driving is used. While it is possible that viewers are uninterested in the uncertainty of the outcome of races, it is also possible that NASCAR racing is so inherently uncertain that the point standings are not particularly informative about who is likely to win. Similarly, we do not find any relationship between anticipated speed (POLE) and audience size in the regressions.

As expected, the audience for Sprint Cup racing is much lower if the race has to be run on a weekday, and is also considerably smaller on days when NFL football games are being broadcast. Having an NFL game at the same time as a Sprint Cup race reduces the size of the viewing audience by roughly 20%, and running a race on a weekday, while many potential viewers are at work, reduces the television audience by over 90%. Both of these effects are quantitatively and statistically significant. We experimented with other possible competition for the NASCAR viewers' attention, but found no evidence that PGA Majors, MLB Playoff games, Triple Crown horse races, the Indianapolis 500, or WWE wrestling events are substitutes for Sprint Cup races in the minds of racing fans. There is no statistically significant difference between the audience sizes for races run on oval tracks and races run on road courses, although the point estimates suggest that road races draw roughly 10% more viewers, all else equal. Of course, all else is not equal; road course races are run at considerably slower speeds. Finally, the results indicate that fans prefer to watch races with more prize money at stake; each additional $1 million in PURSE (slightly more than one half of one standard deviation) increases audience size by about 6%.

When we turn to the results that incorporate the effects of the Chase for the Championship, some important differences emerge. Including the closeness of the competition for the remaining spots in the Chase field requires that we limit attention to the races in those seasons in which the Chase was part of the competition (i.e., 2004–2009) and only to those races leading up to the final determination of the Chase field. In this restricted sample, we cannot reject the hypothesis that CRASHES is exogenous (the estimated Wu–Hausman statistic is only 0.421 and not statistically significant), meaning that two-stage least squares is not necessary. Hence, ordinary least squares regression is used to estimate this model; the results are presented as Model 4 in Table 6.3. Of key interest for this study is the relationship between aggressive driving and television viewership. The effect of aggressive driving on the size of the television audience is reduced greatly in this specification; the coefficient on the number of crashes is smaller by almost an order of magnitude and is no longer statistically significant.

Outcome uncertainty, which had a small and statistically insignificant effect in the larger sample, now has a larger and statistically significant impact on the size of the viewing audience. Recall that the measures of outcome uncertainty, both for the standings at the top of the championship competition and for the last places in the Chase field, are given in terms of point differences between the leader and a close competitor divided by the number of races remaining. Thus, smaller values of the uncertainty measures mean tighter competition, so we would expect a negative coefficient if tighter competition leads to larger television audiences. The magnitude of the effect of a smaller standings lead (i.e., a more uncertain final outcome) depends on how close it is to the end of the season or to the Chase field being determined. A 50-point reduction in the overall points differential with 20 races to go in the season (i.e., with ten races to go before the Chase field is set) produces a 4% increase in the viewing audience (i.e., $-50/20 \times -0.016 = 0.04$, where -0.016 is the estimated coefficient on CLOSE5). The same 50 point reduction with only 13 races remaining in the season, which represents a more significant tightening of the competition, gives rise to a 6.1% increase in the viewing audience (i.e., $-50/13 \times -0.016 = 0.061$). Similarly, a 50-point reduction in the gap between the 10th place car and the 12th place car with ten races remaining before the ten-car

Chase field is set leads to a roughly 1% increase in the television audience (i.e., $-50/10 \times -0.0014 = 0.01$, where -0.0014 is the estimated coefficient on CLOSECH2), but the same 50-point reduction with only three races remaining produces a 2% increase in viewing (i.e., $-50/3 \times -0.0014 = 0.02$).

The effect of competition from NFL football telecasts on the size of the NASCAR viewing audience is smaller and no longer statistically significant in the models that incorporate the Chase for the Championship. One should be cautious about making comparisons between the estimates that include the Chase variable and those that cover the entire sample; the latter do not include the last 10 weeks of the NASCAR season, which overlaps with the later part of the NFL season when division and conference championships are being determined and fan interest is particularly high. However, if the intention behind introducing the Chase concept into Sprint Cup racing was to provide a product that would compete better with NFL games for the television viewers' attention, these results suggest that the increased outcome uncertainty has made Sprint Cup racing a more desirable and less substitutable alternative to NFL broadcasts.

The remaining results do not change particularly when attention is focused on Chase era racing. Although the coefficient on pole qualifying speed is statistically significant in Model 4, the effect remains very small. Races that are run on weekdays continue to have viewing audiences that are roughly 90% smaller than those run on weekends, and there is no statistically significant difference between road course and track races. Finally, the estimated effect of an additional million dollars of prize money continues to be about a 6% increase in viewership.

Summary and Concluding Remarks

Aggressive driving is an inherent feature of auto racing, and nowhere more so than in NASCAR's Sprint Cup Series. To the extent that aggressive driving increases fans' demand for attendance and television viewing, NASCAR has an incentive to design a set of rules, choose tracks, and award prizes that encourage this behavior. In this paper, we have examined a set of models that estimate the impact of aggressive driving, including the accidents that often are its result, on the size of the Sprint Cup television audience. After controlling for the availability of substitutes, the anticipated speed and closeness of competition, and other variables that are likely to affect viewers' choices, we find evidence that the degree of aggressive driving is positively related to the number of people watching Sprint Cup broadcasts in the pre-chase era, and that the effects are both quantitatively large and statistically significant.

Whether the degree of aggressiveness is *optimal* from NASCAR's viewpoint is another matter. It seems clear that while NASCAR prefers a high degree of competitiveness and the risk taking that accompanies it, it is greatly concerned about the health and safety of drivers, crew members, and fans at the track, as evidenced by the required use of the HANS system to prevent drivers from head and neck injuries, safety aspects of the Car of Tomorrow design, pit row speed limits, and track features intended to protect fans from flying debris. The principle of risk compensation suggests that additional safety features added to race cars and tracks creates a moral hazard problem, leading drivers to take more chances in the manner of Peltzman (1975); the magnitude of that effect is of course an open question. Given that our results indicate that the added aggressive behavior can potentially add to profits by increasing viewer demand, the interplay between safety requirements and on-track aggression becomes an interesting decision problem with implications for racing rules and institutions. These are more complex problems and merit further research.

Acknowledgments We are grateful to Craig Depken for valuable comments, Carly Litzenberger of the Nielsen Company for assistance with the data, and Matthias Franzen for diligent research assistance. Peter von Allmen gratefully acknowledges funding support from the Moravian College Amrhein Faculty Development Fund.

References

NASCAR.com (2010) 10-race Chase for the CUP Crowns Series Champion. Posted March 8. Accessed online: http://www.nascar.com.

Aronson E, Wilson TW, Akert RM (2007) Social Psychology. Pearson Education: Upper Saddle River, NJ.

Becker GS, Huselid MA (1992) The Incentive effects of Tournament Compensation Systems. Administrative Science Quarterly 37:336–350.

Berkowitz J, Depken CA, Wilson DP (2010) When Going in Circles is Going Backwards. Unpublished manuscript.

Botchford J (2010) Track is too Fast, Says Head of Luge Federation. Vancouver Sun, May 21. Accessed online: http://www.vancouver sun.com.

Buraimo B (2008) Stadium Attendance and Television Audience Demand in English League Football. Managerial and Decision Economics 29(6):513–523.

Buraimo B, Simmons R (2009) A Tale of Two Audiences: Spectators, Television Viewers, and Outcome Uncertainty in Spanish Football. Journal of Economics and Business 61(4):326–338.

Depken CA, Wilson D (2004a) The Efficiency of the NASCAR Reward System: Initial Empirical Evidence. Journal of Sports Economics 5(4):371–86.

Depken CA, Wilson D (2004b) HYPERLINK "http://ideas.repec.org/a/kap/revind/v24y2004i1p51-72.html" Wherein Lies the Benefit of the Second Referee in the NHL? HYPERLINK "http://ideas.repec.org/s/kap/revind.html" Review of Industrial Organization 24(1):51–72.

Dubner SJ, Levitt SD (2006) How Many Lives did Dale Earnhardt Save? The New York Times, February 19. Accessed online: http://www.nytimes.com.

Associated Press (AP) (2010) Economy Tough on Bristol Speedway. ESPN.com, last updated August 20. Accessed online: http://www.sports.espn.go.com.

Forrest D, Simmons R, Buraimo B (2005) Outcome Uncertainty and the Couch Potato Audience. Scottish Journal of Political Economy 52(4):641–661.

Hagstrom RG (1998) The NASCAR Way: The Business That Drives the Sport. John Wiley and Sons: New York, NY.

Howell MD (1997) From Moonshine to Madison Avenue: A Cultural History of the NASCAR Winston Cup series. Bowling Green State University Popular Press: Bowling Green, OH.

Lazear EP (1989) Pay Equality and Industrial Politics. Journal of Political Economy 97(3): 561–580.

Lazear EP, Rosen S (1981) Rank Order Tournaments as Optimum Labor Contracts. Journal of Political Economy 89(5):841–864.

NASCAR.com (2004) New NASCAR Playoff Structure Announced. NASCAR.com, posted January 20. Accessed online: http://www.nascar.com.

MacGregor J (2005) Sunday Money. Harper Collins: New York, NY.

O'Roark J, Wood WC (2004) Safety at the Racetrack: Results of Restrictor Plates in Superspeedway Competition. Southern Economic Journal 71(1):118–129.

Peltzman S (1975) The Effects of Automobile Safety Regulation. Journal of Political Economy 83(4):677–725.

Pierce DS (2010) Real NASCAR: White Lightning, Red Clay, and Big Bill France. University of North Carolina Press: Chapel Hill, NC.

Schwartz JT, Isaacs JP, Carilli AM (2007) To Race or to Place? An empirical Investigation of the Efficiency of the NASCAR Points Competition. Journal of Sports Economics 8(6):633–41.

Scribbins J (2006) Crashes and Competition: What Drives Television Viewer Estimates for NASCAR's Nextel Cup? unpublished manuscript, University of Iowa.

Sheridan P (2010) Death Comes as No Surprise. Philadelphia Inquirer, February 13, pp. E1& E6.

Sobel RS, Nesbit T (2007) Automobile Safety Regulation and the Incentive to Drive Recklessly: Evidence from NASCAR. Southern Economic Journal 74(1):71–84.

Spencer L (2010) Edwards Goes Too Far in Search of Payback. FoxSports.com, last updated March 8. Accessed online: http://www.msn.foxsports.com. http://msn.foxsports.com.

von Allmen P (2001) Is the Reward System in NASCAR Efficient? Journal of Sports Economics 5(4):62–79.

Chapter 7
Aggression in Mixed Martial Arts: An Analysis of the Likelihood of Winning a Decision

Trevor Collier, Andrew L. Johnson, and John Ruggiero

Abstract Within the last decade, mixed martial arts has become one of the most popular sports worldwide. The Ultimate Fighting Championship (UFC) is the largest and most successful organization within the industry. In the USA, however, the sport is not sanctioned in all states because some politicians view the sport as too violent. The sport consists of many fighting forms and, unlike boxing, winning a decision requires judging in multiple facets including wrestling, boxing, kick boxing, and jiu-jitsu. In this study, we estimate the likelihood of winning a decision in the UFC. Using data on individual fights, we estimate the probability of winning based on fighter characteristics. We emphasize power strikes as it relates to aggression to determine the likelihood of winning. Our results indicate that knockdowns and damage inflicted are all statistically significant determinants of winning a fight and have the largest marginal effect of influencing judge's decisions.

Introduction

The sport of mixed martial arts (MMA) was introduced in the USA with the Ultimate Fighting Championship (UFC) in 1993. Businessman Art Davie and Brazilian jiu-jitsu black belt Rorion Gracie developed a single elimination tournament between various martial art stylists where there were practically no rules; biting and eye-gouging were not allowed. The fighting was similar to Vale Tudo ("anything goes") that appeared throughout the twentieth century in Brazil. UFC 1 was hyped as answering the question about which martial art would win in a real fight. Karate, boxing, wrestling, savate, sumo wrestling, and jiu-jitsu were all represented in the inaugural tournament which allowed fighters across all weight

T. Collier (✉)
University of Dayton, Dayton, OH, USA
e-mail: collier@udayton.edu

R.T. Jewell (ed.), *Violence and Aggression in Sporting Contests: Economics, History and Policy*, Sports Economics, Management and Policy 4,
DOI 10.1007/978-1-4419-6630-8_7, © Springer Science+Business Media, LLC 2011

classes. Brazilian jiu-jitsu black belt Royce Gracie was crowned the first winner, beating boxer Art Jimmerson, shoot wrestler Ken Shamrock, and savate World Champion Gerard Gordeau.

The UFC and MMA received mixed reviews from the USA public regarding the anything goes rules. Senator John McCain, R-Arizona, labeled the sport as "Human Cockfighting" (Sandomir 2007). In 1997, McCain contacted the governors of all 50 states and urged them to ban the sport (Silverman 1998). This criticism caused the UFC to make a series of rule changes to increase the number of state athletic commissions and cable television providers that would be willing to host and air events. However, this public criticism and lack of mainstream appeal, not to mention the costly legal processes to secure sanctioning, placed the owners of the UFC in a difficult financial situation. In 2001, Zuffa, LLC, owned by Frank and Lorenzo Fertitta, bought the UFC. Lorenzo Fertitta was a former member of the Nevada State Athletic Commission and was able to secure sanctioning in Nevada for the UFC in late 2001. During the period between 1997 and 2001, the rules were changed significantly to introduce weight classes and prohibit kicks to the head of a downed opponent, hair pulling, fish-hooking, head butting, and groin strikes. Strikes to the back of the head and neck and small joint manipulation were also banned.

The violence presented to the audience in UFC seems to be particularly appealing. Professional wrestling lead by the World Wrestling Entertainment (WWE), boxing, and the UFC compete in the USA for pay-per-view audiences. Over the past several years, there has been a significant reduction in WWE's pay-per-view numbers as UFC's popularity has grown and boxing's popularity has remained steady. The UFC generated $411 million in revenues and 9.145 million "buys" from the 16 events shown on pay-per-view (Meltzer 2011). The number of UFC buys is up 13.5 percentage points from 2009 sales. The WWE saw decreases year to year in buys between 2008–2009 and 2009–2010 of 19.8 percentage points and 14.4 percentage points, respectively. Some in the media attribute this to people's fascination with violence (Rossen 2010).

The focus of the UFC's competitions has been on striking, grappling, and submissions. Striking is most commonly associated with the fighters that have boxing and kickboxing backgrounds and fighters using this method are often fan favorites because their fights often end in knockouts. Absent a knockout or submission, a fight concludes at the time limit and the winner is determined by a set of three judges. The criteria are clean strikes, effective grappling, octagon control, and effective aggressiveness. Thus, power punches improve the chances of a fighter winning in two ways: power punches may lead to a knockout or they could affect the judges scoring of the rounds.

In this paper, we use UFC data from November 2000 through the end of 2009. Data were provided by FightMetric, a company founded in 2007. FightMetric collects data scientifically, using strict definitions, slow motion, a single scorer per fight, and data validation tests. The company is the official statistics provider for the UFC. More information can be obtained at http://www.fightmetric.com.

Since UFC 28, fights have been governed by a common set of rules. The data include information on fight and fighter characteristics. Fight characteristics include attempted and landed punches and kicks (which we aggregate into total strikes) overall and for power strikes. We analyze the effect of a variety of variables on the win/loss outcome of the fight. Of particular interest, we investigate the effect of power strikes. Our results indicate that knockdowns and damage inflicted are the variables with the largest marginal impact on the probability of winning a fight. This is not surprising for two reasons. One, knockdowns and damage inflicted occur very frequently in a fight relative to the other strikes used in our data, thus we would expect them to have a larger impact. Second, this result is consistent with the story told in Downey (2007), where fighting strategies became more obviously violent in response to the many rule changes in UFC.

Interestingly, we have found no published research analyzing the impact of fighting strategies/characteristics on the probability of winning a professional fight. Some research exists on the theoretical relationship between boxing contracts and the effort exerted by the boxers (Tenorio 2000; Amegashie and Kutsoati 2005; Sanders 2008), but nothing empirical (known to these authors). However, there is a vast history of research modeling the determinants of winning other sporting contests. European football seems to be the most heavily researched.

Carmichael and Thomas (2005) is one example of research on the impact of home-field advantage on the probability of winning a football match. Similarly, de Dios Tena and Forrest (2007) estimated the effect of replacing a manager during the season on the team's chances of winning games following the replacement. Other examples of studies estimating factors impacting the probability of winning a football match include (but are not limited to) Koning (2000), Forrest et al. (2005), and Chumacero (2009). This type of analysis is certainly not limited to football, with other researchers analyzing everything from tennis (Gilsdorf and Sukhatme 2008) to cricket (Allsopp and Clarke 2004).

The remainder of the paper is organized as follows. Section "Methodology" presents a probit regression model to predict winning based on the attributes of the fighters and the fight. Section "Empirical Application" describes the analysis of the FightMetric data focusing on UFC events and discusses the results of our regression model developed in section "Methodology." Two separate regressions are considered depending on the outcome of the fight. We first consider all fights including those that ended either due to submission or knockout. In our second regression, we consider only those fights that were decided by the judges. This allows us to focus on those factors that are most important to the judges in deciding the outcome of each fight. Marginal effects are calculated to determine the marginal impact that each characteristic has on the probability of winning. Section "Conclusions" provides some concluding remarks.

Methodology

Our goal is to determine which aspects of a fight (e.g., head punches versus other body blows) are most important in determining a winner. We use the full sample of all fights in the FightMetric database and a subsample limited to those fights that end in judges' decisions in order to focus on the subjective weight that judges attach to certain acts of aggression. We estimate a binary response model to estimate the impact of fighter characteristics on the probability of winning. The general model takes the form:

$$P(w = 1 \mid X) = G(X\beta), \tag{7.1}$$

where w is an indicator variable for whether the fighter won the fight, X is a vector of fighter characteristics, β is a vector of coefficient estimates, and G is a nonlinear function producing a value between 0 and 1. We specify G as the standard normal cumulative distribution function (called a probit model), which is expressed as the following:

$$G(z) = \Phi(z) = \int_{-\infty}^{z} \phi(v)\mathrm{d}v, \tag{7.2}$$

where $\phi(z)$ is the standard normal density

$$\phi(z) = \frac{1}{\sqrt{2\pi}} \mathrm{e}^{-(1/2)z^2}. \tag{7.3}$$

The coefficient estimates from this model do not give us any meaningful information other than the direction of the effect of x on the probability of winning. We obtain the marginal impact of a change in x on the probability of winning by taking the partial derivative:

$$\frac{\delta p(x)}{\delta x_i} = g(X\beta)B_i, \tag{7.4}$$

where $g(z) = (\mathrm{d}G/\mathrm{d}z)(z)$. For more information on the probit model, the reader may refer to Greene (2008).

The marginal effects that we show and discuss in the results section indicate the change in the probability of winning a fight resulting from a one unit increase in the dependent variable, evaluated at its mean. For example, a finding of a marginal effect of 0.12 on the variable age would mean that increasing a fighter's age by 1 year above the average age would increase the fighter's probability of winning by 12 percentage points. It is important to recognize that the size of the marginal effect will change with the size of the dependent variable in question, which is why marginal effects are typically evaluated at the mean of the dependent variable.

Empirical Application

Data

Data for UFC fights were obtained from FightMetric. We considered only fights that occurred in the UFC under the current rules, which were established in November 2000. Our dependent variable is either 0 (loss) or 1 (win) and we consider numerous

Table 7.1 Descriptive statistics

	All fights ($N=946$)		Fights with decisions ($N=646$)	
Variable	Mean	SD	Mean	SD
Win	0.500	0.500	0.500	0.500
Damage	0.177	0.461	0.268	0.577
Tight Sub	0.079	0.287	0.124	0.365
Clinch knockdowns	0.044	0.227	0.033	0.177
Standups	0.760	1.360	1.423	1.862
Knockdowns	0.183	0.464	0.135	0.434
Jabs to head attempted	14.317	20.698	26.269	26.615
Jabs to head landed	5.079	8.388	9.009	9.844
Power to head attempted	20.096	23.721	35.379	29.116
Power to head landed	6.044	7.794	9.885	8.999
Ground jabs to head attempted	15.125	23.630	27.365	31.285
Ground jabs to head landed	13.361	21.001	24.081	27.756
Ground power to head attempted	8.605	13.578	12.226	16.434
Ground power to head landed	4.966	7.836	6.667	9.062
Jabs other attempted	3.543	7.079	6.426	9.876
Jabs other landed	3.013	6.505	5.469	9.164
Power other attempted	7.586	9.609	12.876	12.450
Power other landed	5.973	7.656	10.033	9.810
Ground jabs other attempted	4.697	10.478	9.056	14.518
Ground jabs other landed	4.666	10.427	9.000	14.452
Ground power other attempted	0.924	2.851	1.729	4.232
Ground power other landed	0.871	2.677	1.627	3.948
Takedowns attempted	2.521	3.591	4.500	4.750
Takedowns successful	1.031	1.645	1.814	2.196
Slam	0.134	0.439	0.217	0.591
Sweep	0.178	0.471	0.308	0.612
Choke	0.365	0.769	0.432	0.900
Lock	0.284	0.709	0.354	0.824
Height	71.526	3.289	71.053	2.885
Weight	186.122	29.300	180.896	26.368
Age	28.793	4.183	28.514	4.009

fighter and fight characteristics to estimate the probability of winning the fight. Among the fighter characteristics, we use fighter height (*height*), weight (*weight*), and age (*age*). Descriptive statistics are reported in Table 7.1.

We would expect that younger fighters would have a higher probability of winning and that this effect would increase with the difference in the two fighters' ages. Weight differences could affect the probability of winning in either direction. A lower weight could proxy speed advantage while a higher weight might indicate more power. We note that advantages in weight are mitigated by weight classes and the fact that too much weight loss can lead to stamina problems. In general, we would expect height to be an advantage.

We also include a number of fight variables. We are forced to aggregate round data into total fight data in order to align with judges' decisions on a fight basis. We include variables measuring performance standing (i.e., boxing and kickboxing) and on the ground (wrestling and jiu-jitsu). Fighter activity is measured by the number of punches and kicks (which we aggregate into strikes) attempted and landed on the feet (*jabs attempted*, *jabs landed*, *power attempted*, and *power landed*) and on the ground (*ground jabs attempted*, *ground jabs landed*, *ground power attempted*, and *ground power landed*). Successful strikes that lead to knockdowns are measured by *clinch knockdowns*, *knockdowns*, and *damage*. Wrestling (and judo and jiu-jitsu) are concerned with taking a fight to the ground in order to submit or to inflict damage via ground and pound. We include *take downs attempted*, *take downs successful*, *slams*, and *sweeps* to measure this part of the fight game. Submissions are reflected by *Choke*, *Tight Sub* (i.e., submission attempts that did not end the fight) and *Lock*. *Standups* reflect the ability of a fighter to stand up after being taken down; the variable does not include noncontested stand ups (e.g., when the controlling fighter voluntarily stands).

Since we observe two fighters in a given fight, we use the difference in fighter characteristics for most of our explanatory variables in the probit model. For each fight, we generate a random number for each fighter and choose the fighter with the higher value as the first fighter with the remaining fighter positioned as the second fighter. This is essentially the same as flipping a coin to randomly position the fighters in our database. We then subtract the second fighter's characteristics from the first fighter's characteristics in each fight (e.g., the difference in age would be the first fighter's age minus the second fighter's age). Finally, we estimate the probit model with the indicator variable for whether the first fighter won the fight as a function of the differenced fighter characteristics.

Our methodology is similar to the method used by Gilsdorf and Sukhatme (2008) in their analysis of the probability of winning a tennis match, only they positioned players based on tournament seed. Much of the analyses of the determinants of winning football matches also use similar techniques, often positioning teams based on home versus away team (Carmichael and Thomas 2005; Forrest et al. 2005; Chumacero 2009).

Before we present our probit results, we first consider differences in fight characteristics for fights that ended in a decision versus those fights that ended via knockout, technical knockout, or submission (nondecision). Summary statistics for the difference in fighter characteristics are presented in Table 7.2. The statistics are defined relative to the winning fighter by subtracting the losing fighter's characteristics from the winning fighter's characteristics. Note that this is different than what we use in our analysis below, but this makes for an easier interpretation here.

Interesting results emerge from the summary statistics. *t*-Tests confirm that the means of some of these variables are statistically different between the two categories. The following variables were found to have a significantly *smaller* difference between the winner and loser of a fight in decisions than in nondecisions: tight submissions, clinch knockdowns, knockdowns, chokes, locks, and fighter height. This means that, for example, on average, the difference between the number of

Table 7.2 Mean differences in explanatory variables

	No decisions (N=323)		Decisions (N=623)		t-Test
Variable	Mean	SD	Mean	SD	$Pr(\|T\|>\|t\|)$
Damage	0.269	0.755	0.127	0.506	0.001
Tight Sub	−0.050	0.490	0.030	0.322	0.003
Clinch knockdowns	0.034	0.253	0.074	0.346	0.068
Standups	−1.087	2.709	−0.098	1.138	0.000
Knockdowns	0.102	0.599	0.340	0.641	0.000
Jabs to head attempted	0.700	23.057	1.894	12.614	0.303
Jabs to head landed	1.003	10.554	1.390	7.790	0.523
Power to head attempted	3.545	20.788	2.315	11.597	0.243
Power to head landed	3.548	7.683	2.589	6.601	0.046
Ground jabs to head attempted	14.409	39.617	7.425	17.314	0.000
Ground jabs to head landed	11.709	35.677	6.705	15.710	0.003
Ground power to head attempted	14.811	20.279	8.048	14.861	0.000
Ground power to head landed	8.084	11.079	5.507	8.928	0.000
Jabs other attempted	1.043	12.418	0.148	5.087	0.118
Jabs other landed	0.845	11.345	0.204	4.581	0.219
Power other attempted	2.303	14.021	1.361	6.315	0.155
Power other landed	2.424	11.349	1.242	5.479	0.031
Ground jabs other attempted	8.570	19.384	1.632	8.947	0.000
Ground jabs other landed	8.520	19.284	1.612	8.897	0.000
Ground power other attempted	2.319	5.188	0.465	2.195	0.000
Ground power other landed	2.176	4.850	0.432	0.000	0.000
Takedowns attempted	1.167	7.996	−0.136	3.209	0.000
Takedowns successful	1.604	3.276	0.276	1.549	0.000
Slam	0.235	0.827	0.067	0.456	0.000
Sweep	−0.009	0.685	0.035	0.430	0.221
Choke	0.015	1.267	0.327	0.912	0.000
Lock	−0.127	1.187	0.202	0.886	0.000
Height	0.136	2.711	0.541	3.779	0.088
Weight	0.344	10.899	0.228	12.443	0.888
Age squared	819.758	245.199	819.461	228.714	0.985
Age difference	−0.354	4.968	−1.156	5.674	0.032

All variables are defined relative to the winner of each fight

knockdowns by the winner and the number of knockdowns by the loser was greater in fights that did not end in a decision. These are not surprising findings, given that most of the maneuvers in this list are all ways to end a fight in a knockout or submission.

What is somewhat surprising is that the difference in the fighters' weights are similar across decisions and nondecisions, while the difference in the fighters' height is larger in fights that end in a knockout or submission. Conversely, the following variables were found to have a significantly *greater* difference between the winner and loser of a fight in decisions than in nondecisions: standups, damage, power landed to the head, power landed to other, ground jabs attempted and landed to both head and other, ground power attempted and landed to both head and other, takedown attempts, takedowns successful, slams, and age. It is interesting here that the difference in the fighters' ages is larger in fights that go to a decision. As a point of caution, we remind the reader that these are simply differences in characteristics of those fights that go to a decision versus those that do not. These differences do not necessarily have any predictive power. We will now discuss our probit results, which can tell us if any of the characteristics make a fighter more or less likely to win.

Probit Results

Our probit model using all 946 fights with complete information results in a pseudo R^2 of 0.634, meaning that our model explains about 63 percentage points of the variation in outcomes of these matches. Our probit model of the 323 fights that went to decisions and have complete information results in a similar pseudo R^2 of 0.701. The complete set of results for all fights are displayed in the first two columns of Table 7.3, while the complete set of results for the fights that went to decisions are displayed in the last two columns of Table 7.3. For the sake of brevity, we will only discuss coefficient estimates that are either statistically significant or surprising results. First, we will discuss the results for the model with all fights. Then we will discuss differences between these results and the results using only fights that went to decisions.

Using the data with all fights, the coefficient estimates on the variables for damage, clinch knockdowns, stand ups, knockdowns, power to head landed, ground power to head landed, power other landed, take downs successful, slams, sweeps, chokes, locks, and height are all positive and statistically significant at the 5 percentage points level. This means that we are at least 95 percentage points sure that these variables have a positive impact on the probability of winning. In addition, the coefficient estimates on jabs to head attempted and ground jabs to head attempted are positive and statistically significant at the 10 percentage points level. Remember, however, that these variables used in our model are measured as the difference between the original values of these variables for the two fighters involved in a particular fight. Thus, the fighter who has a higher value for any of these variables has a greater probability of winning the fight.

Two surprising results, of the statistically significant estimates, are that the fighter with a greater number of jabs to head and ground jabs *attempted* has a higher probability of winning, but the fighter with the greater number of jabs to head or ground jabs *landed* does not. One interpretation of these results is that the number of jabs to head and ground jabs attempted are serving as a proxies for which fighter has greater control of the fight, while actually landing these jabs has no real impact on the outcome.

The most surprising result is that none of our age variables held any statistical significance in the model. We hypothesized that a greater difference in age would increase the probability of winning for the younger fighter and that this effect would increase as the difference became larger. However, our results indicate that, after controlling for all the other variables in a fight, age does not impact a fighter's

Table 7.3 Probit results

	All fights (N=946)		Fights with decisions (N=323)	
Variable	Coefficient	SE	Coefficient	SE
Intercept	−0.019	2.955	−5.683	7.5140
Damage	0.341**	0.134	0.393	0.2400
Tight Sub	−0.140	0.215	0.572	0.3540
Clinch knockdowns	0.695**	0.258	−0.232	0.5460
Standups	0.429**	0.083	−0.048	0.1600
Knockdowns	1.178**	0.145	0.835**	0.3970
Jabs to head attempted	0.009*	0.005	0.009	0.0070
Jabs to head landed	−0.013	0.011	−0.013	0.0140
Power to head attempted	−0.007	0.006	−0.001	0.0080
Power to head landed	0.111**	0.018	0.154**	0.0320
Ground jabs to head attempted	0.043*	0.025	0.111**	0.0560
Ground jabs to head landed	−0.037	0.028	−0.105*	0.0600
Ground power to head attempted	−0.016	0.015	0.069**	0.0330
Ground power to head landed	0.116**	0.029	−0.006	0.0620
Jabs other attempted	0.048	0.037	0.125**	0.0540
Jabs other landed	−0.055	0.040	−0.132**	0.0580
Power other attempted	−0.026	0.025	−0.052	0.0330
Power other landed	0.068**	0.031	0.084**	0.0430
Ground jabs other attempted	0.183	0.282	0.161	0.3650
Ground jabs other landed	−0.168	0.283	−0.151	0.3660
Ground power other attempted	−0.169	0.206	−0.138	0.3020
Ground power other landed	0.271	0.226	0.273	0.3290
Take downs attempted	−0.013	0.019	−0.009	0.0250
Take downs successful	0.359**	0.079	0.014	0.1500
Slams	0.746**	0.149	0.376	0.2430
Sweeps	0.736**	0.150	0.079	0.2930
Choke	0.427**	0.074	0.067	0.1200
Lock	0.377**	0.074	0.081	0.1580
Height	0.054**	0.027	0.026	0.0580
Weight	−0.005	0.006	−0.011	0.0140
Age	0.020	0.202	0.437	0.5200
Age squared	−0.001	0.003	−0.008	0.0090
Age difference	−0.009	0.016	0.044	0.0360
Pseudo R^2	0.634		0.701	

Dependent variable is wins

**Indicates significance at the 5 percentage points level; *indicates significance at the 10 percentage points level

probability of winning. One explanation for this result is that our other variables include measures that are probably accounting for age differences. For instance, a younger fighter is likely to be quicker and thus more likely to be successful in takedowns. We found that the fighter with more successful takedowns has a higher probability of winning. Thus, a younger fighter does have a higher probability of winning, but not just because they are younger. They are more likely to win because they are quicker and more likely to be successful in takedown attempts.

Looking at our results for the sample that only includes fights that went to decisions, we see that seven of our coefficient estimates are positive and statistically significant: knockdowns, power to head landed, ground jabs to head attempted, ground power to head attempted, other jabs attempted, and other power landed. Two variables, ground jabs to head landed and other jabs landed, result in negative and statistically significant coefficient estimates. Thus, it can be said that these are the variables that are most important to the judges.

We find a number of these results to be very surprising. It is extremely curious that ground jabs to head *attempted* and other jabs *attempted* are both positively associated with the probability of winning a decision, while ground jabs to head *landed* and other jabs *landed* are negatively associated with the probability of winning a decision. Similarly, ground power to head *attempted* is positively correlated with winning a decision, while power to head *landed* does not seem to be related to the decision. We have two possible explanations for these results: (a) the difference in punches attempted is a proxy for the fighter that dominated the fight (especially on the ground), or (b) the judges had a difficult time determining which ground and body punches actually landed, thus punches attempted dominated their visibility. As a point of fact, the judges in our sample do not have access to television monitors, leading to a clear lack of vantage point.

The other interesting finding here is that knockdowns, power to head landed, and other power landed are all found to be positively associated with winning a decision. These types of blows seem to be the most obviously violent and harmful of the blows we have accounted for. Thus, it appears that judges are swayed in favor of the fighter who is more successful in these harmful strikes.

Marginal Effects

As we discussed above, the coefficient estimates tell us the direction of the relationship between the explanatory variables and the probability of winning, but their magnitudes do not have any meaningful interpretation. Thus, we transform the coefficient estimates into marginal effects so we can understand the impact of a one unit increase of an explanatory variable (at its mean) on the probability of winning the fight. Table 7.4 displays the marginal effects measured using all available fights and only fights that end in decisions.

Increasing the difference in the number of knockdowns created by the two fighters from its average of –0.026 by one knockdown would increase a fighter's probability of winning by 16.6 percentage points. This is the largest marginal effect (measured at its mean) of all the variables included in our model. The difference in the number of slams and sweeps also have marginal effects estimated to be slightly greater than 10 percentage points and are the next greatest in magnitude, with clinch knockdowns following closely behind at 9.8 percentage points. Although we found that a larger difference in the number of jabs to head and ground jabs to head attempted have positive and statistically significant impacts

Table 7.4 Marginal effects

	All fights (N=946)		Fights with decisions (N=323)	
Variable	Marginal effect	SE	Marginal effect	SE
Damage	0.048**	0.019	0.044*	0.027
Tight Sub	–0.020	0.030	0.065	0.039
Clinch knockdowns	0.098**	0.036	–0.026	0.062
Standups	0.060**	0.011	–0.005	0.018
Knockdowns	0.166**	0.018	0.095**	0.043
Jabs to head attempted	0.001*	0.001	0.001	0.001
Jabs to head landed	–0.002	0.002	–0.001	0.002
Power to head attempted	–0.001	0.001	0.000	0.001
Power to head landed	0.016**	0.002	0.017**	0.003
Ground jabs to head attempted	0.006*	0.004	0.013**	0.006
Ground jabs to head landed	–0.005	0.004	–0.012*	0.007
Ground power to head attempted	–0.002	0.002	0.008**	0.004
Ground power to head landed	0.016**	0.004	–0.001	0.007
Jabs other attempted	0.007	0.005	0.014**	0.006
Jabs other landed	–0.008	0.006	–0.015**	0.006
Power other attempted	–0.004	0.004	–0.006	0.004
Power other landed	0.010**	0.004	0.01**	0.005
Ground jabs other attempted	0.026	0.040	0.018	0.041
Ground jabs other landed	–0.024	0.040	–0.017	0.041
Ground power other attempted	–0.024	0.029	–0.016	0.034
Ground power other landed	0.038	0.032	0.031	0.037
Take downs attempted	–0.002	0.003	–0.001	0.003
Take downs successful	0.051**	0.011	0.002	0.017
Slams	0.105**	0.020	0.043	0.027
Sweeps	0.104**	0.020	0.009	0.033
Choke	0.060**	0.010	0.008	0.014
Lock	0.053**	0.010	0.009	0.018
Height	0.008**	0.004	0.003	0.007
Weight	–0.001	0.001	–0.001	0.002
Age	0.003	0.028	0.049	0.059
Age squared	0.000	0.000	0.005	0.004
Age difference	–0.001	0.002	–0.001	0.001

**Indicates significance at the 5 percentage points level; *indicates significance at the 10 percentage points level. Standard errors are calculated using the delta method

on the probability of winning, the marginal effects are only 0.1 percentage points and 0.6 percentage points, respectively. The former is the smallest marginal effect of all of the variables we find to have statistically significant coefficient estimates. We should note here that the scale of the variables mentioned above is significantly different. The average number of knockdowns for a fighter is 0.183, while the average number of ground jabs to head attempted is 15.125. Thus, knockdowns occur much less frequently and so it is not surprising that one more knockdown for a fighter will have a significant increase in their probability of winning.

The last two columns of Table 7.3 display the coefficient estimates and standard errors for our model of fights that end in decisions. Using this sample of the data, we find that the difference in the number of knockdowns again has the largest marginal increase in the probability of winning a fight. The marginal effects are shown in Table 7.4. Here, a one unit increase in the difference in the number of knockdowns from its average of –0.026 increases a fighter's probability of winning a decision by 9.5 percentage points. The marginal effect of a one unit increase in the difference in damage, from its average, results in a 4.4 percentage points increase in a fighter's probability of winning a decision. Finally, the marginal effects of the other statistically significant characteristics are all less than 2 percentage points. Again, the same caveat about the scale of the variables applies. In addition, we should mention that damage and tight submission are binary indicator variables for each round. This means they can never have a value of greater than one in any round, hence never have a value of greater than the number of rounds in the fight in our aggregated data.

Conclusions

In this chapter, we estimate probit models to identify the effect of fighter and fight characteristics on the probability of winning a fight in MMA. Using data provided by FightMetric, we include only fights from the UFC. We estimated two probit models, using the full sample of fights with complete data and a subsample that only included fights that end in judges' decisions. Most of the results were expected. The only fighter characteristic that was statistically significant was height (only in the full sample of data), but the marginal effect was relatively small. Age and weight were not statistically significant.

The fight variables that were statistically significant in both models were knockdowns, ground jabs to the head attempted, and power strikes landed (both to the head and other parts of the body). Ground power strikes to the head landed were significant in the full sample but not in the subsample; this might result because successful ground power strikes to the head typically end fights. The variables with the largest marginal effects in the subsample of fights that go to a decision were damage and knockdowns, which is not surprising given their limited frequency in a fight.

Acknowledgments The authors thank Alon Cohen and Rami Genauer of FightMetric for providing data and assistance in interpreting variables.

References

Allsopp PE, Clarke SR (2004) Rating Teams and Analyzing Outcomes in One-Day and Test Cricket. Journal of the Royal Statistical Society Series A 167(4):657–667.

Amegashie JA, Kutsoati E (2005) Rematches in Boxing and Other Sporting Events. Journal of Sports Economics 6:401–411.

Carmichael F, Thomas D (2005) Home-Field Effect and Team Performance: Evidence from English Premiership Football. Journal of Sports Economics 6(3):264–281.

Chumacero RA (2009) Altitude or Hot Air? Journal of Sports Economics 10(6):619–638.

De Dios Tena J, Forrest D (2007) Within-Season Dismissal of Football Coaches: Statistical Analysis of Causes and Consequences. European Journal of Operational Research. 181(1): 362–373.

Downey G (2007) Producing Pain: Techniques and Technologies in No-Holds-Barred Fighting. Social Studies of Science 37(2):201–226.

Forrest D, Goddard J, Simmons R (2005) Odds-Setters as Forecasters: The Case of English Football. International Journal of Forecasting 51:551–564.

Gilsdorf KF, Sukhatme VA (2008) Testing Rosen's Sequential Elimination Tournament Model: Incentives and Player Performance in Professional Tennis. Journal of Sports Economics 9(3):287–303.

Greene WH (2008) Econometric Analysis, 6th ed. Prentice Hall: Upper Saddle River, NJ.

Koning R (2000) Balance in Competition in Dutch Soccer. The Statistician 49:419–431.

Meltzer D (2011) Another Record Year for UFC on PPV" Yahoo! Sports, posted January 11. Accessed online: http://www.sports.yahoo.com.

Rossen J (2010) "The Kick Heard 'Round the World. ESPN.com, posted December 20. Accessed online: http://www.espn.go.com.

Sanders S (2008) A Constructive Comment on "Rematches in Boxing and Other Sporting Events." Journal of Sports Economics 9(1):96–99.

Sandomir R (2007) From the Edge of Madness to Fighting's Mainstream. New York Times, posted May 25. Accessed online: http://www.nytimes.com.

Silverman A (1998) John McCain Breaks Up a Fight. Phoenix New Times, posted February 12. Accessed online: http://www.phoenixnewtimes.com.

Tenorio R (2000) The economics of Professional Boxing Contracts. Journal of Sports Economics 1:363–384.

Part IV
International Team Sports

Chapter 8
Aggressive Play and Demand for English Premier League Football

R. Todd Jewell

Abstract This study estimates a demand curve for per-match attendance in the English Premier Football League (EPL), the highest level of professional association football (soccer) in England. An emphasis is placed on the effect of aggressive play on attendance demand. Aggressive play is measured by fouls and cards accumulated by a team during each season. The results indicate that aggressive play by EPL teams has a significant effect on attendance and that this effect varies with team quality and the type of infraction. An increase in normal fouls by the home team appears to decrease attendance for the best teams and increase attendance for the worst teams. However, an increase in yellow-card fouls has the opposite effect on attendance. Interestingly, red cards given for violent play do not seem to be related to EPL per-match attendance, suggesting that fans do not have preferences for seeing violent play.

Introduction

Known as soccer in the USA, the sport of association football is played by amateur and professional athletes around the globe. The current study estimates the relationship between in-match violent and aggressive play and demand in the English Premier League (EPL), the highest level of professional association football in England. In commonly used terminology, the words "violence" and "aggression" are often interchangeable. For the psychologist who studies deviant behavior, violence and aggression mean distinctly different things (Abrams 2010). In the context of this study, "aggressive play" is defined as play that intends to physically intimidate the opponent and "violent play" is defined as crossing the line of physical intimidation to acts that could easily cause injury, whether or not injury is the intent.

R.T. Jewell (✉)
University of North Texas, Denton, TX, USA
e-mail: tjewell@unt.edu

R.T. Jewell (ed.), *Violence and Aggression in Sporting Contests: Economics, History and Policy*, Sports Economics, Management and Policy 4,
DOI 10.1007/978-1-4419-6630-8_8,

The EPL has the reputation as a league in which physically aggressive play is part of the culture, where the game is generally played "hard but fair." Physically aggressive play is considered to be a tactic that, if employed well, can increase the ability of a team of lesser skill to compete with more highly skilled teams. For example, the London-based club Arsenal has a reputation, whether deserved or not, of being a team composed of players that do not like playing against teams with a physically aggressive style of play, indicating that aggressive play can improve a team's chances of winning against Arsenal. However, there is a cost to physically aggressive play if it leads to fouls and misconduct. Nonetheless, the tactical use of physically aggressive play may be fairly widespread in the EPL given the league's reputation.

Limited research exists on aggression within the game, although the English leagues clearly have a history of such play. Consider, for instance, the "hardman," who dishes out punishment to opposing players as a means of retaliation or simply intimidation. Often, the hardman toes the line between aggressive play and physical violence. Some might call this type of play "thuggery," but this type of player is somewhat revered by fans, at least fans of the team on which he plays. The role of the hardman in the top English league has been filled by players such as: Ron "Chopper" Harris of the 1960s and 1970s (his nickname is not due to his love of motorcycles); Graeme Souness of the 1970s and 1980s (possibly the most feared Scotsman since William Wallace); Vinnie Jones (leader of the Wimbledon Crazy Gang) and Stuart "Psycho" Pearce (his nickname says it all) of the 1980s and 1990s; and Robbie Savage (more comedian than hardman) and Roy Keane (truly a scary man when in his normal state of anger) of the 1990s and 2000s. Interestingly, Souness, Stuart, and Keane are or have been managers in England. Anyone who thinks thuggery does not exist in the current game should consider Ben Thatcher's tackle/assault on Pedro Mendes in 2006; this and other reminders of the potential for acts of physical violence in the modern game can be easily viewed on Youtube (http://www.youtube.com).

From the perspective of an economist, aggressive play in football matches is an outcome of the forces of supply and demand, and violence and aggression exist because fans respond positively to them. Football spectators may directly demand aggression because these elements of sporting contests are entertaining. Teams and leagues that wish to maximize profit will optimally respond to spectator preferences by ratcheting up the aggression level. Thus, spectator preferences bid up the monetary return to aggressive play, and the rational response is a more aggressive output. In addition, football spectators are clearly entertained by seeing their favorite teams win, and there may be a relationship between aggressive play and team success. If aggression (and possibly violence) helps football clubs to be successful, then fans will indirectly demand more aggressive play to produce more wins. However, aggressive play may limit a team's success, which will lead fans to indirectly demand less aggression. Thus, spectator demand for wins drives up the monetary return to wins, and the rational response is an output that contains more or less aggression depending on the relationship between wins and aggression.

FIFA (*Fédération Internationale de Football Association*, International Federation of Association Football in English), the sport's world governing body, has over 200 member countries, a quantity that surpasses even the number of United Nations members. FIFA establishes the rules of the game for all competitions that it sanctions, including international matches and professional club leagues in member nations. One of the primary laws of the game (Law 12) involves fouls and misconduct and the penalties for such offenses (FIFA 2010). The penalties range in severity according to the seriousness of the offense, and the referee is responsible for meting out appropriate punishment with input from two assistant referees and a fourth official. The referee may award a free kick (direct or indirect) against the offending team, he may choose to caution the offending player and award a yellow card, or he may take the extreme step of sending off the offending player with a red card if the misconduct is judged to be egregious enough.

Since fouls and cards are clearly observable indicators of aggressive and violent play, data on fouls and cards can be used to measure the level of aggression in a given match. This study estimates EPL attendance demand concentrating on the effect of aggression and violence on demand, utilizing information on total fouls, yellow cards, and red cards. The results indicate that aggressive play by EPL teams has a significant effect on attendance and that this effect varies with the quality of the home team and the type of aggressive play. In general, additional aggressive play by the home team appears to decrease attendance for the best teams and increase attendance for the worst teams. More specifically, the results indicate that home-team normal fouls and home-team red cards for professional fouls follow this general pattern, a negative effect for better teams and a positive effect for worse teams. However, the results with respect to home-team yellow-card infractions indicate that additional cards lead to greater attendance for the best teams and lower attendance for the worst. Further evidence suggests that truly violent play is not related to attendance demand. Finally, the results indicate that normal fouls, yellow-card fouls, and red-card fouls by the away team do not influence attendance demand.

Data and Methodology

At the professional club level, European association football is generally considered to be the highest quality in the world, even though national teams from South America routinely defeat European competition at tournaments such as the FIFA World Cup. Although fans and pundits can argue about the relative strengths and weaknesses of a particular country's domestic league, the EPL is currently the most highly ranked domestic professional league in Europe. Furthermore, the EPL has four of the top five ranked club teams in Europe: Manchester United, Chelsea, Arsenal, and Liverpool, the so-called "Big Four" of English football. This ranking is produced by UEFA (Union of European Football Associations, the governing body of European association football) based on the performance of teams in the UEFA Champions League and the UEFA Cup/Europa League over the previous 5 years.

Table 8.1 Aggressive play: 2,660 English Premier League matches (complete sample: 2003–2004 to 2009–2010)

	Home	Away	Difference (%)
Normal fouls	33,192	35,015	5
Yellow cards	3,426	4,557	33
Red cards	169	262	55
Second yellow card	72	129	79
Serious foul play	45	51	13
Violent conduct	21	42	100
Professional foul	26	32	23
Deliberate handball	5	5	0
Offensive language or gestures	0	3	NA

Note: Home teams have significantly fewer normal fouls, yellow cards, and red cards than away teams

Spain had the highest-rated domestic league from 1999 to 2007. The EPL jumped to first in the rankings in 2008 and has occupied that spot since then. In the current ranking, the top club team in Europe is Barcelona, with Sevilla being the next highest ranked Spanish team at number 7.

The basic data set used in the study contains observations on all matches played in the EPL for seven full seasons from 2003–2004 to 2009–2010. These data are gathered from the ESPN Soccernet Web site (http://www.soccernet.espn.go.com), the EPL Web site (http://www.premierleague.com), and the Soccerbase Web site (http://www.soccerbase.com). It is suggested that the EPL actually consists of three "leagues within-a-league." At the top, the EPL has been dominated by the Big Four. Over this period, only three teams won the EPL championship, Arsenal (2003–2004), Chelsea (2004–2005, 2005–2006, 2009–2010), and Manchester United (2006–2007, 2007–2008, 2008–2009). Furthermore, in every year except 2004–2005 and 2009–2010, the Big Four finished in places one through four, important spots indeed due to the fact that these top four spots give clubs a chance to play in the highly lucrative UEFA Champions League. In any given season, there are a group of approximately a dozen "mid-table teams" that are essentially fighting for fifth place and to avoid being pulled into the relegation zone. At the bottom, there are a handful of teams struggling to avoid relegation. Of the 21 teams relegated over this time period, 14 were in the league less than 2 years between promotion and relegation.

Table 8.1 gives details of the level of aggressive and violent play in the EPL from 2003–2004 to 2009–2010, where aggression and violence is measured by fouls and cards. Over the sample period, EPL referees called a total of 68,207 normal fouls, handed out 7,983 yellow cards, and gave a total of 430 red cards. As shown in Table 8.1, the level of violent or aggressive play experienced over this time period by home and away teams differs in a systematic way. In the light of research on the bias of referees toward the home team (Sutter and Kocher 2004; Garicano et al. 2005; Dawson et al. 2007; Dohmen 2008; Buraimo et al. 2009), it should be no surprise that the home team had 55% fewer red cards, 33% fewer yellow cards,

Table 8.2 Aggressive play by league position: 2,660 English Premier League matches (complete sample: 2003–2004 to 2009–2010)

	Mean	SD	Minimum	Maximum
Normal fouls per team per year				
Top teams (4)	445.7	28.1	368	496
Mid-table teams (8)	492.2	43.2	383	580
Bottom teams (20)	502.5	42.7	402	600
Yellow cards per team per year				
Top teams (4)	52.0	6.5	40	65
Mid-table teams (8)	56.3	8.5	40	81
Bottom teams (20)	60.1	11.5	34	85
Red cards per team per year				
Top teams (4)	2.7	1.7	0	6
Mid-table teams (8)	2.9	1.8	0	7
Bottom teams (20)	3.4	1.9	0	9

Notes:
Top teams have significantly fewer normal fouls, yellow cards, and red cards than both mid-table and bottom teams, and mid-table teams have significantly fewer normal fouls, yellow cards, and red cards than bottom teams
The top-teams group is the Big Four (Arsenal, Chelsea, Manchester United, and Liverpool)
The mid-table group includes all eight EPL teams that are not in the Big Four but spent the entire sample period in the EPL (Aston Villa, Bolton, Blackburn, Everton, Fulham, Manchester City, Tottenham Hotspur, and Portsmouth – note that Portsmouth was relegated after the 2009–2010 season)
The group of bottom teams includes all 20 EPL teams that spent at least 1 year of the sample period in a lower division (Birmingham City, Burnley, Charlton, Crystal Palace, Derby County, Hull City, Leeds United, Middlesbrough, Newcastle United, Norwich City, Reading, Sheffield United, Southampton, Stoke City, Sunderland, Watford, West Bromwich Albion, West Ham United, Wigan, and Wolverhampton)

and 5% fewer normal fouls than the away team. Another explanation could be that the difference in red and yellow cards simply reflects differences in playing style; specifically, the away team generally plays more aggressively than the home team in order to negate a home-field advantage. The most common red-card infraction is a second yellow card (47% of the total), followed by serious foul play (22%), violent conduct (14%), and a professional foul (13%).

Given the distinction between the quality of top and bottom teams in the EPL, it is unsurprising that research suggests that the level of aggressive play in football is influenced by team quality (Jewell 2009). One would expect teams to treat aggressive play as a substitute for quality in producing wins, and teams of lesser quality will have higher levels of aggressive play. The data bear this out; over the period 2003–2004 to 2009–2010, the Big Four had significantly fewer average normal fouls (445.7 compared to 497.6), yellow cards (52 compared to 58.3), and red cards (2.7 compared to 3.2) per team per year than all other EPL teams. Table 8.2 gives more detail on the correlation between team quality and aggressive play. Specifically, the best teams have statistically fewer fouls and cards than mid-table teams, and mid-table teams have statistically fewer fouls and cards than the EPL's bottom teams.

Modeling Attendance Demand in the EPL

Demand for match-day attendance in association football has been studied for some time (Matheson 2006). Recent studies have examined attendance demand for European football at the club level (Garcia and Rodriguez 2002; Simmons 1996), for association football in the USA (Jewell and Molina 2005), and for football in South America (Madalozzo and Villar 2009). Although these studies have concentrated on various aspects of football demand, such as the impact of television (Allen and Roy 2008; Buraimo and Simmons 2006; Forrest and Simmons 2006), the general consensus is that demand for association football is similar to demand for other professional sports. Specifically, demand for professional sports is a function of variables that can be grouped into two major categories: market potential and quality of the teams (Borland and Macdonald 2003). The present study posits an additional category, that of aggressive play, so that a general equation for match-day attendance in the EPL can be stated as the following:

$$D_{ijkt} = \Delta(A_{ijkt}, Q_{ijkt}, M_{ijt}), \tag{8.1}$$

where i indexes the home team, j indexes the away team, k indexes the match number in any given year, and t indexes the year in which the match is played. M_{ijt} is the home team's market potential when playing team j in year t, Q_{ijkt} is absolute and relative quality of the home and away teams in match k of year t, A_{ijkt} is the level of aggressive or violent play that fans expect from each match, and Δ is a function that maps aggressive play, team quality, and market potential to match-day attendance demand. The variables included in each category are described below.

This study measures aggressive play in the EPL in two ways: (1) as an index of disciplinary points associated with both yellow-card fouls and red-card fouls and (2) as the number of normal fouls, yellow-card fouls, and red-card fouls. The English Football Association (EFA) keeps track of the disciplinary records of players and teams through accumulation of disciplinary points assigned to yellow-card and red-card infractions (EFA 2010). Red cards are assigned disciplinary points based on the nature of the infraction. Red cards for second yellow-card fouls are assigned ten disciplinary points, as are red cards for professional fouls and deliberate handballs. Red cards for serious foul play, violent conduct, spitting or offensive, insulting, abusive language, and/or gestures are given 12 disciplinary points, implying that the EFA feels that these are more-serious offenses. A yellow card is assigned four disciplinary points without regard to the specific offense, with the exception that two yellow cards for the same player are counted as a single red-card offense. Given the implicit weights assigned by the EFA, the sum of yellow cards and red cards times their weights results in an index of disciplinary points that can be used to measure aggressive play in each EPL match. No disciplinary points are assigned for normal fouls, so the index does not contain information on that number.

Equation (8.1) is based on the assumption that EPL fans have some preference for or against aggressive play and that these preferences translate into changes in demand for match-day attendance. Given that spectators make their decisions to

Table 8.3 Summary statistics: 1,957 English Premier League matches (estimation sample: 2004–2005 to 2009–2010)

	Mean	SD	Minimum	Maximum
Attendance (per match)	34,964.41	13,252.99	14,007	72,159
Disciplinary points (1-year lag)	252.19	46.77	158	364
Normal fouls (1-year lag)	483.71	47.33	368	600
Yellow cards (1-year lag)	56.49	10.25	34	85
Red cards (1-year lag)	2.93	1.75	0	7
Type-1 red cards (1-year lag)	1.30	1.08	0	5
Type-2 red cards (1-year lag)	0.50	0.74	0	3
Type-3 red cards (1-year lag)	1.12	1.05	0	4
League points (per year)	54.90	16.78	28	95
Match uncertainty (per match)	0.54	0.42	0	2.40
Population (per hectare, per team)	22.31	11.72	10.03	46.38
Income (£ per capita/1,000, per team)	16.09	3.39	13.17	21.33
Local competitors (per year)	4.14	2.05	0	7
Derby match (per match)	0.04	0.21	0	1
Distance (in km, per match)	223.26	142.7	0	548

attend matches prior to the actual match, this study posits that fans take the expectation of aggressive play into account when making the match-attendance decision. Thus, the measure of A_{ijkt} from (8.1) must incorporate indicators of the potential for aggression in any given match. This study uses a 1-year lag of aggressive play per team to proxy the expectation of violence in any given match. Other measures were analyzed, including various lengths of within-season lags, but the 1-year lag proved to be the best fit in the estimation. In addition, measures of the expected aggression of the visiting team showed no significant relationship to attendance demand in the EPL and are, therefore, removed from the estimations reported below for parsimony. Thus, evidence suggests that the best indicator of a team's aggression in a given match in year t is the team's average aggression level for the entirety of year $t-1$ and that expected aggression by the visiting team is unrelated to match-day attendance demand.

Using a 1-year lag reduces sample size, since the first year must be deleted and teams without a recent 1-year history of EPL aggression must be deleted. The resulting estimation sample covers the seasons 2004–2005 to 2009–2010 and includes 1,957 home games of 24 EPL clubs. Since the estimation sample systematically deletes the home attendances of eight low-quality EPL clubs (Burnley, Crystal Palace, Derby County, Leeds United, Norwich City, Sheffield United, Watford, and Wolverhampton), the results reported below can be interpreted as indicative of attendance demand for those teams that are good enough to survive at least a season in the EPL. Summary statistics for the estimation sample are presented in Table 8.3.

Demand for the EPL is measured by per-match attendance. As is the case in many sports contexts, EPL attendance is constrained by stadium size, necessitating the use of a censored-regression technique. With the EPL data, there is an additional complication: there is some variation in reporting of attendances for different matches in the same stadium, so that attendance for a "sellout" is not necessarily equal to maximum stadium capacity. Following Buraimo and Simmons (2006), a sellout is defined as any attendance above 95% of maximum stadium capacity. Using this definition, approximately 55% of EPL matches during the sample period were sellouts. Each of these sellouts is treated as a right-censored observation in the estimation. For observations in the estimation sample, the average of *attendance* is approximately 35,000 spectators. This number is slightly below the raw average, since attendance at sellouts is calculated at exactly 95% of reported capacity.

In the estimation sample of six EPL seasons, the average number of *disciplinary points* per EPL team per year was 252.2 based on a 1-year lag. Over the same period, the average EPL team had 483.7 *normal fouls*, 56.5 *yellow cards*, and 2.9 *red cards* per year. The data also contain information about the reason a red card is given, as is shown in Table 8.1. In order to gain additional insight into the relationship between EPL attendance and red cards, this study creates three red-card categories: *Type-1 red cards* are those given for second yellow-card offenses; *Type-2 red cards* are those given for professional fouls and deliberate handballs; and *Type-3 red cards* are those given for serious foul play, violent conduct, spitting or offensive, insulting, abusive language, and/or gestures. Table 8.3 shows that the average team in the estimation sample had 1.3 *Type-1 red cards*, 0.5 *Type-2 red cards*, and 1.1 *Type-3 red cards* per year, reflecting the information in Table 8.1 that the most often-awarded red card is for a second yellow-card offense.

Absolute team quality is measured by the number of league points the home and away teams accumulate in a given year. Thus, *league points* measures team quality over an entire season. As in all FIFA-sanctioned league competitions, three points are given for a win and one point is given for a tie. In terms of (8.1), this measure posits that fan preferences for match-day attendance are related to the potential quality of the teams involved and not necessarily the potential quality of any given game. As shown in Table 8.3, the average EPL team amassed 54.9 *league points* over the sample period. Research also indicates that the relative quality of the participating teams influences match attendance (Forrest and Simmons 2002). Specifically, the closer in quality that the teams are, the greater attendance will be. This effect is measured with *match uncertainty*, computed as the absolute value of the difference between the points-per-game of the home team and the away team at the point of the match in each year.

Market potential is largely determined by local market size, measured using *population* per hectare and *income* per capita. Population data are measured as of April 2001, and these data are gathered from the UK Office of National Statistics' Web site (http://www.neighbourhood.statistics.gov.uk). Income data are gathered from Linacre (2002, Table 3b) and represent total household income per capita in Pounds Sterling/1,000 for 1999. *Population* and *income* should be positively related to attendance demand, assuming that a larger fan base translates into more paying spectators and assuming that football is a normal good. A greater number of high-quality sides in a given area should lead to less market potential. *Local competitors* are the number of additional EPL teams located in the home team's region in a given year; the measured effect of this variable is expected to be negative.

Attendance demand should be greater when a team is playing a traditional rival, an effect measured with the dummy variable *Derby match*. The home team may also benefit from the attendance of away fans; *distance* in kilometers from a club's home ground to the match location is included, with the expectation that greater distances reduce attendance demand for away fans.

This study assumes a demand form in which both the independent and dependent variables enter linearly. In addition, dummy variables for year and match number of the home team are included to measure yearly changes in demand and changes in demand over a given season that are not picked up by other independent variables. A series of dummy variables for each away team are also included to capture changes in EPL attendance associated with local fan interest in the visiting team. For instance, *attendance* should be greater for a home game against one of the Big Four teams, regardless of the value of the independent variables. Usage of the variables discussed above results in the data-specific equation for estimated attendance demand given in (8.2), where α_0 through α_9, β_{05-06} through β_{09-10}, γ_2 through γ_{38}, and δ_2 through δ_{31} are parameters to be estimated and e_{ijkt} is the error term.

$$\begin{aligned}\text{Attendance}_{ijkt} = {} & \alpha_0 + \alpha_1\text{Aggression}_{it-1} + \alpha_2\text{Home-TeamLeague Points}_t \\ & + \alpha_3\text{Away-TeamLeague Points}_t + \alpha_4\text{Match Uncertainty}_{ijkt} \\ & + \alpha_5\text{Population}_i + \alpha_6\text{Income}_i + \alpha_7\text{Local Competitors}_{it} \\ & + \alpha_8\text{Derby Match}_{ijt} + \alpha_9\text{Distance}_{ij} + \sum \beta_t\text{Year}_t + \sum \gamma_k\text{Match}_k \\ & + \sum \delta_j\text{Away Team}_j + e_{ijkt}. \end{aligned} \tag{8.2}$$

An obvious omission from (8.2) is a measure of ticket price. As is the case in many, if not most, studies of demand in sports, choosing an appropriate proxy for price in EPL football is a tough nut to crack. As stated by Krautmann and Hadley (2006, p. 177): "Although the appeal of using the sports industry to test economic theory is in the breadth and availability of data, it is ironic that the dilemma of choosing a good proxy for price may never fully be resolved." Although not a perfect solution, this study takes the position that much of the information which would be captured by a price variable is also included in the variables *population*, *income*, and *year*. Nonetheless, the reader is advised to keep the issue of missing price information in mind when interpreting the results of this study.

Estimation and Results

This section presents estimates of the effect of violent play on attendance demand in the EPL using equation (8.2). The data represent an unbalanced panel, where the panel unit is the home team. The panel nature of the data suggests that the most appropriate estimation technique would be a fixed-effect or random-effect model. However, the fact that the dependent variable, *attendance*, is a censored variable makes a panel-data estimator problematic. Specifically, censored-regression models with panel data are cumbersome to estimate and require more restrictions than linear panel-data models. Some past research on attendance demand in football use linear panel-data estimators (Garcia and Rodriguez 2002; Forrest and Simmons 2006; Madalozzo and Villar 2009), effectively ignoring the issue of censoring. However, since more than half of the EPL estimation sample is right censored, it would be unwise to ignore this issue with the present data set. It is possible to estimate a panel-data censored regression (i.e., the panel-data tobit model discussed by Wooldridge 2002, pp. 540–544), but models of this type are notoriously difficult to estimate. MLE panel-data tobit models were attempted with the EPL data, but none converged to a maximum. This outcome is unsurprising since the dependent variable is censored on stadium capacity, which will be highly correlated with the team individual-specific effect.

Given the complications with panel data and censoring, this study presents estimates of pooled, censored OLS regressions of *attendance* on the independent variables. Several variations of equation (8.2) are presented. Specifically, models are estimated with different indicators of aggressive play: (1) *disciplinary points*; (2) *normal fouls*, *yellow cards*, and *red cards*; and (3) *normal fouls*, *yellow cards*, and *red card types*. In addition, models are estimated interacting *home-team league points* with measures of aggressive play. Given the clear differences in aggression by league position shown in Table 8.2, one might expect that the influence of aggression on attendance demand would vary by league points. Specifically, EPL teams that are better (i.e., those that have more league points) will be less likely to substitute aggression for skill, and their fans may respond differently to increases or decreases in aggressive play.

Table 8.4 reports the results of censored regressions of EPL per-match attendance on aggressive play, team quality, and market size, where aggressive play is measured as *disciplinary points* for the home team. The results in the first column indicate that EPL attendance is affected by the aggressive play of the home team, with each additional *disciplinary point* lagged 1 year for the home team reducing current *attendance* by approximately 32 fans. Thus, each yellow card reduces *attendance* by 128 fans, and each red card reduces *attendance* by a minimum of 320 fans. The second column of Table 8.4 shows evidence that the effect of aggressive play varies by *home-team league points*, such that the marginal effect of an increase in aggressive play decreases as the average skill level of a club increases. The point of inflection occurs at 32 *league points*, implying that only those teams at the very bottom of EPL league table are expected to increased attendance with increased violent play. The fans of better EPL teams, on the other hand, seem to prefer a less aggressive approach. Perhaps this is related to the type of fan that is attracted to the best teams, or it may reflect the decreased need for teams to rely on aggression as a substitute for skill as skill level increases.

The effect of team quality is as expected, since more league points for either the home or away team leads to higher attendance. However, the effect of *away-team league points* is insignificant in both columns of Table 8.4, most likely due to the inclusion of the dummy variables for the away team. Greater *match uncertainty* leads to greater *attendance*, also as expected. Most of the market potential measures

Table 8.4 English Premier League attendance demand: dependent variable = *attendance (per match)*, violent play = *disciplinary points (1-year lag)*, $N = 1{,}957$ matches

Violent play		
Home-team disciplinary points (1-year lag)	−31.94***	62.77**
	(8.56)	(31.18)
Home disciplinary points × Home points		−1.96***
		(0.33)
Team quality		
Home-team league points	883.88***	1,378.29***
	(28.30)	(160.16)
Away-team league points	22.77	19.53
	(47.02)	(47.02)
Match uncertainty	3,011.96***	2,917.27***
	(967.94)	(967.36)
Market potential		
Derby match	11,809.60***	11,787.89***
	(2,361.66)	(2,361.02)
Local competitors	−2,364.86***	−2,353.65***
	(183.96)	(183.36)
Distance	−0.10	0.36
	(3.05)	(3.04)
Population	259.80***	243.78***
	(37.47)	(37.59)
Income	1,199.56***	1,217.77***
	(135.00)	(134.91)
Constant	−7,172.75	−31,163.72***
	(6,007.29)	(9,726.94)
R^2	0.687	0.695

Notes:
Robust standard errors in parentheses
R^2 is computed using the method of McKelvey and Zavoina (1975), which has been shown to be an appropriate goodness-of-fit measure for censored regression models (Veall and Zimmermann 1995)
Estimation includes dummy variables for match number, year, and opponent. Match fixed-effects are significant at the 5% level in both estimations ($F(37, 1{,}876) = 1.44$; $F(37, 1{,}875) = 1.46$), year fixed-effects are insignificant in both estimations, and away-team fixed-effects are significant at the 1% level in both estimations ($F(30, 1{,}876) = 1.79$; $F(30, 1{,}875) = 1.81$)
The constant term contains information on the excluded categories for match (#1), year (2004–2005), and opponent (Arsenal)
Defining a sellout as above 95% capacity leads to 1,085 censored observations (55.4%)
*Significant at the 10% level; **Significant at the 5% level; ***Significant at the 1% level

perform as expected; *attendance* is higher at matches against traditional rivals, teams with more *local competitors* have lower per-match attendance, and *population* and *income* are positively related to *attendance*. The lone insignificant measure of market potential is *distance*, which, like the effect of *away-team league points*, is most likely insignificant due to the inclusion of away-team dummies.

The EPL's index of disciplinary points does not include information on normal fouls. In addition, the effects of yellow and red cards are combined in this index,

Table 8.5 English Premier League attendance demand: dependent variable = *attendance (per match)*, violent play = fouls and cards, $N = 1{,}957$ matches

Violent play		
Home team normal fouls (1-year lag)	–55.65***	418.28***
	(9.59)	(37.92)
Home normal fouls × Home points		–9.17***
		(0.73)
	–45.75	–532.14***
Home-team yellow cards (1-year lag)	(41.46)	(147.56)
Home yellow cards × Home points		9.77***
		(3.11)
	–135.85	–3,190.35***
Home-team red cards (1-year lag)	(194.81)	(846.02)
Home red cards × Home points		58.51***
		(16.49)
Team quality		
Home-team league points	852.16***	4,464.76***
	(28.52)	(300.21)
Away-team league points	23.06	11.87
	(46.36)	(43.21)
Match uncertainty	2,835.47***	1,660.99*
	(956.59)	(899.14)
Market potential		
Derby match	11,354.95***	10,834.83***
	(2,335.74)	(2,188.77)
Local competitors	–2,286.76***	–2,123.96***
	(181.10)	(168.05)
Distance	–0.69	1.53
	(3.02)	(2.80)
Population	202.27***	270.87***
	(37.90)	(36.56)
Income	964.21***	966.70***
	(136.84)	(127.27)
Constant	–21,550***	–170,848***
	(7,621.60)	(16,915.99)
R^2	0.697	0.780

Notes:
See notes for Table 8.4
Estimation includes dummy variables for match number, year, and opponent. Match fixed-effects are significant at the 5% level in both estimations ($F(37, 1{,}874) = 1.47$; $F(37, 1{,}871) = 1.45$), year fixed-effects are insignificant in both estimations, and away-team fixed-effects are significant at the 1% level in both estimations ($F(30, 1{,}874) = 1.76$; $F(30, 1{,}871) = 1.96$)

which complicates the interpretation since yellow cards and red cards are given for different types of aggressive behavior. Table 8.5 shows results of censored regressions similar to those in Table 8.4, changing the measure of aggressive play to include *normal fouls* and disaggregating the effects of *yellow cards* and *red cards*. The results presented in the first column of Table 8.5 indicate that the relationship between aggressive play and EPL per-match attendance is negative, similar to that shown in Table 8.4. However, only the marginal effect of *home-team normal fouls* is statistically significant. The second column of Table 8.5 shows the importance of interacting fouls and cards with home-team quality, since adding in these interactions results in significant marginal effects for *normal fouls*, *yellow cards*, and *red cards*, which all vary by *home-team league points*.

Normal fouls lagged 1 year for the home team appear to have a positive marginal effect for low-quality teams and negative for high-quality teams (point of inflection, 46 league points), similar to the effect of *disciplinary points* shown in Table 8.4. Conversely, 1-year lagged *yellow cards* and *red cards* appear to have negative marginal effects for low-quality teams and positive marginal effects for high-quality teams (points of inflection, approximately 55 league points for both yellow and red cards). Thus, the results in Table 8.5 lead to a more nuanced conclusion than those from Table 8.4; namely, better EPL teams see lower *attendance* from aggression leading to *normal fouls*, but these same teams get greater *attendance* from aggressive play that results in some sort of card. It is unclear whether these results are due to differences in preferences of the fans of high- and low-quality teams or whether they are due to the relationship between the probability of winning and aggressive play. Note that the coefficients for the remaining variables are of the same signs as in Table 8.4, although some of the magnitudes have changed.

Before further discussing the implications of the estimation results, it may be instructive to investigate the effect of different types of red cards. As discussed previously, red cards can be given for a variety of offenses, some of which are more "violent" than others. Table 8.6 extends the analysis presented in Table 8.5 by disaggregating the number of red cards into three general categories. The results from Table 8.5 are similar to those in Table 8.6 with respect to *normal fouls* and *yellow cards*. The effect of *red cards* on attendance is more complicated. Specifically, the marginal effect of second yellow cards (*Type-1 red cards*) is negative and increasing in home-team quality (point of infection, 56 league points), similar to the effect presented in Table 8.5, while the effect of professional fouls (*Type-2 red cards*) is positive and decreasing in home-team quality (point of inflection, 55 league points). It is worth noting that red cards given for more aggressive or dangerous play (*Type-3 red cards*) do not significantly affect EPL attendance with or without an interaction effect. Perhaps this last result indicates that truly violent play has no impact on EPL attendance.

The results presented in Table 8.6 imply that fans of high-quality EPL clubs prefer to see their team play the type of aggressive football that leads to yellow cards, either a first or a second. However, fans of these same teams do not seem to like for their teams to commit professional fouls which lead to expulsion. Over the sample period, only six teams averaged more than 55 *league points* per year: Chelsea, Manchester United, Arsenal, Liverpool, Everton, and Tottenham Hotspur. Interestingly, these six teams are the only EPL teams that qualified for the UEFA Champions League over the estimation period, so they are clearly the six best teams in the sample.

Table 8.6 English Premier League attendance demand: dependent variable = *attendance (per match)*, violent play = fouls and card types, $N = 1{,}957$ matches

Violent play		
Home team normal fouls (1-year lag)	−50.44***	413.89***
Home normal fouls × Home points	(9.81)	(38.66)
		−8.97***
		(0.74)
Home-team yellow cards (1-year lag)	−28.70	−549.70***
Home yellow cards × Home points	(42.03)	(150.39)
		10.74***
		(3.14)
Home-team type-1 red cards (2nd yellow, 1-year lag)	−811.06***	−6,714.95***
Home type-1 red cards × Home points	(313.39)	(1,213.02)
		120.13***
		(24.15)
Home-team type-2 red cards (prof. foul, 1-year lag)	1,079.72***	4,834.57**
Home type-2 red cards × Home points	(454.90)	(1,967.86)
		−87.19**
		(38.82)
Home-team type-3 red cards (violent play, 1-year lag)	−121.29	−2,313.91
Home type-3 red cards × Home points	(338.41)	(1,721.45)
		41.17
		(34.29)
R^2	0.697	0.775

Notes:
See notes for Tables 8.4 and 8.5
Coefficients for team quality and market potential are suppressed for brevity. These coefficients are similar to those reported in Tables 8.3 and 8.4
Estimation includes dummy variables for match number, year, and opponent. Match fixed-effects are significant at the 5% level in both estimations ($F(37, 1{,}872) = 1.47$; $F(37, 1{,}867) = 1.44$), year fixed-effects are insignificant in both estimations, and away-team fixed-effects are significant at the 1% level in both estimations ($F(30, 1{,}872) = 1.76$; $F(30, 1{,}867) = 2.01$)

The results for the best EPL teams point to the importance of the relationship between wins and aggression in determining spectator preference for or against aggressive play. Aggressive play can increase the probability of winning, but there is also a cost associated with aggression if it leads to player expulsion (Jewell 2009). For the best EPL teams, yellow-card aggression may well enhance the probability of winning a given game, since the best teams are better able to overcome the cost of playing a man down should that aggression lead to an expulsion. Lower-quality teams, however, are less able to overcome an expulsion and have a higher cost of playing aggressively. On the other hand, the value of a professional foul may be much higher for lower-quality teams, since this type of foul negates a scoring chance for the opponent. Since we assume that fans have preferences for a winning team, the worse a team is, the less fans want to see unnecessary yellow cards and the more fans want to see valuable professional fouls, which may lead to expulsion but may also prevent a goal being scored by the opposition.

Elasticity of Attendance Demand for Aggressive Play in the EPL

The results presented in the proceeding tables allow for an analysis of the responsiveness of attendance demand for each EPL team. Table 8.7 presents estimated elasticities of demand for *attendance* with respect to changes in *home-team league points* and with respect to changes in *home-team disciplinary points* for each EPL team. The estimated elasticities are computed from the coefficients in Table 8.4 and are ranked by average *league points*. As expected, attendance demand is significantly increasing in *league points* for all EPL clubs, with elasticities ranging from 0.79 (Newcastle United) to 2.07 (Portsmouth). In general, EPL attendance demand is elastic with respect to home-team quality, suggesting that fans are responsive to changes that teams make to increase their skill level. Following the results in Table 8.4, most EPL teams have negative estimated demand elasticities for changes in *disciplinary points*, with the only exceptions being the four lowest-quality teams that have elasticities that are not significantly different from zero (Reading, Southampton, West Bromwich Albion, and Hull City, each of which are only in the estimation sample for a single season). All EPL teams have attendance that appears to be inelastic with respect to *disciplinary points*, suggesting that fans are relatively unresponsive to changes in this measure of overall aggressive play.

The results presented in Table 8.6 above give a more detailed view of EPL attendance demand, which can be used to generate a clearer picture of the responsiveness of EPL fans to changes in aggressive play. Table 8.8 presents estimated elasticities of demand for *attendance* with respect to changes in disaggregated measures of aggressive play for each EPL team. The estimated elasticities are computed from the coefficients in Table 8.6 and are ranked by average *league points*. Table 8.8 more clearly shows the differences in the responsiveness of fans of high- and low-quality teams to changes in aggressive play. For *home-team normal fouls*, fans of better teams respond negatively to more fouls, and this response is generally elastic; for the top six teams, fan response is highly elastic. Conversely, fans of low-quality teams respond positively to increases in *normal fouls*, and this response is generally elastic. Perhaps fans of the best EPL teams are accustomed to seeing their team win and win with style, so that more fouls simply ruins the spectacle, while fans of the worst EPL teams may not care as much how the team plays, as long as the team tries hard to win.

The demand elasticities with respect to changes in first or second yellow cards also clearly show the difference between fans of good and not-so-good EPL clubs. The estimated demand elasticities for *yellow cards* and for *Type-1 red cards* are negative or insignificantly different from zero for all except the Big Four teams. In addition, fan appear to respond inelastically to changes in yellow cards, so that any change in first or second yellow cards would bring about a proportionally smaller change in *attendance*. For *Type-2 red cards*, fans are even less responsive. Interestingly, the estimated elasticities with respect to *normal fouls* are generally larger than those for card offenses, suggesting that the relationship between per-game attendance demand and aggressive play in the EPL is largely driven by the most common type of fouls rather than by yellow or red cards.

Table 8.7 Elasticity of demand for aggressive play (from estimates in Table 8.4): ranked by average league points

Home team	Estimation sample years	Total matches	Attendance per match	League points per year	League-points elasticity	Disciplinary points per year	Disciplinary-points elasticity
Chelsea	04/05–09/10	114	39,590	87.2	1.95***	254.3	–0.69***
Manchester United	04/05–09/10	114	69,539	85.2	1.12***	235.7	–0.35***
Arsenal	04/05–09/10	114	50,391	74.7	1.43***	236.3	–0.41***
Liverpool	04/05–09/10	114	42,675	71.7	1.68***	194.0	–0.35***
Everton	04/05–09/10	114	36,274	59.7	1.47***	250.6	–0.37***
Tottenham Hotspur	04/05–09/10	114	34,492	57.3	1.50***	239.7	–0.35***
Aston Villa	04/05–09/10	114	37,234	54.2	1.34***	235.0	–0.27***
Manchester City	04/05–09/10	114	42,660	51.5	1.09***	239.3	–0.22***
Blackburn Rovers	04/05–09/10	114	22,902	51.0	1.69***	323.0	–0.56***
Bolton Wanderers	04/05–09/10	114	23,348	47.8	1.70***	281.0	–0.35***
Stoke City	09/10	19	26,844	47.0	1.22***	346.0	–0.38***
Newcastle United	04/05–08/09	95	48,900	44.4	0.79***	262.4	–0.13***
Fulham	04/05–09/10	114	22,145	44.3	1.78***	253.0	–0.28***
Middlesbrough	04/05–08/09	95	28,501	44.0	1.36***	262.8	–0.19***
West Ham United	06/07–09/10	76	33,360	43.3	1.04***	291.0	–0.20**
Birmingham City	04/05, 05/06, 09/10	57	26,936	43.0	1.37***	266.0	–0.23**
Portsmouth	04/05–09/10	114	18,954	42.8	2.07***	237.0	–0.25**
Charlton Athletic	04/05–06/07	57	25,555	42.3	1.72***	175.3	–0.14*
Sunderland	08/09, 09/10	38	40,165	41.5	0.85***	287.0	–0.13*
Wigan Athletic	06/07–09/10	76	18,357	40.5	1.83***	285.5	–0.26*
Reading	07/08	19	22,818	36.0	1.64***	174.0	–0.06
Southampton	04/05	19	30,209	32.0	0.97***	238.0	0.00
West Bromwich Albion	05/06	19	24,615	30.0	1.19***	204.0	0.03
Hull City	09/10	19	23,948	30.0	0.96***	310.0	0.05
Average					1.48***		–0.31***

Notes:
Elasticities are predicted values for each match and averaged over matches for each team
*Significant at the 10% level; **Significant at the 5% level; and ***Significant at the 1% level

Table 8.8 Elasticity of demand for aggressive play (from estimates in Table 8.6): ranked by average league points

Home team	Normal fouls per year	Normal-fouls elasticity	Yellow cards per year	Yellow-card elasticity	Type-1 red cards per year	Type-1-red-card elasticity	Type-2 red cards per year	Type-2-red-card elasticity
Chelsea	445.7	−4.16***	55.0	0.53***	1.2	0.11***	0.3	−0.02*
Manchester United	440.8	−2.21***	53.3	0.28***	1.5	0.07***	0.3	−0.01*
Arsenal	440.3	−2.37***	53.2	0.28**	1.2	0.05***	0.7	−0.03
Liverpool	443.8	−2.36***	45.5	0.23**	1.0	0.04***	0.0	–
Everton	501.8	−1.67***	54.0	0.14	1.7	0.01	0.7	0.00
Tottenham Hotspur	452.8	−1.34***	52.8	0.10	1.2	0.03	0.3	0.01
Aston Villa	524.5	−0.90***	53.3	0.04	0.7	0.00	0.2	0.00
Manchester City	473.8	−0.52***	52.3	0.00	1.5	−0.03*	0.5	0.00
Blackburn Rovers	549.7	−1.17***	70.3	0.01	2.3	−0.05*	1.2	0.02
Bolton Wanderers	512.0	−0.17**	66.7	−0.15	0.8	−0.05**	0.3	0.00
Stoke City	524.0	−0.15	73.0	−0.12	1.0	−0.04***	0.0	–
Newcastle United	499.2	0.16	58.6	−0.09	1.0	−0.02***	1.0	0.02*
Fulham	477.0	0.36	55.5	−0.19	2.0	−0.10***	0.5	0.02*
Middlesbrough	501.6	0.40	61.8	−0.20	1.0	−0.04***	0.0	–
West Ham United	516.5	0.39	67.0	−0.16*	1.0	−0.05***	0.5	0.01*
Birmingham City	509.0	0.54	57.3	−0.18*	0.7	−0.05***	1.7	0.06*
Portsmouth	495.7	0.75	54.8	−0.28*	1.7	−0.19***	0.2	0.01*
Charlton Athletic	474.0	0.66**	39.7	−0.16*	1.0	−0.07***	0.7	0.02**
Sunderland	441.0	0.48***	66.0	−0.17**	1.0	−0.05***	0.5	0.01**
Wigan Athletic	483.0	1.37***	62.8	−0.40**	1.5	−0.15***	0.8	0.06**
Reading	402.0	1.60***	38.0	−0.27***	2.0	−0.21***	1.0	0.07**
Southampton	450.0	1.89***	52.0	−0.36***	1.0	−0.10***	0.0	–
West Bromwich Albion	500.0	2.94***	40.0	−0.37***	2.0	−0.25***	2.0	0.08***
Hull City	565.0	3.42***	70.0	−0.67***	1.0	−0.13***	0.0	–
Average		−0.68***		−0.01		−0.03		0.01

Notes:
Elasticities are predicted values for each match and averaged over matches for each team
*Significant at the 10% level; **Significant at the 5% level; and ***Significant at the 1% level

Conclusion

This study shows evidence that per-game attendance in the English Premier League is related to the level of aggressive play of the home team. The results suggest that different types of fouls (normal fouls, yellow-card fouls, and red-card fouls) are related to EPL attendance in different ways. First, increases in normal fouls lead to lower attendance at better clubs and greater attendance at worse clubs. Furthermore, fans appear to be highly responsive to changes in normal fouls. Second, yellow cards, whether given for a first or second offense, lead to higher attendance at the best EPL clubs and lower attendance or insignificant changes in attendance at all other clubs. Third, red cards given for professional fouls have a small effect on EPL attendance, with the effect varying by league points. Fourth, red cards given for violent offenses do not appear to be related to EPL per-match attendance.

The relationship between demand for football attendance and aggressive or violent play can be direct, where fans have preferences for seeing aggressive play no matter what the outcome of the game, or indirect, where fans have preferences to see their home team win and the probability of winning is positively related to aggressive play for some teams. Although no firm distinction can yet be made between a direct or indirect connection, the results in this study suggest that EPL fans may not have a preference to see violent and aggressive play in and of itself. Instead, the fans of teams with less skill appear to respond to aggressive play differently than fans of better teams, a result which reflects the tradeoff between skill and aggression in producing wins. Further research is needed to clarify the pathways that connect demand for attendance to demand for aggressive play, but the results in this study provide a starting point.

No matter what the theoretical basis for the relationship between attendance demand and aggressive play, there are interesting policy implications for EPL clubs. Table 8.8 suggests that the each EPL club may have an incentive to change their level of aggression in order to maximize per-game attendance. Teams at the top of the league (like the Big Four) sell out many of their matches, so the only way they can increase attendance would be to increase stadium capacity. However, consider teams in the next tier of the league; conditional on team quality, teams like Everton, Aston Villa, and Manchester City can actually increase attendance by decreasing the number of normal fouls they commit. Given the tradeoff between team quality and aggression, this further suggests that these teams might consider spending more money on quality players, thereby reducing the need for aggressive play. Now consider the teams at the bottom of the league; conditional on quality, these teams can increase attendance by increasing the number of normal fouls and decreasing the number of yellow-card fouls. In as much as yellow-card fouls are normal fouls taken to an extreme, this implies that EPL teams like Sunderland and Wigan can increase attendance by scaling back the aggressive play a bit. In this way, they are not much different from the better teams in the league.

Acknowledgments The author thanks Megan Dorman, Brittany Causey, Andrea Maloy, and Ashley Hanisko for excellent research assistance.

References

Abrams M (2010) Anger Management in Sport: Understanding and Controlling Violence in Athletics. Human Kinetics: Champaign, IL.

Allen G, Roy G (2008) Does Television Crowd Out Spectators? New Evidence from the Scottish Premier League. Journal of Sports Economics 9:592–605.

Borland J, Macdonald R (2003) Demand for Sport. Oxford Review of Economic Policy 19:478–502.

Buraimo B, Forrest D, Simmons R (2009) The Twelfth Man? Refereeing Bias in English and German Soccer. Journal of the Royal Statistical Society A 173:431–449.

Buraimo B, Simmons R (2006) Market Size and Attendance in English Premier League Football. Lancaster Management School Working Paper #2006/002.

Dawson P, Dobson S, Goddard J, Wilson J (2007) Are Football Referees Really Biased and Inconsistent? Evidence on the Incidence of Disciplinary Sanction in the English Premier League. Journal of the Royal Statistical Society A 170:231–250.

Dohmen TJ (2008) The Influence of Social Forces: Evidence from the Behavior of Football Referees. Economic Inquiry 46:411–424.

English Football Association (EFA) (2010) FA Regulations 2010–2011: Disciplinary Procedures. EFA, London, England. September 2009. Accessed online: http://www.thefa.com/TheFA/RulesandRegulations.

FIFA (2010) Laws of the Game 2010/2011. FIFA, Zurich, Switzerland. July. Accessed online: http://www.fifa.com/worldfootball/lawsofthegame.html.

Forrest D, Simmons R (2002) Outcome Uncertainty and Attendance Demand in Sport: The Case of English soccer. The Statistician 51:229–241.

Forrest D, Simmons R (2006) New Issues in Attendance Demand: The Case of the English Football League. Journal of Sports Economics 7:247–266.

Garcia J, Rodríguez P (2002) The Determinants of Football Match Attendance Revisited: Empirical Evidence from the Spanish Football League. Journal of Sports Economics 3:18–38.

Garicano L, Palacios-Huerta I, Prendergast C (2005) Favoritism under Social Pressure. Review of Economics and Statistics 87:208–216.

Jewell RT (2009) Estimating Demand for Aggressive Play: The Case of English Premier League Football." International Journal of Sport Finance 4:192–210.

Jewell RT, Molina DJ (2005) An Analysis of the Relationship between Hispanics and Major League Soccer. Journal of Sports Economics 6:160–177.

Krautmann A, Hadley L (2006) Demand Issues: The Product Market for Professional Sports. In Handbook of Sports Economic Research, ed. Fizel J, pp. 175–189. ME Sharpe: Armonk, NY.

Linacre A (2002) Regional, Sub-Regional, and Local Area Household Income. UK Office for National Statistics.

Madalozzo R, Villar RB (2009) Brazilian Football: What Brings Fans to the Game? Journal of Sports Economics 10:639–650.

Matheson VA (2006) European Football. In Handbook of Sports Economic Research, ed. Fizel J, pp. 118–135. ME Sharpe: Armonk, NY.

McKelvey R, Zavoina W (1975) A Statistical Model for the Analysis of Ordinal Level Dependent Variables. Journal of Mathematical Sociology 4:103–120.

Simmons R (1996) The Demand for English League Football: A Club Level Analysis. Applied Economics 28:139–155.

Sutter M, Kocher MG (2004) Favoritism of Agents: The Case of Referees' Home Bias. Journal of Economic Psychology 25:461–469.

Veall MR, Zimmermann KF (1995) Comments on 'Goodness-of-Fit Measures in Binary Choice Models.' Econometric Reviews 14:117–120.

Wooldridge JM (2002) Econometric Analysis of Cross Section and Panel Data. MIT Press: Cambridge, MA.

Chapter 9
Violence in the Australian Football League: Good or Bad?

Ross Booth and Robert Brooks

Abstract In this chapter, the trend in violence in the Australian Football League (AFL) is examined for the period 2000–2009. We begin with a brief history of the league and the key features of the game. A distinction is made between controlled aggression and unsanctioned violence. The potential effects of both forms of violence on the future of the AFL are discussed along with the responses by the league in terms of programs to increase participation, changes to the laws of the game and their interpretation, and implementation of the tribunal system. Tribunal data for the period 2000–2009 is analyzed to see whether these changes have had any impact on both the level of violence and of attendance.

Introduction

Since its inception, Australian rules football has been a popular source of entertainment for its spectators. It is a game with significant physical contact, which many fans enjoy. However, in a time where numerous sports and other entertainments compete for the attention and involvement of the general public, it is important that the Australian Football League (AFL) does not let violence rise to a level that will discourage participation, attendance, viewership, and general interest in the game.

Brief History of the AFL

The fully professional and national AFL comprised 16 clubs in 2010 and developed from the Victorian Football League (VFL) formed in 1897. The VFL began

R. Booth (✉)
Monash University, Melbourne, VIC, Australia
e-mail: ross.booth@buseco.monash.edu.au

R.T. Jewell (ed.), *Violence and Aggression in Sporting Contests: Economics, History and Policy*, Sports Economics, Management and Policy 4,
DOI 10.1007/978-1-4419-6630-8_9,

in 1897 with eight clubs: Carlton; Collingwood; Essendon; Fitzroy; Geelong; Melbourne; St Kilda; and South Melbourne. Seven of these clubs were based in the Melbourne metropolitan area with Geelong located about 75 km southwest of Melbourne. Over time, the number of clubs in Melbourne grew, and in the 1980s and 1990s clubs from cities outside Victoria were admitted. The league became the AFL in 1990. Richmond and University were admitted in 1908, but University disbanded before the start of the 1915 season. In 1925, Footscray, Hawthorn, and North Melbourne joined to make a 12-team competition that continued until 1987. South Melbourne moved to Sydney for the 1982 season and became Sydney (Swans) in 1983.

The VFL expanded nationally with the inclusion of the Brisbane Bears and the Perth-based West Coast (Eagles) in 1987, Adelaide in 1991, and Fremantle in 1995, making a league of 16 teams. In 1997, Port Adelaide joined the AFL, while the formation of the Brisbane Lions as a merger of the Brisbane Bears and Fitzroy kept the number of clubs at 16. In addition, two Victorian clubs changed trading names in an attempt to become more attractive to (national) spectators and corporate sponsors. Footscray began trading as the Western Bulldogs in 1997 and in 1999 North Melbourne became the Kangaroos, only to revert to North Melbourne in 2009 following a change from private to member-ownership (Booth 2004). The league is now in an expansion phase with a new team on the Gold Coast in 2011 and another in Western Sydney in 2012.

Analysis of 16 clubs' finances and stated objectives suggest that the clubs are win-maximizers (subject to breaking even financially) rather than profit-maximizers. The win-maximizing objective stems from the nature of club ownership. Of the 16 clubs, 11 are owned by their members, 4 are owned by their respective state football Commissions, and the other license remains with the AFL (Booth 2004).

The VFL was incorporated as a company limited by guarantee in 1929 and traditionally operated under a delegate system. Each league club, as the "members" of the company, nominated an equal number of delegates, later known as directors, who collectively formed the board of directors – the ultimate decision-making body of the League. Following the 1993 Crawford report, the AFL clubs voted to abolish the club board of directors in order to transfer the bulk of decision-making authority to the AFL Commission – an independent board of between six and nine individuals, including the AFL CEO and any other executive commissioners who are appointed by the Commission. The AFL clubs are the only members of the AFL and save for some retained voting rights by the clubs relating to the admission, relocation, merging, or expulsion of clubs, the AFL Commission has the right to exercise all the powers of the League, including the formulation of policy and implementation of strategy (Macdonald and Booth 2007).

The AFL's mission statement is to make the league the most successful national elite sports competition for the benefit of key stakeholders (AFL clubs, players, and the public); promote player participation at all levels; promote public interest in the game; attract and develop the most talented athletes and sports administrators; and foster good citizenship on and off the field (AFL, various years).

Key Features of the Game

The distinctive features of modern Australian football include teams of 18 players (plus four interchange players) playing with an oval-shaped ball on an oval-shaped playing surface (135–185 m in length and 110–155 m in width), but with no offside rule. A match is played over four quarters each of 20 minutes. A goal worth six points is scored by a team member kicking the ball between the two goal posts, and a behind worth one point is scored either when the ball is kicked between the goal posts and the behind posts (the two of which are positioned on the outer side of each of the goal posts), or "rushed" by any player between the behind posts. Players are allowed to tackle each other between the shoulder and the knee, to run while bouncing the ball and to catch or "mark" the ball, the latter allowing a player to take a "free" kick. However, throwing the ball is not permitted, instead it must be either kicked or "handballed" or "handpassed" (punched with a clenched fist).

Australian rules football is renowned for being one of the most physically demanding and intense of contact sports. Sanctioned and unsanctioned physical violence has been a common part of the sport since its inception. In addition to the dramatic fitness demands of the game, players must endure frequent physical contact from opposing players (and without wearing any form of protective equipment, save for the odd player who wears a protective "bicycle" helmet). The lack of an offside rule exposes players to significant contact from all sides. As a result there is considerable exposure to both accidental and deliberate violent conduct by opposing players that can result in injury.

The most common kind of violence in the AFL occurs in the form of controlled aggression, or sanctioned violence, where players concentrate on winning the ball in the challenge, and challenging for the ball as aggressively as possible in a hard but fair way (Grange and Kerr 2008). Tackling (below the shoulder and above the knee) and bumping are allowed in Australian rules football, and the ideas of being "hard at the ball," "hard in the contest," and "tackling fiercely" are some of the most sought after and heralded attributes in football players. One of the key statistics in AFL, aside from the goals and behinds, is "contested possessions," 50–50 contests between opponents to win the ball. Often the winner is the one who throws his body in first, who has the strength to break his opponent's tackle, or who beats his opponent "one on one" in a show of strength and speed (Roberts 2010). These physical contests can easily lead to injuries and reckless conduct. The AFL wants to encourage these spirited contests, but at the same time the league wants to minimize any serious injuries to players.

The other notable kind of aggression that occurs in the AFL is that of unsanctioned violence. This kind of violence operates outside the laws of the game and may be a result of accidental or deliberate violent conduct. It is expected that this form of violence would have a negative effect on team performance if players are suspended as a result. In recent times, there has been a well-publicized push by the AFL Commission to address some of the negative effects of excessive violence in the game and to protect the players from unnecessary injury. For long-term expansion of the game, the AFL feels this is an issue it needs to address (AFL, various years). But whilst doing so, they must ensure a balance between attracting new fans and maintaining the current fan base. Characteristics such as hardness, aggression, and stoicism are commonly accepted and celebrated throughout the AFL community, and the AFL faces a difficult balancing act (Hickey and Fitzclarence 2004).

AFL supporters are among some of the most passionate fans in the world, yet if the AFL implements too many rule changes, it could potentially lose a large number of fans. By way of example, fierce rivalries exist between certain AFL clubs, such as Carlton and Collingwood, and more recently, Essendon and Hawthorn. On average, these marquee, rivalry games in the AFL fixture, draw in excess of 70,000 spectators. Thus, they are huge revenue raisers for the involved clubs and for the AFL itself. Aside from the even contest and high standards of play, these fixtures are often known for their "melees" and/or violent clashes. This is a significant feature which contributes toward the high match attendance. Sports broadcasters also take advantage of this rivalry, by building up the drama and providing viewers with flashbacks of the incidents that happened in past games.

A pertinent example of violence that captures the interest of the public and media would be the recent Hawthorn–Essendon rivalry. In 2010, this match drew a crowd of over 61,000 (which was in the top-ten crowd figures for the 2010 season), despite both teams being placed in the bottom half of the league table at the time (Quayle 2010). The primary reason for this attendance was the violent clashes that had occurred between these two teams in the past. In particular, the "line in the sand" Round 11 match between Hawthorn and Essendon at the Melbourne Cricket Ground in 2004 was the catalyst for this modern day rivalry. Between 2002 and 2006, Essendon toyed with Hawthorn, not only beating them on the scoreboard, but punishing them physically. But in the 2004 clash, Hawthorn struck back in a brutal fight, with 18 players in all facing the tribunal. Hawthorn was once again soundly beaten on the scoreboard that day, but they would never be humiliated by the physical dominance of Essendon again, and a great rivalry was born (Hinds 2004).

While violence on a sporting field can add an extra element of adrenalin and intensity to the viewing experience of a sporting match, injuries and negative publicity can in turn provide a disincentive to view and participate in that particular sport. The AFL needs to strike an appropriate balance between the action the spectators want to see, and violence and serious injury to players and any associated long-term harm to the game.

Physical Contact, Violence, and Its Effect on Participation

In terms of attendance, revenue, and television ratings, the AFL is Australia's premier sporting league (Macdonald and Booth 2007). But for the game to continue to grow, the AFL needs to win the hearts and minds of the young. One of the main factors that contribute to youth participation in any sport or recreational activity is the child's parents. It is often mothers or guardians who have considerable influence over the decisions as to which activities are ultimately pursued (Hickey and Fitzclarence 2004). Parents or guardians have reported concerns over injury and safety as the reason for discouraging their children from playing sport. In comparison with other contact sports such as rugby league and rugby union, the AFL is more highly participated in, and less frequently discouraged by parents and guardians. Yet in comparison with association football (soccer), its closest rival in terms of expansion and participation rates, AFL football is not viewed as favorably, since it is perceived as having more physical contact and violence and more likely to result in injury (Boufous et al. 2004).

The AFL has addressed this issue through its Auskick program of modified rules aimed at primary school children between the ages of 5 and 12. The main attraction to this form of the game, especially for parents, is the focus on friendship, fun, participation, and the noncompetitive environment where the aim is to keep violence and injuries to a minimum. Modified rules at Auskick level, including restrictions on tackling, are designed to foster learning and encourage fun in a safe environment, and this program has had a strong appeal with parents, especially mothers (AFL, various years).

The Tribunal System 2000–2009: Introduction of the Match Review Panel

An independent tribunal was created in 1913 (Pascoe 1995). A player reported for some act of violence was forced to attend a tribunal hearing where (typically) the umpire provided evidence in support of his report and the relevant players and witnesses were cross examined. A player who was found guilty would normally be suspended for a number of matches, with the number depending on the severity of the charge. Changes to the laws of the game and to the tribunal system made between 2000 and 2009 are detailed in the Appendix. A key change was the introduction of a new tribunal system for penalizing on-field player misconduct, which included a new match review panel (MRP). The MRP system was established in 2005 primarily to increase efficiency, credibility, and transparency, and to stamp out the financial burden of appeals. But even in the years prior to introduction of the MRP, new rules were administered to further protect players. These included, among others, more stringent classifications of rough conduct, harsher penalties for head high contact to players on opposing teams, the outlawing of tackles with two motions, and the pinning of players' arms in the tackle where the player is subsequently driven into the ground. All of these steps were publicized as an effort to increase safety and to promote a better public image for the game.

The introduction of the MRP was just part of a redesign of the system of reporting and punishing players for on-field violence. The MRP was introduced to review the footage of all games to find any reportable behavior. Each offense is now judged according to a scale of seriousness – conduct ranges from negligent to intentional, impact is from low to severe, and contact is either high or to the body. Each category draws a certain number of activation points, which correspond to the number of games for which the player will be suspended. In addition, a new penalty was created: a reprimand. If the activation points accrued for a particular offense are less than 100, a player can accept a reprimand and will not miss any matches through suspension, but these points will be taken into consideration should the player commit another reportable offense. Reprimands are generally given for negligent, low-body contact, according to the AFL's categorization of offenses.

The overhaul of the AFL tribunal system was aimed at making the sentences handed down more consistent and to promote the transparency of the match review process. By allocating activation points to categories, in theory, similar offenses should draw the same penalties. The system was also aimed at making the system more efficient, by enabling players not to have to appear at the tribunal if they wanted to accept a penalty. This is encouraged by offering an "early guilty plea" – if a player decides not to challenge the MRP's findings, they can receive a 25% discount on their sanction. The new system is also trying to reduce violence by issuing harsher penalties to repeat offenders, especially those players who have been suspended in the past 3 years. For each match suspended in the past 3 years, the player will receive a 10% loading for any new offenses, with the maximum loading capped at 50%. This is designed as a disincentive for repeat offenders: players who have been suspended in the past 3 years will be more conscious of their behavior on the field, as their penalties will be increased because of their previous offenses.

The impact of harsher penalties for repeat offenders was evidenced by the Steven Baker (St. Kilda) case in Round 13, 2010. Baker received a 9-week suspension for three counts of striking, and one of making unreasonable or unnecessary contact with an injured player. In 2007, Baker had received a 7-week suspension for rough conduct, and since this was within 3 years of the 2010 offense, Baker received the maximum 50% loading. In the same circumstances, a player who did not have a bad record would have received a 6-week suspension with an early guilty plea (Matthews 2010).

Tribunal and MRP Data Analysis: 2000–2009

We obtained data on an annual basis of AFL tribunal outcomes on a club basis for the period from 2000 to 2009 (AFL, various years). This is an interesting period to study as the AFL introduced the MRP system for the 2005 season. Thus, we have five full seasons of data before the introduction of the new system and five full seasons of data since the introduction of the new system. The data set includes the number of players charged (Players); the number of charges (Charges); the number of players suspended (Suspended); the number of matches players were suspended (Matches); the number of players fined (Fined); and the Australian dollar value of fines (Dollars in thousands). Since the 2005 season, we also have data on the number of players who have MRP total points under the threshold for a one-match suspension (UnderMatch). Using the dataset, we also construct two new variables: the

Table 9.1 Comparison of tribunal outcomes: before and after the introduction of the match review panel system

	Full sample (2000–2009)	Pre-MRP (2000–2004)	Post-MRP (2005–2009)	*p*-Value: *t*-test Pre vs. post
Players	118.0	125.6	110.4	0.17
Charges	157.2	172.0	142.4	0.14
Suspended	47.4	52.4	42.4	0.02
Matches	83.5	94.0	73.0	0.02
Matches/susp	1.76	1.80	1.73	0.62
UnderMatch			31.2	
UM+susp	63.0	52.4	73.6	0.00
Fined	59.3	59.4	59.2	0.99
Dollars	118.7	145.9	91.5	0.11

average number of matches a suspended player is suspended for (Matches/Susp); and the aggregate of the number of players suspended and the number of players who have MRP total points under the threshold for a one-match suspension (UM + Susp).

For each season, we aggregate the results across clubs, and Table 9.1 presents the average of each of these variables for the whole sample period and for each of the two subperiods either side of the introduction of the MRP system. In addition, Table 9.1 also reports the *p*-value of the *t*-test of differences in the means assuming equality of variances across the two subsamples. The results in Table 9.1 reveal the following patterns. First, there are no statistically significant changes in the number of players charged, number of charges, players fined, dollars fined, or average length of suspensions for players suspended comparing the periods before and after the introduction of the MRP system. Second, there are statistically significant decreases in number of players suspended and matches suspended after the introduction of the MRP system. Third, if you aggregate together the number of players suspended and the number with a reprimand (UnderMatch) in the MRP system, there is a statistically significant increase in the total number of players penalized for bad behavior with the introduction of the MRP system. Under the MRP system, players carry forward previous offenses as their previous track record (good or bad) contributes to their points outcome. Thus, the system introduces features where players are rewarded for past good behavior and penalized for past poor behavior. In this setting, having more players carrying forward points creates incentives for better future behavior and, therefore, is consistent with the significant reduction in the number of suspensions.

In Figs. 9.1–9.3, we show the time-series patterns in the number of players charged (Players); the number of charges (Charges); the number of players suspended (Suspended); the number of matches players were suspended for (Matches); the number of players fined (Fined); the dollar value of fines (Dollars); the number of players who have MRP total points under the threshold for a one-match suspension (UnderMatch); and the aggregate of the number of players suspended and the

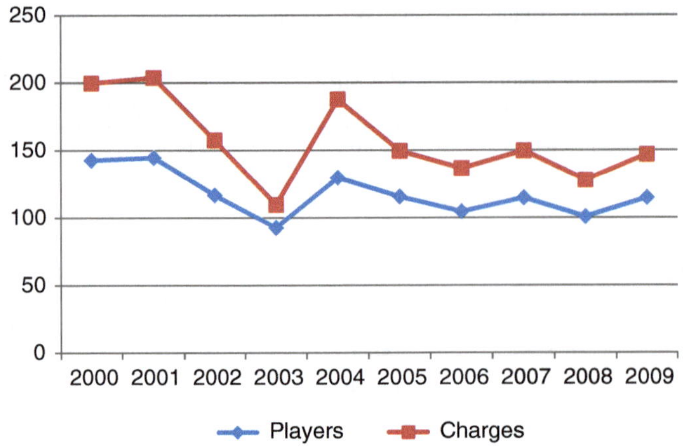

Fig. 9.1 Players charged, 2000–2009

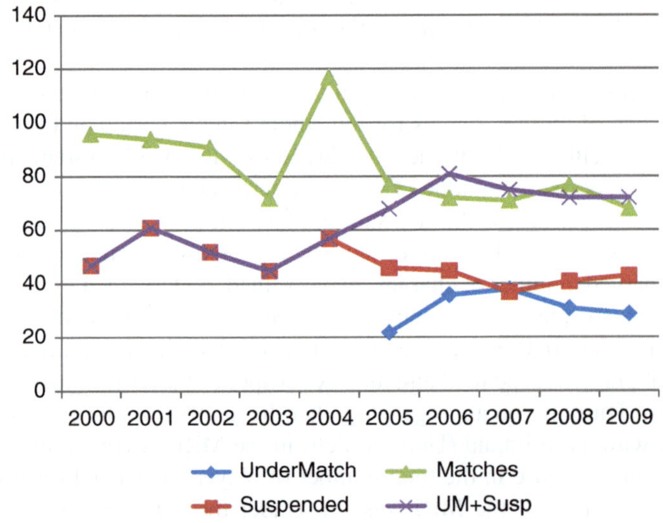

Fig. 9.2 Players suspended, 2000–2009

number of players who have MRP total points under the threshold for a one-match suspension (UM + Susp) over the period from 2000 to 2009. The figures show a sharp increase in the number of players charged, number of charges, dollar amount fined, and matches suspended in 2004. This was primarily due to a large number of charges from two individual matches in 2004: the round 11 Essendon vs. Hawthorn home and away games, and the Brisbane vs. Port Adelaide Grand Final, in which Brisbane's Alastair Lynch received a 10-match suspension and $15,000 in fines after being reported a record-equaling seven times for exchanging punches in a fight with Port Adelaide's Daryl Wakelin.

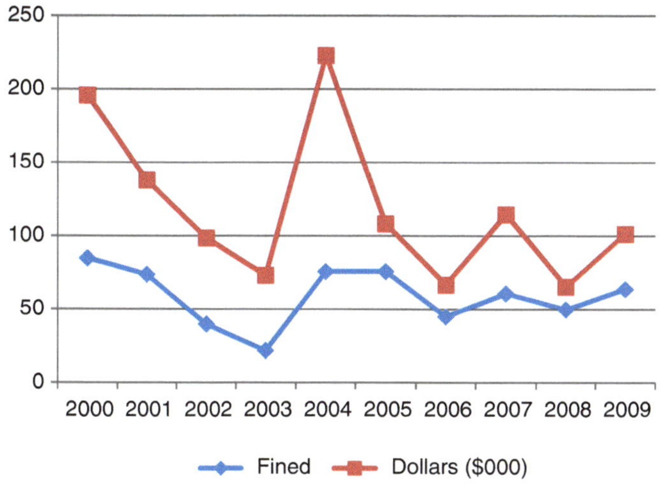

Fig. 9.3 Players fined, 2000–2009

Modeling Attendance Demand

There are a number of previous studies of attendance at Australian rules football. While most studies focus on modeling attendance in the AFL competition and its preceding competition in the VFL, a small number of papers also analyze data for the South Australian state-based competition prior to the introduction of Adelaide-based teams into the AFL [for details see Drever and McDonald (1981) and Fuller and Stewart (1996)]. It should be noted that Fuller and Stewart (1996) also include attendance at VFL matches in their modeling. Borland (1987) conducts a long-term time-series analysis of aggregate attendance in the VFL over the period 1950–1986 focusing on economic variables (income and prices) as well as habit persistence in consumption (lagged attendance) and uncertainty of outcome.

Borland and Lye (1992) model attendance at the match level in the VFL over the period 1981–1986. Their model makes allowance for habit persistence in consumption, match uncertainty, team performance, and stadium size. Pinnuck and Potter (2006) model attendance at the match level in the AFL over the period 1989–2002 as part of a larger exercise of determining the relationship between on-field performance of clubs and off-field financial success. Lenten (2009) uses a structural time-series model to explore the relationship between competitive balance and average match attendance in VFL/AFL football over the period 1945–2005, finding that improvements in competitive balance are associated with increased attendance. This finding is especially interesting given that Booth (2004) finds that labor market arrangements for players have impacted competitive balance in VFL/AFL football.

A summary of attendance and club membership data over our sample period is provided in Table 9.2. The data in Table 9.2 show an increase in both match attendance levels and membership levels across the last decade. The annual data for these

Table 9.2 Comparison of attendance and membership data: before and after the introduction of the match review panel system

	Full sample (2000–2009)	Pre-MRP (2000–2004)	Post-MRP (2005–2009)	*p*-Value: *t*-test Pre vs. post
Attendance	34,621	33,055	36,187	0.000
Membership	31,328	28,667	33,990	0.002

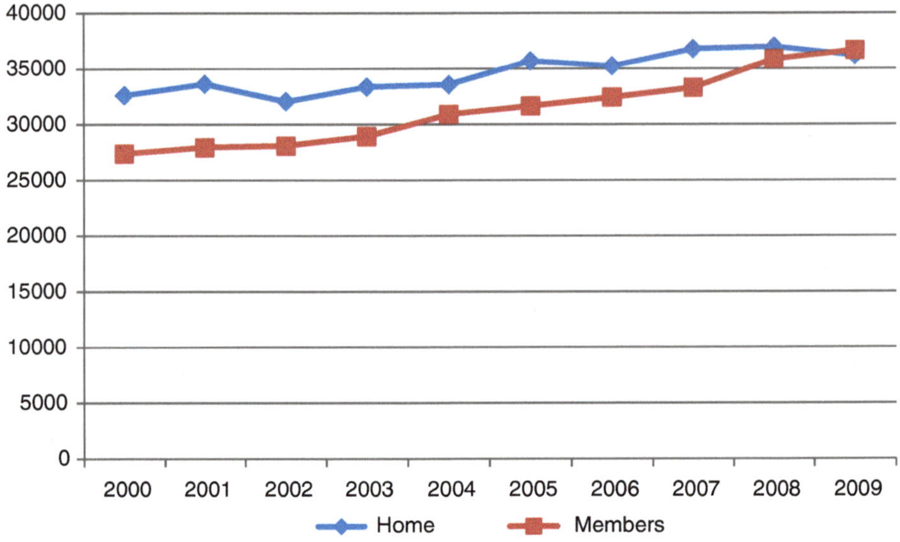

Fig. 9.4 Attendance and membership, 2000–2009

variables are reported in Fig. 9.4, which shows the same pattern and a narrowing gap between average attendance levels and club membership.

The previous literature on modeling attendance at Australian rules football has not considered the potential influence of variables for aggressive or violent play. Jewell (Chap. 8 of this book) includes an aggressive play variable in his study of attendance in the English Premier League. Based on the number of fouls in the previous season, the author is able to obtain a reasonable measure of aggressive play by team and year. It is more difficult to construct a comparable measure for the AFL, as free kicks in matches are awarded for a large number of rule infringements that are not related to aggressive play. Thus, we use our tribunal data from the previous section to measure the club's aggressive play at a season level by their tribunal outcomes for that season.

Our analysis of attendance is provided at the season level. Our base model for attendance reflects team performance and habit persistence through the inclusion of variables for the number of wins per team per season and the number of registered club members in a given season. The base model specification is:

$$\text{ATTENDANCE}_{it} = \beta_0 + \beta_1\text{WINS}_{it} + \beta_2\text{MEMBERSHIP}_{it} + \beta_3\text{TRIBUNAL}_{it} + u_{it}.$$

Table 9.3 Home game attendance: base model specification

	Wins	Membership	Tribunal	R^2
Players	226.96	0.576	185.614	0.377
	(0.061)	(0.000)	(0.202)	
Charges	228.225	0.574	126.278	0.379
	(0.059)	(0.000)	(0.161)	
Suspended	243.11	0.569	−79.019	0.371
	(0.046)	(0.000)	(0.735)	
Matches	240.04	0.570	−30.508	0.371
	(0.048)	(0.000)	(0.780)	
UnderMatch	578.56	0.573	−681.90	0.334
	(0.739)	(0.000)	(0.194)	
Fined	243.26	0.568	458.12	0.411
	(0.038)	(0.000)	(0.001)	
Dollars	235.02	0.579	123.03	0.391
	(0.049)	(0.000)	(0.024)	

Rows corresponds to the use of that measure as the tribunal variable
p-Values are given in parentheses

$ATTENDANCE_{it}$ is the average home game attendance for club *i* in season *t*; $WINS_{it}$ is the number of wins by club *i* in season *t*; $MEMBERSHIP_{it}$ is the membership of club *i* in season *t*; $TRIBUNAL_{it}$ is the measure of tribunal outcomes for club *i* in season *t*. For the tribunal measure, we consider the seven different measures discussed in the tribunal data analysis section of the paper. Specifically, these tribunal measures are: the number of players charged (Players); the number of charges (Charges); the number of players suspended (Suspended); the number of matches for which players were suspended (Matches); the number of players fined (Fined); the Australian dollar value of fines in thousands (Dollars); and the number of players who have MRP total points under the threshold for a one-match suspension (UnderMatch). For the UnderMatch variable, we only model the data since the introduction of the MRP system.

Estimation Results

In Table 9.3, we report the results of a panel-data, least-squares regression of the base model. We include the model specifications with the seven different tribunal outcome measures. Our results show a consistently positive and significant coefficient on the number of wins across all of the specifications of the model that imply a marginal increase in average match attendance of over 200 for each win, although the estimate is lower for the UnderMatch specification that only includes the five most recent seasons. The membership variable is consistently positive and significant across all of the specifications of the model, and the coefficient magnitude

Table 9.4 Home game attendance: fixed effects specification

	Wins	Membership	Tribunal	R^2
Players	482.504	0.329	−17.496	0.878
	(0.000)	(0.000)	(0.844)	
Charges	480.174	0.325	4.416	0.878
	(0.000)	(0.000)	(0.938)	
Suspended	480.089	0.322	29.903	0.878
	(0.000)	(0.000)	(0.822)	
Matches	481.433	0.319	26.846	0.878
	(0.000)	(0.000)	(0.649)	
UnderMatch	531.527	0.420	120.297	0.918
	(0.000)	(0.000)	(0.620)	
Fined	478.775	0.323	30.679	0.878
	(0.000)	(0.000)	(0.723)	
Dollars	482.902	0.330	−15.736	0.878
	(0.000)	(0.000)	(0.618)	

Rows correspond to the use of that measure as the tribunal variable
p-Values are given in parentheses

suggests an increase in average match attendance of approximately 570 for every additional 1,000 members.

The significance of the tribunal measures as proxies for aggressive play depends upon the particular measure. Most of the variables are not significant. Exceptions are found using Fined and Dollars, where statistically significant and positive impacts on attendance are found. In the AFL, most fines are administered as a response to melees in which a large number of players push and shove each other and grab at each other's shirts. In general, these melees are not characterized by acts of violence that lead to suspensions. However, they may remind supporters of past famous brawls but in a safer setting where players assert their authority. This finding is comparable to the differential impacts of the different levels of penalties in the National Hockey League (NHL) (for a discussion, see Coates and Grillo (2009) and Chap. 4 of this book).

Because our model is on a season basis, we are not able to include a match uncertainty measure at the match level along the lines of studies such as Borland and Lye (1992) and Pinnuck and Potter (2006). In addition, we do not include a competitive balance measure along the lines of Lenten (2009). As an alternative, we estimate our models with fixed effects for both seasons and clubs. Thus, these fixed effects capture an amalgam of match uncertainty and competitive balance effects, along with any role played by changing economic variables. Because there are not significant right-censoring constraints in attendance at AFL stadia, we do not have the problems of using fixed effects estimators noted by Jewell in Chap. 8 of this book.

In Table 9.4, we report the results of panel-data, fixed-effects estimation for our base model augmented with club and season fixed effects. The inclusion of season fixed effects should capture any general time trend in attendance that might arise independent of our aggressive play and violence variables. As before, we include

Table 9.5 Home game attendance: fixed effects specification with finals interaction

	Wins	Membership	Tribunal	Finals × Tribunal	R^2
Players	389.618	0.339	−77.163	118.570	0.879
	(0.000)	(0.000)	(0.449)	(0.237)	
Charges	420.215	0.331	−25.065	57.692	0.878
	(0.000)	(0.000)	(0.707)	(0.407)	
Suspended	457.668	0.322	−3.770	73.903	0.878
	(0.000)	(0.000)	(0.981)	(0.709)	
Matches	433.556	0.319	−17.914	87.880	0.879
	(0.000)	(0.000)	(0.818)	(0.375)	
UnderMatch	503.778	0.422	38.155	127.991	0.918
	(0.000)	(0.000)	(0.915)	(0.753)	
Fined	413.887	0.332	−57.492	164.424	0.879
	(0.000)	(0.000)	(0.609)	(0.219)	
Dollars	418.504	0.336	−54.544	80.384	0.880
	(0.000)	(0.000)	(0.184)	(0.141)	

Rows correspond to the use of that measure as the tribunal variable
p-Values are given in parentheses

model specifications with the seven different tribunal outcome measures. Our results show a consistently positive and significant coefficient on the number of wins across all of the specifications of the model that suggest a marginal increase in average match attendance of approximately 480 for each win, which is more than double that found without fixed effects. As in Table 9.3, the estimated coefficient on wins is higher on the UnderMatch specification. The membership variable is consistently positive and significant across all of the specifications of the model and the coefficient magnitude suggests an increase in average match attendance of approximately 320 for every additional 1,000 members, quite a bit smaller than in Table 9.3 without fixed effects. In general, the tribunal measures as proxies for aggressive play are not significant. This indicates that any aggressive play feature that these variables were capturing in the previous specification have now been captured by the fixed effects.

In Chap. 8 of this book, Jewell finds that the impacts of aggressive play on EPL attendances depends on team quality with a positive impact for low-quality teams and a negative impact for high-quality teams. To explore whether such an impact might also be present in the AFL, we augment our base model with an interactive dummy variable allowing the impacts of tribunal outcome on attendance to vary depending on whether the club reached the finals in that season. Thus, our augmented model is:

$$\begin{aligned}\text{ATTENDANCE}_{it} &= \beta_0 + \beta_1\text{WINS}_{it} + \beta_2\text{MEMBERSHIP}_{it} + \beta_3\text{TRIBUNAL}_{it}\\ &+ \beta_4\text{FINALS}_{it} \times \text{TRIBUNAL}_{it} + u_{it}.\end{aligned}$$

In Table 9.5, we report the results of fixed effects estimation for our model augmented with an interactive dummy on final qualification and tribunal outcomes.

Table 9.6 Home game attendance: fixed effects specification with wins interaction

	Wins	Membership	Tribunal	Wins × Tribunal	R^2
Players	446.740	0.328	−65.379	4.321	0.878
	(0.007)	(0.000)	(0.765)	(0.810)	
Charges	471.493	0.325	−4.046	0.789	0.878
	(0.000)	(0.000)	(0.975)	(0.943)	
Suspended	462.197	0.319	−30.000	5.552	0.878
	(0.000)	(0.000)	(0.933)	(0.857)	
Matches	434.340	0.312	−63.196	8.170	0.878
	(0.000)	(0.000)	(0.697)	(0.551)	
UnderMatch	690.256	0.419	950.068	−72.759	0.920
	(0.000)	(0.000)	(0.172)	(0.202)	
Fined	462.254	0.323	−11.559	3.796	0.878
	(0.000)	(0.000)	(0.956)	(0.821)	
Dollars	464.447	0.329	−38.316	2.040	0.878
	(0.000)	(0.000)	(0.579)	(0.713)	

Rows correspond to the use of that measure as the tribunal variable
p-Values are given in parentheses

Note that over the sample period, 8 of the 16 teams qualified for the finals/playoff series at least once. As above, we include the model specifications with seven different tribunal outcome measures. Our results show a consistently positive and significant coefficient on the number of wins across all of the specifications of the model that suggest a marginal increase in average match attendance of over 400 for each win, and the estimate is a bit higher on the UnderMatch specification. Thus, we find little change regarding the wins variable. The membership variable is consistently positive and significant across all of the specifications of the model and the coefficient magnitude is approximately the same as in Table 9.4.

As in Table 9.4, the tribunal measures as proxies for aggressive play are not significant in Table 9.5. Interestingly, the point estimates of our parameters reveal the opposite pattern to Jewell's results; we find a negative coefficient for teams that do not make the finals and a positive coefficient for the teams that do make the finals. However, the importance of this result should not be overstated given the lack of statistical significance in the estimated parameters. As a further exploration of the relationship between aggressive play and team quality, we estimate a model with an interactive dummy variable between wins and tribunal outcomes. The results of estimation of this model are reported in Table 9.6. In general, the results are qualitatively similar to those reported in Table 9.5 for the finals and tribunal interactive variables.

Coates and Grillo (2009) explore changes in the NHL rules around physical play and their impacts on scoring and team revenues. The rule changes happened during the NHL lockout period in 2004/2005 and provide a sample for either side of this period in which to examine the impacts of the rule changes. The analysis demonstrates a positive impact on scoring as a result of the rule changes, although the

Table 9.7 Home game attendance: fixed effects specification with MRP interaction

	Wins	Membership	Tribunal	MRP × Tribunal	R^2
Players	494.980	0.310	−131.454	327.651	0.881
	(0.000)	(0.000)	(0.204)	(0.038)	
Charges	498.758	0.296	−87.851	272.696	0.884
	(0.000)	(0.000)	(0.175)	(0.007)	
Suspended	477.438	0.327	−153.420	513.119	0.882
	(0.000)	(0.000)	(0.330)	(0.037)	
Matches	480.388	0.327	−60.800	234.914	0.882
	(0.000)	(0.000)	(0.399)	(0.039)	
Fined	506.282	0.298	−103.458	390.792	0.883
	(0.000)	(0.000)	(0.311)	(0.018)	
Dollars	505.808	0.307	−41.859	204.001	0.883
	(0.000)	(0.000)	(0.203)	(0.016)	

authors also find that easier scoring may have created a greater return from better defensive play strategies. In addition, the authors find a significant impact of the penalty variables on team revenues, although the impact appears to differ between USA and Canadian teams and the impact seems to have changed as a result of the rule changes. In the AFL context, there has also been a significant rule change to the tribunal system with the introduction of the MRP system. Following the example of Coates and Grillo (2009), we now explore whether the impacts of the tribunal variables vary with the introduction of the MRP system. In this setting, we augment our fixed effects model with an interactive dummy variable for the post-MRP period. Our model becomes:

$$\begin{aligned}\text{ATTENDANCE}_{it} &= \beta_0 + \beta_1\text{WINS}_{it} + \beta_2\text{MEMBERSHIP}_{it} + \beta_3\text{TRIBUNAL}_{it} \\ &\quad + \beta_4\text{MRP}_{it} \times \text{TRIBUNAL}_{it} + u_{it}.\end{aligned}$$

The results of the estimation of this model are reported in Table 9.7. Our results show a consistently positive and significant coefficient on the number of wins across all of the specifications, with a marginal increase in average match attendance of approximately 500 for each win. The membership variable is consistently positive and significant across all of the specifications, with a marginal increase in average match attendance of approximately 300 for every additional 1,000 members. Interestingly, the results show radically different impacts of the tribunal measures in the pre-MRP period as compared to the post-MRP period. In the pre-MRP period, all of the tribunal measures are negative and insignificant, similar to the results found in other tables. However, for the post-MRP period, all of the tribunal measures are positive and significant. Recall that the MRP system was designed to reduce aggressive play; to the extent that the tribunal measures proxy for aggressive play, we find an additional premium to aggressive play *after* the introduction of a system designed to curtail such play. In this setting, our results are comparable to those obtained by Coates and Grillo (2009) for the NHL.

Summary and Conclusions

The physicality of AFL football is what draws many fans to its games. But the AFL is aware that violence and injuries must not rise to a level that will discourage attendance, membership, viewership, and ultimately participation. During the period 2000–2009, the AFL changed the tribunal system (most notably with the introduction of the MRP in 2005) in the belief that the new system would not only be more efficient, transparent, and certain, but that the system would reduce the incidence of violence and injuries and help improve its public image as a sport for the young.

Overall, our results suggest that the MRP system has been effective in reducing the level of violent play given the statistically significant reductions in the number of players suspended and total matches suspended in the season. This has been achieved without any significant change in the average number of matches per suspension, and would appear to be related to three factors: (1) the set of changes in the rules of the game to reduce the likelihood of violent play as detailed in Appendix; (2) the greater transparency in the penalty system; and (3) the carry over system that rewards previous good behavior and sets higher penalties for repeat offenders. Interestingly, despite the reduction in violent play, there does appear to be a greater attendance premium from aggressive play after the introduction of the MRP system.

Acknowledgments The authors wish to thank Scott Taylor from the AFL for the provision of data on tribunal outcomes. The authors also wish to thank Col Hutchinson from the AFL for provision of data on attendances, memberships, and team performance. The authors also wish to thank some of the Clayton 2010 sports economics class for their insights into this topic.

Appendix: Key Changes to the Laws of the Game

[Sources: AFL (various years); Lovett (2011)]

2000

- New definition of "charging" introduced: "A charge means an act of colliding with an opposition player where the amount of physical force used is unreasonable or unnecessary in the circumstances, irrespective of whether the player is or is not in possession of the football or whether the player is within 5 m of the football."
- Players could choose to accept automatic fixed penalties when reported for minor offenses – could plead guilty and receive a monetary penalty for a first offense on any of the following charges: abusive language, disputing a decision, interfering with a player kicking a goal, pinching, spitting, wrestling, shaking the goal post, deliberately kicking the ball into the roof of a stadium or time wasting.

2001

- Given that the AFL's view is that the Grand Final is the showpiece game of the year and must be decided by skill rather than on-field violence, any player found guilty of a reportable offense in the Grand Final would receive a more severe penalty than if he had been found guilty of a similar offense during the home and away season.

- Any player found guilty of a reportable offense in a home and away or finals match, and subsequently suspended, may not necessarily be allowed to serve that suspension during the preseason competition only.
- Spitting was deleted from the list of charges where a player may take an automatic fine.

2003

- Concern about situations where players bent over the ball are subject to heavy front-on approach by a player intending to bump or tackle. Greater emphasis on protection is given to a player on the ground, preventing any other player sliding into him with his knees.

2004

- A significant change was made to the AFL judicial process with the appointment of the game's first Video Reports Officer whose role was to review all video footage of incidents forwarded to him to decide if a report should be laid. Previously, this was the task of the umpires officiating in a particular match.

2005

- In November 2004, the AFL Commission approved a new structure for the AFL tribunal designed to promote efficiency, transparency, and certainty (see below).
- Almost all clubs supported significant change to the current system and were overwhelmingly supportive of penalties to be offered before a tribunal hearing.
- Improved efficiency by allowing players to accept the penalties without facing a tribunal hearing.
- Improved transparency and certainty by introducing a publicly available table of offenses.
- The table of offenses is graded according to: whether the offense was intentional, reckless or negligent; whether the impact was severe, high, medium, or low; whether the incident was in play or behind play; and whether the contact was high or to the body.
- All reports (umpire, video reports officer, etc.) would be channeled through a MRP which would review all reports and determine what penalty on an offense a player could accept. Under the previous system, field umpires could make a report on the day of the match or after reviewing the video, and the AFL Investigations Officer could report players after a video review. These reports went straight to the AFL tribunal without reference to any panel.
- A Chairman would control the tribunal hearing while a three-panel jury would determine the guilt or innocence of the player and also decide the length of suspension.
- Players would face a jury of their peers if they chose not to accept the penalty offered by the MRP.

- Reduce damage done to the credibility of the tribunal process by not requiring victim players to attend and give evidence at Tribunal hearings.
- Legal representation is permitted.
- The cost of Appeals Board hearings reduced but an appeal will be restricted to certain grounds. Formerly, the cost of lodging an appeal was $15,000 ($7,500 nonrefundable), now reduced to $5,000 and $2,500, respectively.
- Melees and second and subsequent wrestling fines added to the list of penalties with a set of monetary penalties.
- Rules regarding public comment on tribunal decisions to be refined.
- Updated and improved technology available to the MRP and tribunal.

2006

- The overhaul of the MRP and the AFL tribunal system received great support at the end of its first year (2005) and was fine-tuned on the basis of feedback on its first year of operation.

2007

- Rule 15.4.5 was changed to protect a player from forceful front-on contact when that player had his head down over the ball.
- Under Rule 19.2.2, "intentionally recklessly or negligently bumping or making forceful contact to an opponent from front-on when that player has his head over the ball" will be a reportable offense and strict sanctions will be applicable.
- The above change was made to provide greater protection for players who are playing the ball and to minimize the likelihood of serious spinal injury.
- There were also stricter interpretations dangerous tackles such as by unnecessarily and dangerously driving an opponent into the ground with their arms pinned.

2008

- The new law relating to bumping a player with his head over the ball and the interpretation for policing dangerous tackles received tremendous support and continued in 2008.

2009

- Introduction of a free kick for misconduct, such as interfering with an injured player – previously players could be reported but a free kick could not be awarded.
- During the season, clubs raised concerns with the increased prevalence of prohibited contact as a tactic before matches and in between quarters. As this tactic is against the current laws and not in the spirit of the game, all umpires were instructed to closely monitor this practice and award free kicks against players who forcefully bump, push, or strike their opponents when the ball is more than 5 m away.

References

Australian Football League (AFL) (various years) AFL Annual Report, 2000, 2001, 2002, 2003, 2004, 2005, 2006, 2007, 2008, 2009. AFL Publishing: Melbourne, Australia.

Booth, R (2004) The Economics of Achieving Competitive Balance in the Australian Football League, 1897–2004. Economic Papers 23:325–344.

Borland J (1987) The Demand for Australian Rules Football. Economic Record 63:220–230.

Borland J, Lye J (1992) Attendance at Australian Rules Football: A Panel Study. Applied Economics 24:1053–1058.

Boufous S, Finch C, Bauman (2004) Parental Safety Concerns: A Barrier to Sport and Physical Activity in Children? Australian and New Zealand Journal of Public Health 28(5).

Coates D, Grillo AS (2009) Does Crime Pay? Evidence from the NHL. Unpublished manuscript.

Drever P, McDonald J (1981) Attendances at South Australian Football Games. International Review for the Sociology of Sport 16:103–113.

Fuller M, Stewart M (1996) Attendance Patterns at Victorian and South Australian Football Games. Economic Papers 15(1):83–93.

Grange P, Kerr J (2008). Physical Aggression in Australian football: A Qualitative Study of Elite Athletes. Psychology of Sport and Exercise 11:36–43.

Hickey C, Fitzclarence L (2004) 'I Like Football When it Doesn't Hurt': Factors Influencing Participation in Auskick. ACHPER Healthy Lifestyles Journal 51(4).

Hinds R (2004) Bombers, Hawks to Face 27 Charges. Sydney Morning Herald Online, posted June 9. Accessed online: http://www.smh.com.au.

Lenten L (2009) Unobserved Components in Competitive Balance and Match Attendances in the Australian Football League, 1945–2005: Where is All the Action Happening? Economic Record 85:181–196.

Lovett M (2011) AFL Record Guide to Season 2011. AFL Publishing: Melbourne, Australia.

Macdonald R, Booth R (2007) Around the Grounds: A Comparative Analysis of Football in Australia. In The Political Economy of Football in Australia, ed Stewart B. Melbourne University Press: Melbourne, Australia.

Matthews B (2010) Saint Nick's Rule Taps Baker – Finals Only Hope of Playing This Season. Herald Sun, June 29, p. 82.

Pascoe R (1995) The Winter Game: The Complete History of Australian Football. Text Publishing: Melbourne, Australia.

Pinnuck M, Potter B (2006) Impact of On-Field Football Success on the Off-Field Performance of AFL Football Clubs. Accounting and Finance 46:499–517.

Quayle E (2010) Bombers Too Hard for Hawks. The Age Online, posted May 2. Accessed online: http://www.theage.com.au.

Roberts P (2010) Stats Incredible: The Tackling Myth. MelbourneFC.com.au, posted June 22. Accessed online: http://www.afl.com.au.

Part V
Spectator Violence and Criminal Activity

Chapter 10
The Effect of Hooliganism on Greek Football Demand

Vassiliki Avgerinou and Stefanos G. Giakoumatos

Abstract This study estimates the effect of spectator violence on football demand based on the information of spectator disorder incidents in Greek football stadia. The results indicate that more serious incidents of spectator violence in and around stadia have a significant negative effect on attendance demand. These incidents involve stadium damages, violence toward players, referees, fans, and the police and resulting injuries. Less serious manifestations of stadium disorder do not have a negative effect on demand but have increased dramatically in the last years. The big five clubs Olympiakos, PAOK, Aris, AEK, and Panathinaikos seem to create the most incidents of spectator violence. Our results imply that there are economic gains to football clubs from effective spectator violence control.

Introduction

Football has been historically associated with violence. Interestingly, violence in football was not always perceived as a social problem. In the thirteenth century, playing ball served as an opportunity to settle old scores and land disputes between the young men of neighboring villages and towns in England. As early as the fourteenth century though, there were calls for controls of the game not for moral, but for commercial reasons: business suffered as ordinary citizens were driven away from market towns on match days (Marsh et al. 1996). In 1303, an Oxford student was killed, allegedly by Irish fellow students, while playing football. By 1314, the mayor of London issued a proclamation on the King's behalf forbidding rumpuses with large footballs in the public fields. In the next three centuries, football was officially banned in England by more than 30 royal and municipal laws.

V. Avgerinou (✉)
University of Peloponnese, Sparta, Greece
e-mail: vasavg@uop.gr

R.T. Jewell (ed.), *Violence and Aggression in Sporting Contests: Economics, History and Policy*, Sports Economics, Management and Policy 4,
DOI 10.1007/978-1-4419-6630-8_10,

Not only did the kings believe that recreational sports were impeding the progress of archery which was necessary for war, but also mayhem was caused by football in towns. During the eighteenth century, football was sometimes a symbol of resistance to authority or to change (Birley 1993). In 1740, a football match was played at Kettering, of 500 men per side, but the real purpose was to loot a local food store (Marsh et al. 1996). Football in its recognizably modern form came largely as a result of urbanization and industrialization which confined the battlefield game into smaller play areas. The incidence of spectator disorderliness has varied considerably over time but Dunning et al. (1988) report that it has always been present on a greater or lesser scale since the 1870s.

It is obvious that when one refers to football violence a distinction must be made between violence on the field, in the sense of aggressive play, and violence among spectators. Violence on the field is an inherent feature of the sport, falls under the rules of the game and is penalized accordingly by the referee. It is acceptable and even desirable to an extent for the entertainment of watching the game. Spectator violence is considered a threat to the sport and a social problem.

The term "hooliganism" has been used to describe spectator violence in football. It is not a scientific concept and has no precise definition. The word possibly stems from the "Houlihans," an Irish family that lived in London in the late nineteenth century and loved fighting (Pearson 1983). Dunning et al. (1988, 2000) describes the disorderliness that attracts the label football hooliganism as complex and many-sided. It takes place in football-related contexts and embraces verbal violence, throwing of missiles at players and officials (ranging from various objects as coins and broken seats to fireworks and crude incendiary devices), pitch invasions deliberately engineered to halt the match or attack players, vandalizing of club, private and public property, fights between opposing fans or with the police in, around, or far away from football stadia, attacking vehicles carrying rival supporters, dodging in and out of moving traffic, etc. Pearson (2007) distinguishes between two specific types of disorder that have been labeled hooliganism: (a) spontaneous and usually low-level disorder caused by fans at or around football matches; and (b) deliberate and intentional violence involving organized gangs who attach themselves to football clubs and fight firms from other clubs, sometimes a long way in time and space from a match. A tragic example synonymous to football hooliganism is the Heysel Stadium disaster in Brussels, Belgium in 1985, where 39 fans lost their lives and 600 more were injured at the European Cup Final between Juventus and Liverpool FC, as a result of rioting before the match.

Significant academic research has been devoted to identifying and explaining the causes of football hooliganism. The dynamics of the working class in relation to the "bourgeoisification" of football (increase of middle-class spectators and superstar status of players), the ritualization of human aggression, the advertising of the game by the media as a context where fights and "exciting" incidents regularly take place, subcultural characteristics that legitimize violent behavior, cultural and historical forces, and major "fault-lines" of particular countries. Some explanations of the phenomenon are: social class and regional inequalities in England; religious sectarianism in Scotland and Northern Ireland; linguistic subnationalisms in Spain; and city

Table 10.1 Football-related arrests and injuries

	Greece		England
	A and B divisions		EPL and championship
Year	Arrest	Injuries	Arrests
2003–2004	117	122	2,048
2004–2005	135	120	2,031
2005–2006	124	109	2,098
2006–2007	108	120	2,102
2007–2008	88	93	2,099
2008–2009	162	123	2,041

particularism in Italy (Dunning et al. 1988, 2000; Armstrong 1998; King 1997; Marsh et al. 1996). In a study of Greek hooliganism, Courakis (1998a, b) suggests that hostile fanaticism is more likely attributed to deeper socioeconomic, cultural, and/or geographic differences (e.g., between teams of Thessaloniki and Athens) than to factors stated by the "hard core" supporters, i.e., the provocative behavior of the opposing team's fans (25.8%), unjust decisions by the referees (14.2%), and the presence and/or provocative attitude of police officers (13.7%).

Hooliganism seems to be a European and Latin American, and to a lesser extent an Australian, phenomenon. In North America, there is no equivalent of hooliganism, although spectator violence exists, but more in the form of common assault, drunken, and disorderly behavior (Spaaij 2006). The reasons are differences in the historical development of football, the sports and supporter culture, and the demographic composition of sports crowds, i.e., middle-class, college-educated spectators and almost half women (Roberts and Benjamin 2000; Roadburg 1980). It is worth noting that isolated incidents of football-related crowd disorder have been reported in countries as diverse as the USSR, Nigeria, Hungary, and India (Dunning 2000).

Tolerance of hooliganism manifestations by governments and football governing bodies has varied in different periods and different countries. The Heysel Stadium tragedy that resulted in the indefinite ban of English clubs from European competitions by UEFA led to the implementation of drastic control measures by the English government. While the English suffered the most (hooliganism has been called the "British disease"), they were forced to deal with hooliganism, and although the phenomenon has not disappeared, crowd disorder in and around English stadia has reduced spectacularly. While Greek football never faced the severity of English hooliganism, with four related deaths in 30 years, spectator violence in football stadia is a persistent problem and a cause of headaches for politicians and governing bodies.

Table 10.1 presents numbers of arrests and injuries during a 6-year period for Greek A and B Divisions (the top two divisions) and arrests for the respective English competitions. Police statistics on football-related arrests, wherever available and detailed, only offer a rough indication of recent changes in hooliganism. Changing police tactics significantly influence the number of arrests making variations in yearly data difficult to interpret (Marsh et al. 1996; Spaaij 2006). Total attendance in Greek Super League (formerly the A Division) in 2009–2010 season was 1,802,365, and the number of arrests was 123 (Super League, 2009–2010), i.e., 0.068%, or 1 in 14,705 spectators. Total attendance in the English Premier League for 2009–2010 season was 12,977,251, and arrests were 1,225 (UK Home Office, 2010) , i.e., 0.094% or 1 in 10,638 spectators. One needs to bear in mind that police tactics in the two countries differ vastly.

In their report on football violence in Europe, Marsh et al. (1996) refer to some quantitative data for various European countries that experienced problems of football-related violence at the end of the 1980s. The available data indicate that incidents occurred at around 10% of matches throughout Europe. In Italy, violent incidents occurred in 9.5% of the matches in Serie A and Serie B. In Belgium, serious incidents occurred in 5% of matches, "serious" defined as those resulting in large numbers of arrests and people seriously injured, and less serious incidents occurred at 15% of matches. In the Netherlands, there was some form of fan disorder at 10% of matches. Around 10% of German fans were regularly involved in violence, but no quantitative data are available. In France, one or two aggressive incidents would be recorded for every dozen or so matches, which may not involve actual violence or injuries. In Sweden, one-seventh of the games were affected by fan violence, although the type is not defined. The definition of "serious" seems to be problematic, as when it is not defined it does not necessarily mean violent. However, when an incident is defined as serious, it usually involves injuries.

Although hooliganism has been researched extensively from a sociological and psychological point of view, there seems to be limited research on the economic aspects of spectator violence. Dunning et al. (1988) suggest that although hooliganism cannot be regarded as the sole or even major cause of falling attendances in England, it has undoubtedly been an important contributory factor. Bird (1982) tests a dummy variable for hooliganism in his football demand model, but finds no significant results, probably because of choosing a poor proxy of hooliganism based on a personal impression, as noted by the author. In any case, the absence of systematic recording of football-related violent incidents in any European country complicates the construction of a hooliganism variable.

Hooliganism affects the utility a football fan derives from the stadium experience. Injury from missiles or proximity to fights, delays during the match, policing and surveillance cameras, and a variety of club-level punishments (like games behind closed doors or bans on travel to away matches) are some of the direct and indirect consequences of hooliganism. This study estimates the effect of spectator violence on football demand based on information on spectator disorder incidents in Greek football stadia. The results indicate that more serious incidents of spectator violence in and around stadia have a significantly negative effect on attendance demand. Less serious incidents of stadium disorder do not appear to have a negative effect on demand, even though they have increased dramatically in the last several years. The definition of "seriousness" used in this study is based on the legal treatment of the incidents and the resulting damage to property and public safety.

The majority of the incidents are caused by the fans of the five biggest Greek teams, and there appear to be three clusters of clubs, categorized according to their fans' misbehavior. While in other countries away matches attract more trouble than home matches, Greek fans are more violent at home games. Games of the second half of the season are more violent than those in the first half, as each game becomes more crucial for the league title, qualification for European competitions, and avoidance of relegation.

Data and Methodology

Our data on hooliganism are based on the decisions of the Sports Court regarding matches of the Greek First National Division for 23 seasons from 1986–1987 to 2008–2009 (EPAE Sports Court 1986–2006; Super League Sports Court 2006–2009). We analyze 1,430 decisions on 4,426 incidents of fan misbehavior, ranging from swearing to violent clashes outside stadia, recording the incidents of fan misbehavior upon which the cases against the clubs were built. Football clubs are punished for the inappropriate behavior of their fans inside and in the vicinity of stadia. According to the Sports Law and the Disciplinary Code, teams are obliged to take precautionary measures against actions of their players, coaches, and fans that "damage the reputation of the football game" (Disciplinary Code 2010). Punishments involve monetary fines, games behind closed doors, and bans on the broadcast of matches depending on the severity of the incidents (Law 2725/1999).

Defining Fan Misbehavior

Incidents of fan misbehavior are classified into 11 categories: (1) swearing or inappropriate chanting; (2) lighting of flares, smoke bombs, fireworks, etc. or use of laser pointers, etc.; (3) throwing of missiles; (4) pitch invasion; (5) stadium damages; (6) incidents that necessitate police intervention outside stadium; (7) incidents that necessitate police intervention inside stadium; (8) violence outside stadium; (9) violence inside stadium; (10) injuries; and (11) deaths. The following examples provide an idea of the incidents: (1) yelling "(club name)'s fans are whore's sons!" to the rival supporters (2006); (2) lighting of 47 flares (2009); (3) firing flares at rival supporters (1986); (4) pitch invasion by fans attempting to attack referee (2008); (8) burning of police vehicles and a public bus outside stadium (1991); (9) violent clash inside the stadium between rival fans using broken seats, wooden sticks, rocks, chains, and bats as weapons (2005); player head injury from thrown rocks and coins (1988); (11) death of supporter from flare coming from rival fans' gate (1986). This was the only death related to spectator violence inside a Greek stadium during the sample period.

Data Limitations

A first limitation of our data is that decisions refer to the incidents of fan disorder *that were recorded or brought to the attention of the court.* There is no certainty that all incidents that occurred during the match are mentioned in the decision. In earlier years of the sample, cases were built on a variety of evidence from the match sheet (filled out by the referee), the report of the match observer, the report of the Permanent Committee against Violence, the police report, the video of the game, and press reports. More recently, cases have been based only on the match sheet and the match observer's report, and it is highly likely that some information on fan violence is missing. Cases of misreporting by referees revealed later through videos and press reports are investigated by the Sports district attorney.

A second limitation of our data is that, as football clubs are by law responsible only for the actions of their fans inside and around stadia, no information can be extracted about the violence away from stadia. Such violent actions fall into the category of common crime rather than football-related crime. Thus, our data on hooliganism are limited to incidents in and around stadia. Although an important part of the phenomenon cannot be investigated, this presents no serious problem for the main objective of this study. We believe that the disorder and violence during the match and at the time fans enter and exit the stadium are more likely to influence the decision to buy a ticket than the violence that takes place away from stadia, even if the distant violence is somehow related or influenced by the game.

Overview of the Data

Table 10.2 presents the percentage of matches that are affected per incident for the 23-year period. We use the percentage, rather than the number, of incidents as the number of matches played per year during this period differs significantly, from 182 to 306 per season. The size of the first division varied from 14 to 18 teams, while in the last two seasons playoffs were introduced to the competition. To get the percentages, the number of incidents is divided by the total number of games played per year.

On average, fans engage in swearing and inappropriate chanting in 19.88% of total matches per year, light fireworks/flares, etc. in 12.61% of matches, throw missiles in 20.46% of matches, invade the pitch in 2.93% of matches, create stadium damages in 4.35% of the matches, the police have to intervene around the stadium in 0.65% and inside the stadium in 2.93% of matches, respectively, fans create violent incidents around the stadium in 1.26% of matches, and violent incidents inside the stadium occur in 2.76% of matches. Light or more serious injuries happen in 3.72% of the matches. A closer look at Table 10.2 reveals that "less serious" incidents, like verbal violence, the lighting of flares, etc., and the throwing of missiles have

Table 10.2 Percentage of matches affected

Year	Swearing	Lighting/ objects	Throwing of missiles	Pitch invasions	Stadium damages	Police outside	Police inside	Violence outside	Violence inside	Injuries
1986–1987	5	0.83	3.33	1.25	0	0	0	0.83	0	0.83
1987–1988	12.92	1.67	7.08	1.25	1.25	0	1.67	2.08	3.33	1.67
1988–1989	23.33	2.92	25.83	4.58	5.83	**2.08**	4.17	**6.25**	7.08	**12.5**
1989–1990	15.03	1.96	17.32	4.58	2.29	0.65	1.96	1.96	2.94	3.59
1990–1991	6.86	1.63	11.44	1.96	1.96	0	2.94	1.31	4.25	4.25
1991–1992	7.19	3.27	9.15	0.33	0.98	0.98	1.31	0.98	1.31	4.25
1992–1993	6.86	1.31	5.56	0.98	0.33	0.65	1.31	0.65	0.33	1.31
1993–1994	16.99	6.86	15.03	0.65	0.65	0.65	1.63	0.65	0.98	3.27
1994–1995	32.68	15.36	24.18	2.61	2.94	0	1.31	0	1.31	1.96
1995–1996	23.20	7.19	18.30	2.29	2.61	0	1.63	0.33	1.63	3.92
1996–1997	23.86	14.71	25.49	1.63	1.96	0	0.98	0.33	1.63	3.27
1997–1998	22.22	11.11	17.97	2.29	3.92	0.98	4.58	1,31	3.59	2.61
1998–1999	29.41	21.57	31.05	2.61	4.58	0.98	4.58	0.98	3.59	4.9
1999–2000	17,65	17.32	28.76	1.31	3.59	0.65	2.61	2.61	2.61	4.58
2000–2001	4.17	9.58	20	1.25	9.58	0.83	1.67	1.25	1.25	4.58
2001–2002	7.14	20.33	29.12	4.40	14.29	1.1	4.95	1,1	4.40	6.59
2002–2003	7.92	26.67	32.92	**8.75**	**20.83**	1.67	**9.58**	2.08	**7.50**	9.58
2003–2004	4.17	14.58	17.92	3.33	8.33	**2.08**	5.83	2.5	3.33	5
2004–2005	29.17	17.92	22.92	5.42	5,00	0.42	5.83	0.42	4.58	4.58
2005–2006	47.08	28.75	27.5	4.17	6.25	1.67	4.17	2.08	3.33	2.08
2006–2007	22.92	25.83	26.67	7.50	5.42	0	2.92	0	2.5	042
2007–2008	32.54	13.49	17.86	2.78	1.19	0	0.79	0	0.79	0
2008–2009	**55.95**	**34.52**	**40.08**	4.37	4.37	0	3.17	0	3.17	1.19
Number of incidents	1,230	780	1,266	181	269	40	181	78	171	230
Mean (%)	19.88	12.61	20.46	2.93	4.35	0.65	2.93	1.26	2.76	3.72

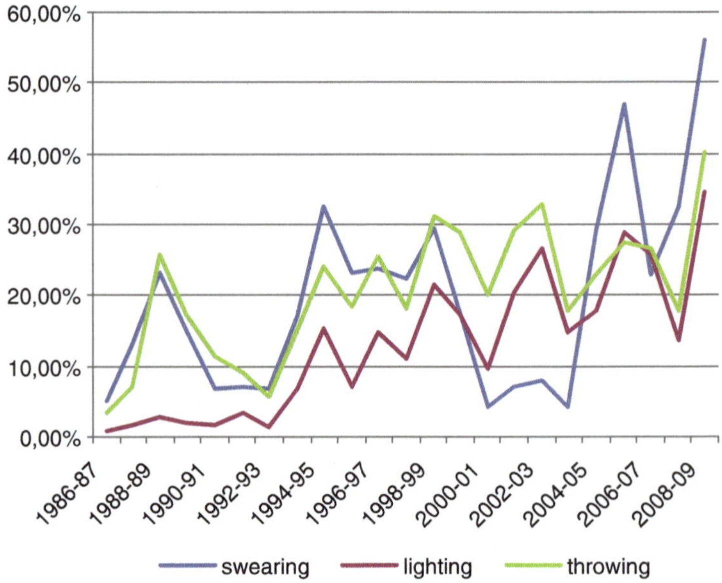

Fig. 10.1 Incidents Type 1 to Type 3

increased dramatically during the last few years. Figure 10.1 presents the three columns of Table 10.1 graphically, showing the increasing trend. Incident types four to ten occur on a lower scale but are persistent, and peaceful seasons are followed by more turbulent ones. This is in line with the unexpected factor incorporated in hooliganism (Marsh et al. 1996).

One interesting feature is that while in other countries fans cause more trouble at away matches (Marsh et al. 1996), Greek fans create more disorder at home than at away matches. That might be expected after 2003 when fan movement bans were imposed but home disorder is higher than away disorder during the first decade as well. Also of interest is the difference in violence in the first and second half of seasons: Games in the first half of the season are more peaceful than games in the second half, when the league title and European Championship qualification for the big clubs and relegation for the small clubs are at stake. For instance, pitch invasions are 70% higher on average in the second half of a season, stadium damages are 47% higher, and injuries are 64% higher.

Violence in Greek Football by Year

To capture the effect of spectator violence on demand, we base the construction of the violence variable on the assumption that some incidents are less serious than others and, thus, less of a nuisance to peaceful fans. The classification of "seriousness" is in line with the legal treatment of the incidents, although the sports law has "overlaps" of seriousness between incidents depending on the resulting damage to property and public safety. For example, the throwing of a missile will be regarded as more serious and result in a heavier punishment of the club if it results in the death of a fan than violent clashes that result to light injuries.

Swearing and inappropriate chanting are a form of verbal violence that can range from insults to threats and be directed toward referees, players, and rival fans. The clubs whose fans engage in such behavior can receive a fine, but individual fans almost never get arrested. Nonhooligan fans might be annoyed by insults and swearing, especially if they bring family members to the stadium. The spontaneous engagement in offensive chanting by thousands of peaceful fans, not just by hardcore fans, raises questions about the level of nuisance this practice creates and whether it influences attendance.

Lighting of various objects is potentially dangerous but presents more of a threat to the hardcore fans than to the rest of the spectators because of its local character. Hardcore fans are usually sitting together in a specific part of the stadium. *Throwing of missiles* can be very dangerous depending on the type of missile. The use of a flare gun in 1986 resulted in the only death inside a Greek stadium, when a fan was hit by a flare in the throat. However, not all flares are lit or thrown with aggressive purpose. Many flares are lit when the team scores a goal, as a form of celebration and an expression of joy. Decisions do not distinguish between violent or celebratory intention. *Pitch invasions* range from celebratory to those with a purpose to halt the game, attack referees, or attack players. Understandably, identifying the intent of any pitch invasion and its perception by the rest of the fans is not straightforward.

Incidents 5–11 have a clear intention of, or are a clear result of, violence: *stadium damages* are violence against property, and *violent clashes with fans or the police inside and around the stadium* are straightforward manifestations of violence. *Intervention of the police* means that incidents happen on a relatively large scale and need to be contained. Police intervention transforms the image of the game into a "war zone" and no doubt have a negative effect on the enjoyment of peaceful fans. *Injuries*, whether light or serious, and *deaths* are a measure of the severity of violence and are likely to drive peaceful fans away from stadia. We expect incidents 5–11 to influence demand negatively.

Table 10.3 shows the percentage of games that have at least one event of Type 5 or higher by year, and Fig. 10.3 illustrates the time trend. In the 6,188 matches played in 23 years by clubs that competed in the first division for at least five seasons during this time, in 8.21% or 510 matches an incident Type 5 or higher occurred. From Table 10.2 and Fig. 10.2, we can attribute the two peaks in Fig. 10.3 mainly to stadium damages in 2002–2003 (20.83%) and injuries in 1988–1989 (12.5%).

Violence in Greek Football by Club

Based on the violent behavior of their fans, clubs can be classified as more or less violent. For this purpose, we use cluster and factor analysis (Johnson and Wichern 1998; Raykov and Marcoulides 2008). Cluster analysis is a statistical technique to

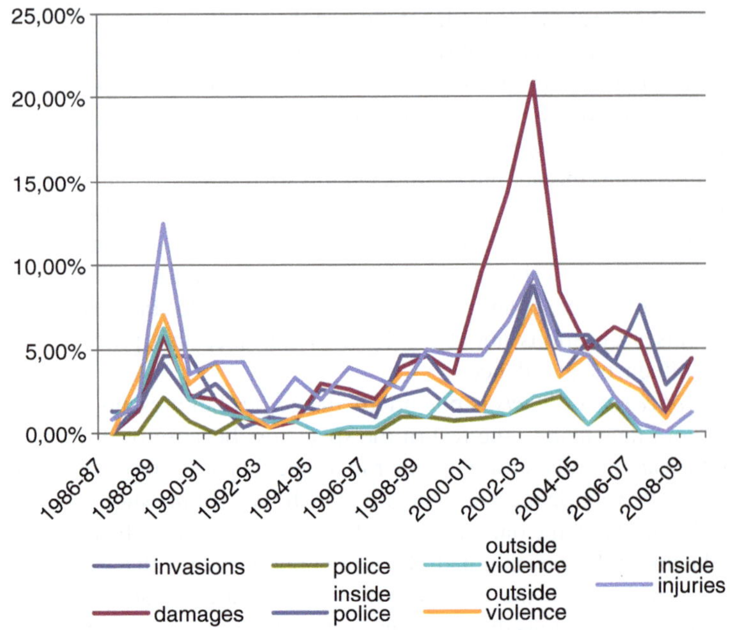

Fig. 10.2 Incidents Type 4 to Type 10

build groups (clusters) from multivariate data. The groups are constructed in order to be as homogeneous as possible and so that the differences among the various groups are as large as possible. Our dataset for the cluster analysis includes 26 clubs that played five or more seasons in the first division and the corresponding percents for each of the ten types of events of fan violence for the 1986–1987 to 2008–2009 seasons. The cluster analysis reveals that Greek clubs appear to be divided into three main groups. Based on the classification resulting from cluster analysis, the total percentages for each type of event are calculated per cluster of clubs. Table 10.4 lists the three groups, and Fig. 10.4 presents these percentages graphically.

The first cluster contains the big five clubs in regards to number of fans, league position, and ticket sales in the Greek championship: AEK, Aris, Olympiakos, Panathinaikos, and PAOK. The fans of teams in this cluster create violent events much more frequently than fans of clubs in the other two clusters. Fans of clubs in the second cluster seem to produce violent events rarely, and fans of clubs of the third cluster can be considered as the average of the other two clusters. Like other countries, Greek football seems to have its share of troublemaking fans. These troublemakers are largely represented by the fans of the big five teams, traditional rivals located in the capital of Athens (AEK, Olympiacos, and Panathinaikos) and the second largest city, Thessaloniki (Aris and PAOK).

Table 10.3 Violence in Greek Stadia (matches with at least one violent event of Types 5 to 10/total matches)

Year	Matches with violent event	% of matches
1986–1987	4	1.67
1987–1988	9	3.75
1988–1989	43	17.92
1989–1990	17	5.56
1990–1991	22	7.19
1991–1992	20	6.54
1992–1993	9	2.94
1993–1994	14	4.58
1994–1995	18	5.88
1995–1996	19	6.21
1996–1997	19	6.21
1997–1998	25	8.17
1998–1999	27	8.82
1999–2000	30	9.80
2000–2001	29	12.08
2001–2002	36	19.78
2002–2003	61	25.42
2003–2004	28	11.67
2004–2005	21	8.75
2005–2006	21	8.75
2006–2007	18	7.50
2007–2008	5	1.98
2008–2009	15	5.95
Mean	22.17	8.21

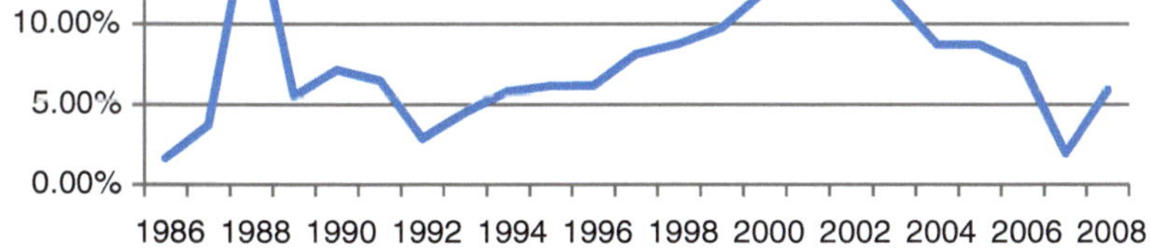

Fig. 10.3 Violence in Greek Stadia

Factor analysis is a statistical technique that uncovers unobserved factors in multivariate data. The point of factor analysis is to reveal the unobserved factors that explain most of the overall variability of the data. We apply factor analysis to the Greek dataset, and discover that a single factor explains 89% of the total

Table 10.4 Cluster analysis

Cluster 1	Cluster 2	Cluster 3
AEK	Apollon Athinon	Egaleo
Aris	Apollon Kalamarias	Ionikos
Olympiakos	Athinaikos	Iraklis
Panathinaikos	Doksa Dramas	Kalamata
PAOK	Edessaikos	Kavala
	Ethnikos	Larissa
	Panachaiki	Levadiakos
	Paniliakos	OFI
	Xanthi	Panionios
		Panserraikos
		Proodeytiki
		Veria

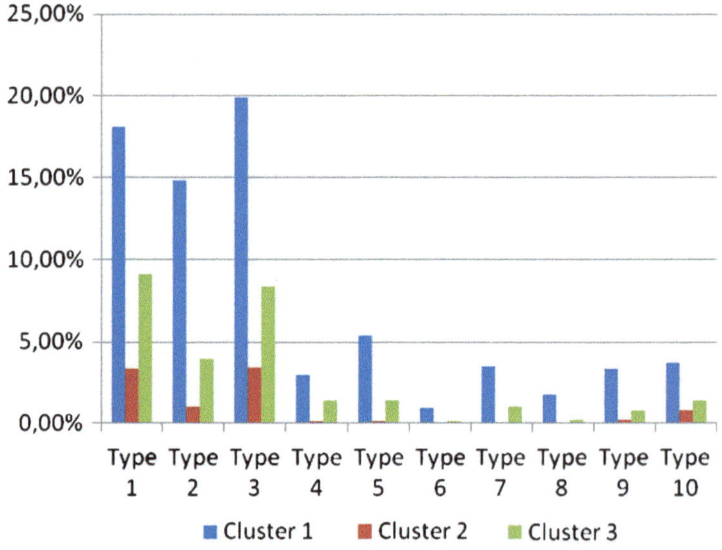

Fig. 10.4 Incidents per cluster

variability, when considering each of the ten event types separately. The analysis also produces a series of loadings for the unobserved factor by event, which can be used as weights to estimate factor scores for each club. The revealed unobserved factor could be considered as a measure of the "tendency to violence" of the fans of each of the 26 clubs, and the estimated values of the factor scores can be used to rank the clubs based on the violent behavior of their fans. Table 10.5 presents the estimated factor scores for each of the 26 clubs. As expected, the big five clubs appear in the first five positions of the ranking. The fans of Olympiakos, the league champion club in 13 out of our 23-season period (and 12 of the 14 last seasons), create the most incidents of disorder.

Table 10.5 Rankings of clubs according to factor scores

Club	Factor scores
Olympiakos	2.54284
PAOK	2.08600
AEK	1.96125
Aris	1.40023
Panathinaikos	1.31160
Panionios	0.28345
Iraklis	0.15815
Ionikos	0.09923
Larissa	0.08514
OFI	–0.09620
Egaleo	–0.31038
Kalamata	–0.35134
Levadiakos	–0.43078
Panachaiki	–0.43676
Proodeytiki	–0.51289
Kavala	–0.54968
Veria	–0.58615
Paniliakos	–0.59008
Panserraikos	–0.61681
Xanthi	–0.65189
Apollon Kalamarias	–0.69288
Ethnikos	–0.73996
Apollon Athinon	–0.76333
Doksa Dramas	–0.82054
Edessaikos	–0.87734
Athinaikos	–0.90089

Demand Model and Results

The literature on professional team sports demand is rich and dates back to 1974. Cairns (1990), Downward and Dawson (2000), and Borland and Macdonald (2003) provide extended surveys of the studies conducted in various sports, especially football. As economic theory suggests demand depends on determinants such as (a) price (plus travel costs), (b) size of the market, (c) income and other macroeconomic factors (such as the rate of unemployment), (d) availability and price of substitutes, and (e) consumer preferences. In sports, we should add uncertainty of outcome (closeness of the competition), quality of the team and the stadium, success of the team, and the weather.

The relationship between the economic determinants and attendance tends to be ambiguous (Dobson and Goddard 2001), as some of the most well-supported teams are located in areas of low per capita income and high unemployment. Madalozzo and Villar (2009) find a price elasticity for Brazilian football of –0.244, and Dobson and Goddard (2001) find a price elasticity of –0.114 for English football, while Bird (1982) finds a price elasticity of –0.22 and an income elasticity of –0.62, suggesting that football in an inferior good. Simmons (1996) finds that the attendance of casual spectators is more price elastic than that of season-ticket holders and finds no evidence of an inferior good effect, while for some clubs attendance is found to be a luxury good. Empirical findings confirm that measures of *market size* have the expected positive sign and are statistically significant, although it is difficult to define the market ("catchment area") of a certain team. Studies indicate that the *quality of the team*, as measured by league rank in current and previous seasons, has a positive effect on attendance with significant coefficients on both home-team and away-team performance.

In the present study, the main objective is to examine whether spectator violence associated with football matches influences attendance in Greek first division football. The other explanatory variables include price, income, playing success, and short-term fan loyalty. A measure for market size is not included due to the difficulty of defining the catchment areas of Greek football clubs. With six teams located in Athens and three teams located in Thessaloniki, half of the league is concentrated in two cities, as is almost half of Greece's population. Our dataset contains a combination of time-series and cross-sectional data. The time-series component covers a period of 23 years from the 1986–1987 to 2008–2009 seasons, and the cross-sectional component includes 30 football clubs that competed for at least three seasons in the first division.

Demand is measured by average annual attendance per club. Spectator *violence* is measured by the percentage of matches with violent events of Types 5–10 in total matches for each club. Preliminary experimentation with the data confirmed our assumption that incidents of Types 1–4 have no significant effect on demand. For each club, the percentage of violent home and away matches created by the club's fans is calculated. A 1-year lag of spectator violence per club is used. The *short-term loyalty* effect is incorporated by using the previous season's attendance. Following Dobson and Goddard (2001), the coefficient on this lagged dependent variable measures the strength of persistence of attendance from one season to the next, and is therefore interpreted as a measure of fan loyalty over a short time period. *Playing success* is measured by the team's finishing position in the league (the champion finishing in position one, etc.).

Average *admission price* is calculated by dividing the gross ticket revenue of each club per year by the club's total number of tickets per year. *Income* is measured by the GDP per capita. Admission price and income are expressed in constant Euro prices (Drachmas were converted to Euros for years 1986–2002). We include one dummy variable to control for the effect of hooliganism-related *deaths*, in and out of stadia. During our 23-year period, one hooliganism-related death has occurred inside stadia and two deaths that are clearly connected to hooliganism outside stadia. The final dataset includes 360 observations.

In general, let $y^{i,t}$ be a variable of our dataset. Variables have been recorded for each club (subscript i) and for each year (subscript t) under consideration. The optimum way to analyze such a dataset is to apply panel data analysis. Panel data models are a class of econometrics models that describe datasets with both cross-sectional and time-series components (Wooldridge 2002). In general, panel models produce more accurate inference of model parameters because they contain more degrees of freedom and more sample variability than cross-sectional data which may be viewed as a panel with $T=1$, or time-series data which is a panel with $N=1$, hence improving the efficiency of econometric estimates. In addition, they have greater capacity for capturing the complexity of our dataset than a single cross-section or time-series data (Hsiao 2007). To model attendance, a linear dynamic panel-data model is applied (Baltagi 1995; Wooldridge 2002). The term "dynamic" comes from the fact that the model includes one or more lags of the dependent variable as covariates. In our case, the dynamic behavior of the dependent variable derives from the fact that the annual attendances for each club are not independent values but associated to each other through a fan loyalty effect.

Concerning the estimation methodology of this model, we must note that the unobserved panel-level effects (by construction) are correlated with the included lagged dependent variables, making standard estimators like OLS inconsistent. For this reason, the Arellano and Bond's (1991) suggestion is adopted that derives a consistent generalized method-of-moments (GMM) estimator for the parameters of this model. Where possible, the natural logarithm of variables are used to facilitate elasticity comparisons. The full specification of the applied model is:

$$y_{i,t} = a + \theta y_{i,t-1} + b_1 \text{pos}_{i,t} + b_2 \text{pr}_{i,t} + b_3 \text{viol}_{i,t-1} + b_4 \text{gdp}_t + b_5 d_t + \varepsilon_{i,t},$$

where:

- $y_{i,t}$ is the natural logarithm of the average attendance, $y_{i,t} = \ln(A_{i,t})$, and $A_{i,t}$ is the average number of tickets per game for each club i in season t.
- $\text{pos}_{i,t}$ is team i's position in season t.
- $\text{pr}_{i,t}$ is the natural logarithm of team i's average admission price in season t, $\text{pr}_{i,t} = \ln(\text{Pr}_{i,t})$, and $\text{Pr}_{i,t}$ is the average price of ticket for club i in season t.
- $\text{viol}_{i,t-1}$ is the percent of violent events in period $t-1$, $\text{viol}_{t-1,i} = \text{NV}_{i,t-1} / \text{NG}_{i,t-1}$, $\text{NV}_{i,t-1}$ is the number of games with violent events for club i in period t, and $\text{NG}_{i,t-1}$ is the number of games for club i in period $t-1$.
- gdp_t is the natural logarithm of the Greek gross domestic product at year t, $\text{gdp}_t = \ln(\text{GDP}_t)$, and GDP_t is the Greek gross domestic product in constant prices obtained from the EC's Web site (http://www.ec.europa.eu).
- d_t is a dummy variable for seasons 1986/1987, 1991/1992, and 1994/1995, when deaths as a result of spectator violence, in and outside stadia, have occurred.
- $\varepsilon_{i,t}$ is the error term.

Table 10.6 shows summary statistics for the estimation sample, and Table 10.7 reports the coefficients from the panel data estimation. Based on the results reported in Table 10.7, we infer that the assumption of dynamic attendance behavior is valid since the parameter on lagged attendance is statistically significant. The position of the club in the league table positively affects attendance. That means that better performing clubs have greater average attendances. Violent events of the previous period have a negative impact on attendance in the present period. Income is positively

Table 10.6 Summary statistics

	Mean	SD	Minimum	Maximum
Average attendance	5,795.16	5,775.15	573.53	38,589.80
Deflated admission price	10.53	4.07	2.58	22.83
GDP (€ per capita/1,000) at constant prices	12.15	1.94	9.99	16.30
Percent of games with violent events of Types 5–10	8.21	0.0002	0.0000	40.00
Percent of games with events of Types 1–4	55.65	0.0007	0.0000	63.33

Greek Super League Football clubs: 30
Time period: 1986–1987 to 2008–2009
Number of matches: 6,212
Number of incidents: 4,426
Summarized data by club and by year: 360 observations

Table 10.7 Greek Super League attendance demand

	Coefficient	SE	*t*-Value	*P*-Value
$y_{i,\,t-1}$	0.309589*	0.054503	5.68	0.000
$\text{pos}_{i,t}$	−0.0311009*	0.0076187	−4.08	0.000
$\text{viol}_{i,t-1}$	−1.206566*	0.3919943	−3.08	0.002
d_t	0.0268836	0.0636061	0.42	0.673
gdp_t	0.968526*	0.2004606	4.83	0.000
$\text{pr}_{i,t}$	−0.467089*	0.076584	−6.10	0.000
Constant	−1.929697	1.879679	−1.03	0.305

Dependent variable = *attendance (annual average per club)*
Spectator violence = *% of violent matches per club (1-year lag)*
$N = 360$
The overall R^2 under fixed effect (Wooldridge 2002) is computed as 0.79
*Significant at 1% level

related to attendance, while price has a negative effect on attendance. The dummy variable d_t (which takes value 1 for the periods when deaths are associated with football matches and 0 otherwise) is not statistically significant.

The dynamic panel model includes the lagged term $y_{i,t-1}$ to capture the dynamic behavior of the dependent variable, but this approach results in estimated coefficients that are difficult to interpret. Following the approach of Dobson and Goddard (2001), we set the values of all variables equal to their steady-state values (the dummy variable d_t is set to 0) and adjust the model to derive an equivalent steady-state model. In detail, we assume:

$$y_{i,t} = y_{i,t-1} = \cdots = y_{i,1} = y_i^*,$$

$$\text{pos}_{i,t} = \text{pos}_{i,t-1} = \cdots = \text{pos}_{i,1} = \text{pos}_i^*,$$

$$\text{pr}_{i,t} = \text{pr}_{i,t-1} = \cdots = \text{pr}_{i,1} = \text{pr}_i^*,$$

$$\text{viol}_{i,t} = \text{viol}_{i,t-1} = \cdots = \text{viol}_{i,1} = \text{viol}_i^*,$$

$$\text{gdp}_{i,t} = \text{gdp}_{i,t-1} = \cdots = \text{gdp}_{i,1} = \text{gdp}_i^*.$$

Then by setting $a^* = a/1-\theta$ and $b_i^* = b_i/1-\theta$ for $i = 1, \ldots, 4$, we can conclude the following.

$$y_i^* = a^* + b_1^* \text{pos}_i^* + b_2^* \text{pr}_i^* + b_3^* \text{viol}_i^* + b_4^* \text{gdp}^*.$$

By applying the above transformation, the following equation defines the steady-state model, which can be used to infer marginal effects.

$$y_i^* = \alpha^* - 0.0448\text{pos}_i^* - 0.672\text{pr}_i^* - 1.73\text{viol}_i^* + 1.39\text{gdp}^*.$$

The coefficients of the steady-state model are statistically significant at the 1% significance level and the correspondent standard errors are 0.091, 0.092, 0.47, and 0.24, respectively.

Based on the estimated parameters of the steady-state model, we conclude that:

- An improvement of one place in the final position of the club in the league will increase its average attendance by 4.48%.
- The price elasticity of attendance is –0.67, implying that clubs are not maximizing profits since attendance is priced at the inelastic portion of demand.
- A decrease of 1% in violence will increase the average attendance of clubs by 1.73%.
- The income elasticity of football demand is positive, 1.39, which means that Greek football is a normal good.

Conclusion

The objective of this study is to examine the effect of spectator violence on attendance demand for Greek first division professional football. Our analysis, based on the decisions of the Sports Court for 23 seasons, reveals that violent incidents occur in 8.21% of matches. Violent incidents refer to stadium damages, violent clashes, intervention of the police, and injuries. If at least one of these events occurs during a match, this study considers that the match was violent. All these events take place inside or around football stadia. After a sharp increase a decade ago, when approximately one in four matches was affected by spectator violence, during the last seasons around 6% of the matches were affected. Historical data show that spectator violence in Greece is persistent and that declines are followed by unexpected re-escalations, or at least it appears that way without deeper analysis of the causes. "Lighter" manifestations of hooliganism, like swearing and inappropriate chanting, lighting of fireworks, etc., and throwing of missiles have risen dramatically, increasing the risk of injury especially for players. Certainly the lack of effective and consistent control measures regarding the objects spectators can bring into the stadia has not helped in this direction.

Our analysis reveals that the spectators of the big five clubs, with respect to positions, fans, and attendances, create the majority of the events with fans of the dominant club Olympiakos being the most violent. Fans are more violent and destructive at home than at away matches, revealing that they have no respect for their stadium. This applies also to the seasons before 2003 when restrictions on fan travel to away matches were imposed as a control measure for violence. The fact that only two out of the big five clubs (Olympiakos and Aris) enjoy their own, modern stadium, while two big clubs (AEK and Panathinaikos) use the Olympic Stadium may be contributing to this behavior. Matches of the second half of the season that are more crucial for the title, the European competitions, and relegation are more violent than those in the first half of the season. Pitch invasions increase 70% in the second half, violent clashes inside the stadium 38%, and injuries 64%. Our results indicate that spectator violence measured as the percentage of matches in which stadium damages, police intervention, violent clashes, and injuries occur has a significant negative effect on attendance.

Ticket sales remain the largest source of revenue for Greek professional football clubs. Total revenues of the 16 football clubs of the Greek Super League amounted to €125 million in the 2005–2006 season, 31% came from ticket sales, 19% from advertising, 18% from TV rights, 12% from subsidies, 11% from other sources, and 8% from sponsorships (Kyriakos 2007). Capacity usage in 2005–2006 was only 32.3%, which translates to three million unsold tickets. Our estimates show that Greek football is a normal good, and the current financial crisis has already affected football attendances. Average attendance in 2010–2011 is already 10.64% lower than in the 2009–2010 season. The financial crisis is also expected to affect the main revenue sources of football clubs. The media market is facing financial problems, as advertising budgets have declined dramatically. This will certainly affect TV rights paid to football clubs. Subsidies are also expected to decrease if the state-controlled betting company, OPAP, is sold as part of the privatization scheme for the repayment of public debt. On the positive side, this study shows evidence that there are economic gains to football clubs from the effective control of spectator violence.

We would like to add a final note in respect to the development of hooliganism. As Marsh et al. (1996) suggest, there seem to be some similarities in the stages of hooliganism development: at an *initial stage* there is sporadic violence inside the stadium directed mainly at referees and players; at a *second stage* there are aggressive encounter between opposing groups of fans and between fans and police/security officers (pitch invasions) within the confines of the stadium, and at a *third stage* there is significant increase in violence outside the stadium. Our data on Greek hooliganism reveal that the first two stages of spectator violence have occurred simultaneously. No clear distinction between these stages can be drawn.

A crucial parameter that needs to be considered is the degree to which violence control measures are used. In Greece, hooliganism in football stadia has not been contained effectively. As a result, hooliganism has had no pressing reason to escape from its "home." In 2003, fan movement bans were imposed which forbid the sale of tickets to away fans in "potentially dangerous" games. As a result, there are seasons in which 50% of the matches have no rival fans (Super League, 2008–2009, 2009–2010). The absence of a distinct rival group within the stadium directs the aggression toward the players and match officials. It is obvious that the policing of hooliganism, or the lack thereof, is one of the determining factors in its development. As we have no quantitative data about incidents far away from stadia from which to draw comparisons, we cannot answer the question of whether Greek hooliganism is in the process of moving outside stadia. We can only say with confidence that disorder and violence within the confines of Greek football stadia are still very much present.

Acknowledgment The authors wish to thank Emmanuel Petrou for his research assistance.

References

Arellano M, Bond SR (1991) Some Specification Tests for Panel Data: Monte Carlo Evidence and an Application to Employment Equations. Review of Economic Studies 58:277–298.

Armstrong G (1998) Football Hooligans: Knowing the Score. Berg: Oxford, UK.

Baltagi BH (1995) Econometric Analysis of Panel Data. Wiley: New York, NY.

Birley D (1993) Sport and the Making of Britain. Manchester University: Manchester, UK.

Bird P (1982) The Demand for League Football. Applied Economics 14:637–649.

Borland J, Macdonald R (2003) Demand for Sport. Oxford Review of Economic Policy 19(4): 478–502.

Cairns (1990) The Demand for Professional Team Sports. British Review of Economic Issues 12:1–20.

Courakis N (1998a) Violence in Greek Stadia: Between Theory and Reality. Proceedings of the 2nd Legal Conference of the Athens College Alumni Association, pp. 153–188 (in Greek).

Courakis N (1998b) Football Violence: Not Only a British Problem. European Journal of Criminal Policy and Research 6:293–302.

Disciplinary Code (2010) Hellenic Football Federation.

Dobson S, Goddard J (2001) The Economics of Football. Cambridge University: Cambridge, UK.

Downward P, Dawson A (2000) The Economics of Professional Team Sports. Routledge: London, UK.

Dunning E, Murphy P, Williams J (1988) The Roots of Football Hooliganism: A Historical and Sociological Study. Routledge and Kegan Paul: London, UK.

Dunning E (2000) Towards a Sociological Understanding of Football Hooliganism as a World Phenomenon. European Journal of Criminal Policy and Research 8:141–162.

EPAE Sports Court (various dates) Sports Court Decisions, 1986 to 2006, No. 3/22.09.1986 – No. 440/2006

Johnson RA, Wichern DW (1998) Applied Multivariate Statistical Analysis. Prentice Hall: Upper Saddle River, NJ.

King A (1997) The Postmodernity of Football Hooliganism. British Journal of Sociology 48(4):576–593.

Kyriakos G (2007) Interview of Super League's Commercial Director. Accessed online: http://www.tovima.gr/sports/article/?aid=180181 (in Greek).

Hsiao C (2007) Panel Data Analysis: Advantages and Challenges. Test 16:1–22.

Marsh P, Fox K, Carnibella G, McCann J, Marsh J (1996) Football Violence in Europe. Social Issues Research Center: Oxford, UK.

Madalozzo R, Villar R (2009) Brazilian Football: What Brings Fans to the Game? Journal of Sports Economics 10(6):639–650.

Pearson, G (1983) Hooligan: A History of Respectable Fears. Macmillan: London, UK.

Pearson G (2007) University of Liverpool FIG Factsheet. Football Industry Group, University of Liverpool, last viewed March 31, 2010. Accessed online: http://www.liv.ac.uk.

Raykov T, Marcoulides GA (2008) An Introduction to Applied Multivariate Analysis. Routledge: New York, NY.

Roadburg A (1980) Factors Precipitating Fan Violence: A Comparison of Professional Soccer in Britain and North America. British Journal of Sociology 31(2):256–276.

Roberts J, Benjamin C (2000) Spectator Violence in Sports: A North American Perspective. European Journal of Criminal Policy and Research 8:163–181.

Simmons R (1996) The Demand for English League Football: A Club-Level Analysis. Applied Economics 28:139–155.

Spaaij R (2006) Understanding Football Hooliganism. A Comparison of Six Western European Football Clubs. Vossiuspers UVA: Amsterdam, Netherlands.

Super League (various dates) Violence Reports, 2008–09, 2009–10. Accessed online: http://www.superleaguegreece.net (in Greek).

Super League Sports Court (various dates) Sports Court Decisions, 2006 to 2009, No. 01/05.10.06 – No. 202/2009.

UK Home Office (2010) Football-Related Arrests Data, 2003–04 to 2009–10. Accessed online: http://www.homeoffice.gov.uk.

Wooldridge JM (2002) Econometric Analysis of Cross Section and Panel Data. MIT: Cambridge, MA.

Chapter 11
Sport Events and Criminal Activity: A Spatial Analysis

Stephen B. Billings and Craig A. Depken II

Abstract This chapter investigates spatial crime patterns associated with events taking place in two downtown venues in Charlotte, NC: an open-air football stadium and an enclosed multipurpose arena. The evidence suggests neither venue's events contribute to an overall increase in reported total, property, or violent crimes in the city. However, both venues experience an increase in crimes within one-half mile from the venue on event days relative to nonevent days. For the arena, violent crimes increase up to a mile away while property crimes decrease for up to 2 miles away on event days compared to nonevent days. For the stadium, violent crimes decrease up to 2 miles away while property crimes increase up to 1 mile away on event days compared to nonevent days. Combined, the evidence suggests that events in these two arenas shift the pattern of reported crime, but in different ways. The results help inform public safety concerns during events and contribute to the debate over public subsidies for venues.

Introduction

Violence in sport is an interesting topic that has been investigated by a number of authors in a variety of contexts including general violence in sport (Guttmann 1998), violence in specific sports such as hockey (e.g., Jones et al. 1996; Paul 2003; Depken and Wilson 2004), the attraction and regulation of boxing (Orbach 2009), and the impacts of cheating through performance enhancing drugs (Osborne 2005) or rules breaking such as match-fixing and sabotage (Preston and Szymanski 2003). A different question, which is the focus of this chapter, is to what extent the concentration of sports fans themselves attract "violence," manifested through crimes against their

C.A. Depken II (✉)
University of North Carolina at Charlotte, Charlotte, NC, USA
e-mail: cdepken@uncc.edu

R.T. Jewell (ed.), *Violence and Aggression in Sporting Contests: Economics, History and Policy*, Sports Economics, Management and Policy 4,
DOI 10.1007/978-1-4419-6630-8_11,

persons or property. Focusing on a metropolitan area in the Southern US, we test whether the spatial pattern of reported criminal activity alters on days during which events are held in two professional-style sports venues: an open-air football stadium (home to a NFL franchise) and an indoor arena (home to a NBA franchise).

Specifically, we gather reported crimes from Charlotte, NC from January 2005 through December 2009. Located approximately 250 miles north-northeast of Atlanta, Georgia, near the border of North and South Carolina, the city was the 34th largest in the USA in 2009 with a metro-area population of 1.7 million. Comprising 242.9 square miles, the city is home to the NFL's Panthers and the NBA's Bobcats; the former of which plays in Bank of America Stadium (hereafter THE STADIUM), an open-air stadium built in 1995 with a capacity of 73,298 and 5,000 stadium-affiliated parking spots, the latter of which plays in Time-Warner Cable Arena (hereafter the Arena), a multipurpose arena built in 2005 with a capacity of 19,026 and an unspecified number of arena-affiliated parking spots. The two arenas are within one and one-half miles of each other and share approximately 30,000 off-street parking spots within a 15 minutes walk of either venue. The reported crimes are sorted into "property" crimes and "violent" crimes and each crime's geospatial location is used to determine the distance from the reported crime to both venues in the city. We then sort each crime into four distance bands which allow for testing whether the spatial pattern of reported crimes changes on days when an event is held in one or the other venue.

The empirical results suggest that the pattern of criminal activity does change on days when an event is held in either venue. While for both venues, crime in the immediate vicinity (within one-half mile) increases on an event day, the nature of the pattern changes in a one-half to one mile band from each venue: reported crime in this distance band decreases around the Arena but increases around the Stadium. For both venues, the total number of reported crimes that occur between 1 and 2 miles away declines and the total number of reported crimes that occur beyond 2 miles from the venue does not change.

Motivation

The analysis of the amount of reported crime that occurs in the vicinity of a sports venue on an event-day is motivated by two primary factors. First, sporting and cultural events are an obvious temptation to would-be criminals. Event attendees are concentrated in a relatively small geographic area, carry considerable sums of cash and expensive accessories including cell phones and cameras, and are often somewhat distracted with the anticipation of attending the event. Team owners, event promoters, and venue operators respond to these increased temptations by hiring and disbursing additional police and security personnel in an attempt to deter criminal activity. The extent to which this response is effective is one empirical question addressed in this study. A second empirical question is whether the increased security presence in the immediate vicinity of the venue influences the pattern of criminal activity some distance away from the venue; that is, does crime increase around the venue or is it displaced to other parts of the city.

Event promoters hire extra security personnel to the point where the expected marginal benefit equals the expected marginal cost. Event promoters arguably consider the expected attendance to the event when determining how many additional security personnel to deploy before, during, and after the event; however, anecdotal evidence suggests that the number of security personnel employed for the vast majority of events in a given venue is relatively stable. On the one hand, the event promoter wishes to protect the person and property of event attendees because in the short-run, that is, on the event day, resources taken from an attendee might reduce the revenues received by the event promoter, especially in the form of concessions and memorabilia. In the longer-term, if the event promoter fails, on a regular basis, to provide adequate security in and around the venue, then the venue might earn a reputation for being dangerous, thereby dissuading attendance and reducing revenue, both in the form of concessions and memorabilia but also in absolute ticket sales.

However well-intentioned the event promoter, it is unlikely that all criminal activities will be dissuaded by the level of security hired to patrol the venue and its immediate vicinity before, during, and after the event. Moreover, venues in which parking is spread over a much greater area, which have fewer affiliated parking lots, have a greater tendency for fans to spend multiple hours before and after the event tailgating, and venues with more entry points might provide greater challenges for security personnel and therefore the pattern of crime might increase in the immediate vicinity of the venue on an event day, all else equal. On the other hand, venues that have more vertical parking structures have parking lots affiliated with the venue (which are therefore easier to patrol by security personnel), have less tailgating, and have fewer entry points might be easier to patrol and therefore might experience less crime on event days as the security personnel deter criminals from engaging in illegal behavior in the immediate vicinity of the venue.

Thus, one approach is to consider reported criminal activity in the vicinity of a venue on a nonevent day compared to an event day, controlling for other factors. However, the above intuition suggests that there might be different changes in crime patterns depending on the venue and also upon distance from the venue. For instance, a change in criminal activity in the immediate vicinity of the sporting event might represent a net increase in criminal activity in the host city. That is, the number of reported crimes in the rest of the city might remain the same while there is an increase in criminal activity localized around the event venue. On the other hand, any increase in criminal activity around the event venue might represent a substitution from criminal activity farther from the event venue, that is, overall crime in the city might not change with only a shift in the geographic areas of where the crimes take place. A final possibility is that, regardless of what happens near the event venue, the overall crime activity in the host city might actually fall.

It is possible that the increase in police presence in the immediate vicinity of the sporting event provides a displacement effect. That is, certain criminal activity might actually increase distant from the event venue because of an actual or perceived reduction in police presence in the rest of the host city. Therefore, to fully identify the impact of a sporting event on criminal activity, it is necessary to consider the effects of the sporting event on reported crimes in locations that are close to the venue as well as in locations that are some distance away from the venue.

Our empirical analysis focuses on the impact of hosting professional sporting events on reported criminal activity. The increase in population density relative to a nonevent day can attract individuals' intent on engaging in criminal activity. However, not all crimes are expected to be associated with professional sporting events. For instance, there is no *ex ante* reason to suspect that arson, murder, or white-collar crime, such as extortion, would be associated with a normal professional sporting event, yet there are good reasons to suspect that robbery, vandalism, assault, or larceny (e.g., selling counterfeit tickets on the secondary market) would be.

Existing Literature

There are several studies that make a connection between sporting events and crime. Several studies purport to find a correlation between sporting events and domestic violence, e.g., Card and Dahl (2011) find a positive correlation between watching American football on television and domestic violence. A number of studies have focused on spectator violence at association football (soccer) matches, especially in Europe (Dunning et al. 1986; Zani and Kirchler 1991; Carnibella et al. 1996). In the case of North American sports, Baumann et al. (2009) investigate whether US cities that host a franchise from the NHL, NBA, MLB, or NFL, and which hosted the Olympics or World Cup matches experience any difference in their crime rates than other cities. They find no evidence that property crimes or violent crimes are impacted by hosting a franchise or a mega-event. Baumann et al. use the reported crime data provided by the Federal Bureau of Investigation's Uniform Crime Reports. However, the UCR data have been criticized as being potentially inaccurate because often not all agencies within a given jurisdiction report their data in a given year.

While Baumann et al. find no evidence that aggregate crime rates are impacted by hosting franchises, their study does not investigate the pattern of crimes within a city as it relates to hosting events. One such study that does this is Rees and Schnepel (2009), who cleverly test for differences in crime patterns associated with US college football games. They find significant and economically meaningful increases in crime rates in towns in which the games are played but no change in crime rates in the hometown of the visiting team. They also show that close games and unexpected outcomes also influence criminal behavior in the town in which the game is played. The evidence strongly suggests that emotional fervor and alcohol consumption combine to create a rather combustible situation when combined with college football.

Beyond the aforementioned literature focusing on association football and fan violence, to date there has been relatively little research tying attendance to various sporting events to crime patterns or crime rates. Messner and Blau (1987) find a positive relationship between reported crime rates and the availability of "non-household leisure activities" which include the local provision of sports. While they do not tie crime directly to attendance, their empirical evidence suggest that there is more crime in cities in which household undertake more leisure activities outside of the home (e.g., attending a professional sporting event) than inside the home (e.g., watching television).

Data and Empirical Specification

Detailed crime data were provided by the Charlotte-Mecklenburg Police Department and cover all reported crimes in the city of Charlotte as well as most of Mecklenburg County, NC. The Charlotte-Mecklenburg jurisdiction contains approximately 750,000 people and average crime rates relative to other medium and large US cities. According to the FBI Uniform Crime Reports, Charlotte had 7.2 violent crimes per 1,000 people and 44.9 property crimes per 1,000 people in 2009. Other US cities with between 250,000 and 1,000,000 people averaged 6.4 violent and 42.3 property crimes per 1,000 people in 2009. Our data include the date and physical address of each reported crime between January 2005 and December 2008. The original data set contains 1,042,559 observations but this is reduced to 983,157 usable observations after removing observations corresponding to crimes that were designated noncriminal, suicide/accidental death, missing person, or runaway. These data classify crime into one of the 39 categories, which we aggregate into total reported crime, total violent crime, and total property crime. Violent crimes include arson, assault, homicide, and rape. Assault represents more than 70% of violent crimes. Property crime includes auto theft, fraud, larceny, hit and run, burglary, and vandalism. Larceny represents about 50% of property crimes.

We identify each crime's geospatial location and relate it to the geospatial location of both the Stadium and the Arena; that is, for each crime it is possible to calculate the distance from the reported crime to each of the Charlotte venues. For each venue, we identify four distance bands: within one-half mile, between one-half and one mile, between 1 mile and 2 miles, and more than 2 miles. Each crime is sorted into one of these four distance bands for each venue (yielding eight dichotomous variables which take a value of one if the crime's location falls within the particular distance band). Because of the relatively close proximity of the Arena and the Stadium (see Fig. 11.1), it is possible for a particular crime to fall, say, within one-half mile of the Arena and within 1 mile of the Stadium. In this case, the particular crime would be sorted into the appropriate bin for each venue.

For each day of the sample period, we identify whether a professional or college football game was played in the Stadium and whether a game or concert was held in the Arena. A dichotomous variable is created that takes a value of one if an event occurs in any of the two venues and interaction terms between whether an event occurs and the distance-band dummy variables are created.

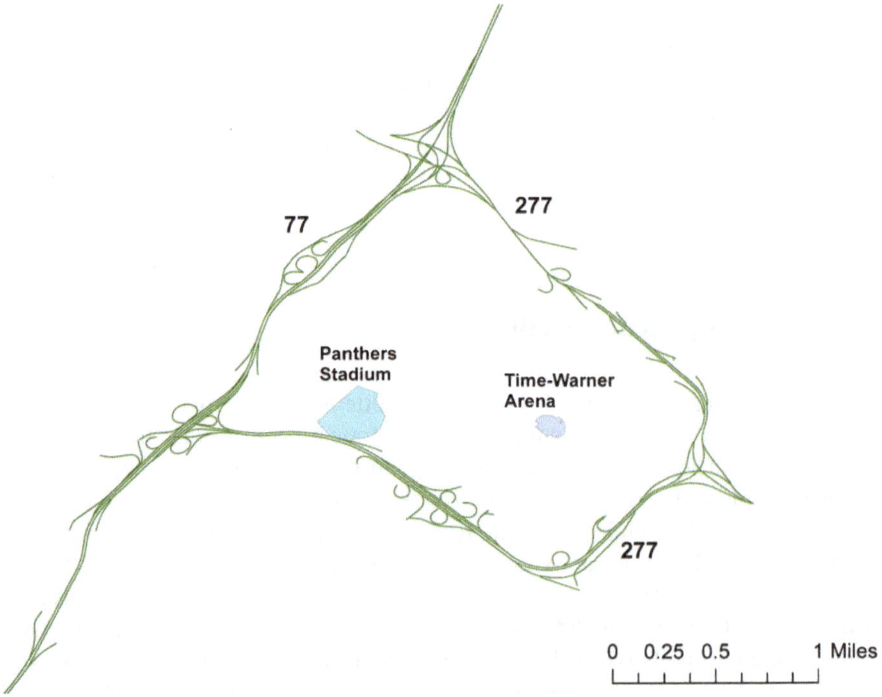

Fig. 11.1 The two venues in city center of Charlotte, NC

The empirical strategy entails estimating the following general form:

$$\begin{aligned} \text{DEP}_{i,j.t} &= \alpha_{i,j} + \beta\text{EVENT}_t + \delta\text{DISTANCE}_j \\ &+ \varphi\text{DISTANCEVENUE}_t + \phi\text{TIME}_t + \varepsilon_{i,j,t}, \end{aligned} \tag{11.1}$$

where the dependent variable DEP is the number of crimes of type i on day t in distance band j, i = total, violent, and property. The explanatory variables include a dummy variable that takes a value of 1 if an event is held in the city on day t (EVENT), a vector that describes the distance band in which the reported crime's geoposition falls relative to either venue (DISTANCE), the interactions between the dummy variables that comprise DISTANCE and two dummy variables that comprise the vector VENUE, BOA, and TWCA, which equal one for the Stadium and the Arena, respectively, and zero otherwise. The vector TIME contains year, month, and day of week dummy variables. A fixed effects model is applied to the data with standard errors clustered by distance band.

The proximity to a venue is distinguished as being "near" or "far" from the event. Admittedly, it is somewhat arbitrary as to where to draw the line between near and far. Here crimes are sorted as falling into four possible bands of concentric circles around a particular sports venue: between zero and a half mile, between a half mile and one mile, between 1 mile and 2 miles, and beyond 2 miles. These distance

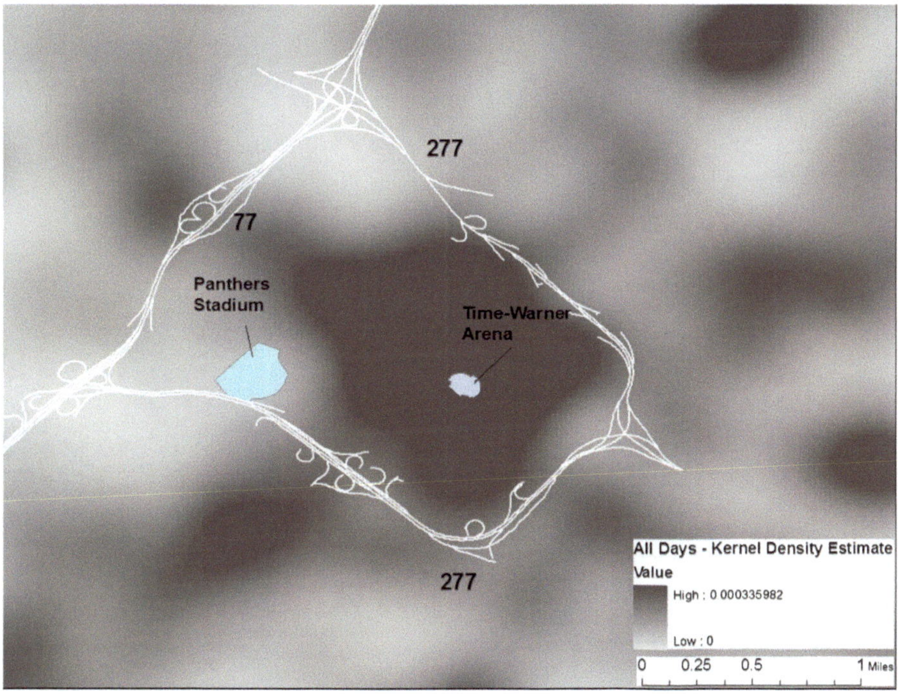

Fig. 11.2 Kernel density estimator depicting distribution of total crime in Charlotte, NC from January 1, 2005 through December 31, 2008

bands were chosen after looking at the distribution of crimes around the venue sites. Figures 11.2 and 11.3 depict two alternative distributions of total reported crime in the city of Charlotte. These figures show the distribution of total reported crimes based on a kernel density estimator (KDE).

The KDE transforms point data for crimes into a continuous measure of crime intensity across our study area. Specifically, we use a bivariate kernel density to estimate the intensity of crime at each location in our study area. The bivariate KDE provides an estimate of point intensity at a given location by taking into account neighboring points in all directions surrounding a given reported crime. We primarily use this estimator as a visualization tool and thus are not concerned about our choice of bandwidth equal to 1,000 m or other issues related to estimating KDE on the edge of a study area. Scholars often use KDEs to transform discrete data into continuous measures of concentration in order to address any biases related to the modifiable areal unit problem. Silverman (1986) provides an excellent treatment of this literature. Weighting is based on inverse distance and follows a Gaussian distribution. This provides a moving window estimate of crime at any location and thus a smooth estimate of crime intensity across our study area. The kernel then standardizes the data such that summing kernel density across the entire study area is equal irrespective of the total number of crimes. This allows us to compare the

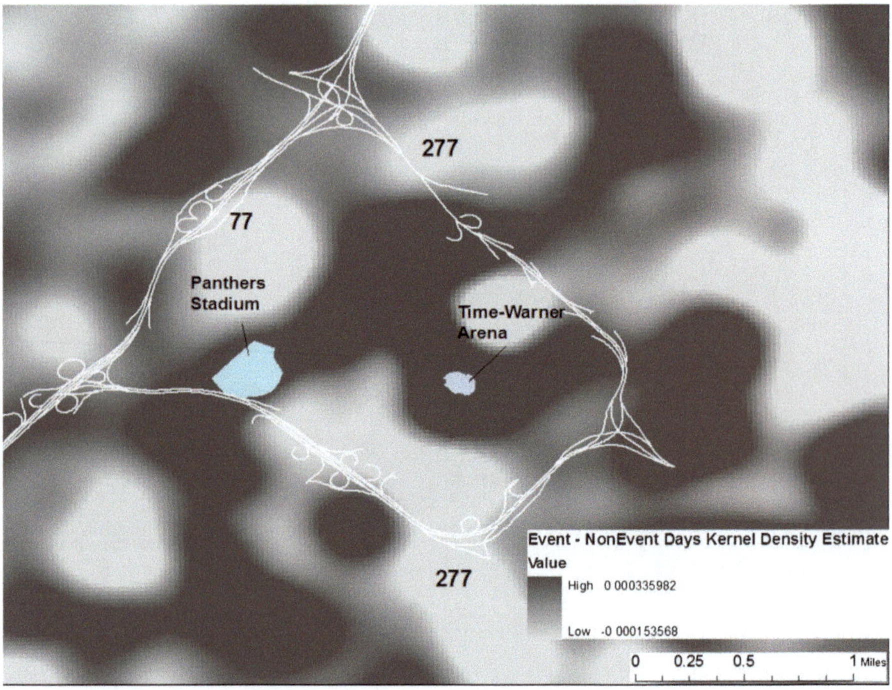

Fig. 11.3 Kernel density estimator depicting distribution of difference in total reported crime in Charlotte, NC on event days and nonevent days from January 1, 2005 through December 31, 2008

location of crime between crime groupings irrespective of their size. For example, in aggregate there are considerably more crimes on nonevent days then event days. Therefore, the KDE only changes in value at a given location if the relative geospatial pattern of crime changes more than fluctuations in crime across all locations.

Figure 11.2 shows relatively more crime in the city center near the Arena and the Stadium, than outside the inner loop (I-277). Figure 11.3 shows the KDE distribution of the *difference* in reported crime on event days and nonevent days. As can be seen, around the two venues there seems to be more crime on event days with the remaining area of the city experiencing a decline in crime on event days. Of course, this does not control for differences between event and nonevent days due to seasonality of sports seasons or the day of week.

Table 11.1 reports the average daily reported number of crimes by type. On an average day during the sample period between January 1, 2005 and December 31, 2008, there were approximately 510 total crimes reported with approximately 360 of these crimes involving property crimes and 98 involving violent crimes, the remainder falling into neither category (e.g., drug-related crimes). Table 11.2 reports the frequency of event types across the two venues. During the sample period, there were 198 NBA Bobcats games and 35 concerts at the Arena, and 34 NFL Panthers games and 5 college football bowl games at the Stadium.

Table 11.1 Daily reported crimes in Charlotte, NC

	Mean	SD	Minimum	Maximum
Total crimes	508.9	66.2	262	788
Property crimes	358.8	54.7	146	584
Violent crimes	97.8	19.4	44	170

Daily crime counts for 1,461 days from January 1, 2005 through December 31, 2008

Table 11.2 Frequency of event types in Charlotte, NC

Event type	Frequency	Percentage
NBA Bobcats game	189	71.9
College football bowl game	5	1.9
Concert at Time-Warner Arena	35	13.3
NFL Panthers game	34	12.9
Total	263	100

Empirical Results

We estimate (11.1) treating the dependent variable as a count variable. As can be seen in Fig. 11.1, there appears to be under-dispersion in the data, as the variance is less than the mean for all three categories of reported crime, thereby rendering the Poisson model inappropriate. We initially estimate a simple model based on daily crime counts for the entire city of Charlotte to test if days with sporting events at either venue have more or less crime than nonevent days. These results are given in Table 11.3, and insignificant coefficients for the dummy variables for *Event at Stadium* and *Event at Arena* highlight that there is no change in crime on event days. This limits concern that crime may increase or decrease as a results of criminals substituting criminal activity to other days. Since geographical displacement is of primary interest to us, we apply the negative binomial estimator to the data, clustering standard errors on distance band, and estimation results are reported in Table 11.4.

Stadium Events

On event days at the Stadium, which are professional or college football games, total reported crime increases within one-half mile of the Stadium and also in the band of one-half to one mile from the Stadium. Coefficients indicates that a Panthers Stadium event increases crime by a factor of 2.44 and 1.08 for less than half mile and half to one mile, respectively. The relative incidence rates are calculated as exp(β) for the coefficients reported in Table 11.4. However, in the band representing 1 mile to 2 miles from the Stadium, the total number of reported crimes actually decreases by a factor of 0.96. Finally, there is no statistically meaningful change in total reported crime beyond 2 miles from the Stadium. The pattern of total crime around the football stadium is very interesting; as overall reported crime in the city does not increase, it seems that the increase in total reported crimes in the immediate vicinity

Table 11.3 Negative binomial estimation results: dependent variable is daily number of reported crimes

Variables	(1) Total crime	(2) Violent crime	(3) Property crime
Panthers Stadium event	0.018	0.011	0.022
	(0.029)	(0.034)	(0.031)
Time-Warner Arena event	0.001	0.000	–0.000
	(0.010)	(0.015)	(0.012)
Constant	6.012***	4.459***	5.676***
	(0.013)	(0.023)	(0.015)
Model chi-square	861	572	763
Pseudo R^2	0.360	0.373	0.353
Observations	1,461	1,461	1,461

Notes:
Dependent variable is the number of reported crimes in Charlotte for each day from January 1, 2005 through December 31, 2008
Each model estimated using a negative binomial specification and includes annual fixed effects, month of year fixed effects, day of week fixed effects
Robust standard errors are given in parentheses
***$p<0.01$

of the stadium is substituting for crimes that might have otherwise taken place in those parts of the city a little further away from the stadium.

The other two specifications in Table 11.4 show that the changes in the pattern of overall reported crimes are somewhat nuanced. Reported violent and property crimes increase close to the stadium on event days. However, when looking at the one-half mile to one mile distance band, the number of reported violent crimes declines while the number of reported property crimes increases on event days in this distance band. When looking at the 1-mile to 2-mile distance band, both reported violent and property crimes fall. This suggests that those who engage in violent crimes are more proximate to the stadium and might correspond with drinking and associated aggressive behavior on the part of fans (Roberts and Benjamin 2000). On the other hand, those who are engaged in property crimes, such as robbery (including breaking and entering cars and buildings) and larceny (which might include scalping counterfeit tickets), seem to move away from the immediate vicinity of the stadium on event days, as might be expected.

Arena Events

Table 11.4 also reports the results corresponding to the events taking place in the Arena. For the one-half mile distance band nearest the Arena, the pattern of reported crime is very similar to that of the Stadium: reported violent, property, and total crime increases in this band on event days. However, the pattern changes when moving to the one-half to one-mile distance band from the Arena. In this band, the total

Table 11.4 Negative binomial estimation results: dependent variable is daily number of reported crimes by distance band

	(1)	(5)	(9)
Variables	Total crime	Violent crime	Property crime
Panthers Stadium event < 1/2 mile	0.894***	1.083***	0.852***
	(0.016)	(0.017)	(0.014)
Time-Warner Arena event < 1/2 mile	0.077***	0.119***	0.049***
	(0.010)	(0.006)	(0.010)
1/2 mile < Panthers Stadium event < 1 mile	0.075***	−0.245***	0.147***
	(0.016)	(0.017)	(0.014)
1/2 mile < Time-Warner Arena event < 1 mile	−0.036***	0.113***	−0.062***
	(0.010)	(0.006)	(0.010)
1 mile < Panthers Stadium event < 2 miles	−0.073***	−0.125***	−0.085***
	(0.016)	(0.017)	(0.014)
1 mile < Time-Warner Arena event < 2 miles	−0.038***	−0.047***	−0.042***
	(0.010)	(0.006)	(0.010)
2 miles < Panthers Stadium event	0.015	0.024	0.011
	(0.016)	(0.016)	(0.014)
2 miles < Time-Warner Arena event	0.001	0.001	−0.001
	(0.010)	(0.006)	(0.010)
Event in the city	0.001	−0.004	0.003
	(0.010)	(0.005)	(0.010)
Constant	2.699***	1.133***	2.370***
	(0.018)	(0.011)	(0.015)
Pseudo R^2	0.361	0.374	0.354
Model chi-square	41,929	28,645	38,142
Observations	11,688	11,688	11,688

Notes:
Dependent variable is the number of reported crimes in one of the four distance bands around each venue in Charlotte: Panthers Stadium, Time-Warner Arena
Each model estimated using a negative binomial specification and includes annual fixed effects, month of year fixed effects, and day of week fixed effects
Each model includes eight fixed effects to indicate one of four distance bands for each venue
Standard errors clustered by distance band and venue and reported in parentheses
$*p<0.1$; $**p<0.05$; $***p<0.01$

number of reported crimes falls by a factor of 0.78. However, the decrease in total reported crimes is net of an increase in reported violent crime and a fall in reported property crime in this distance band. One contributing factor to the differences in reported crime patterns might be the nature of parking and tailgating associated with the two venues: around the Arena parking tends to be more vertical and concentrated and there is less tailgating, whereas around the Stadium parking tends to be more horizontal and less concentrated and tailgating for many hours before and after the event is more common. In areas with concentrated buildings and vertical parking, there might be less breaking-and-entering, for instance, and more assaults (especially in and around bars proximate to the Arena). When moving to the 1 mile to

2 miles distance band from the Arena, the number of reported violent and property (and therefore total crimes) declines. Finally, beyond 2 miles from the Arena, there is no difference in reported crime rates on event days relative to nonevent days.

Conclusions

This chapter provides a geospatial analysis of how the pattern of reported crime in Charlotte, NC, changes when there are sporting and cultural events in one or both of the downtown venues: Bank of America Stadium, home of the NFL Panthers, and the Time-Warner Cable Arena, home of the NBA Bobcats. Using a data set describing all reported crimes in the city from 2005 to 2008, the evidence suggests that events in the two venues correspond with a change in the pattern of reported crimes in the city on event days. For events held in the Stadium, violent and property crimes both increase in the immediate vicinity of the stadium but property crimes increase on event days in the one-half to one-mile distance from the Stadium, whereas violent crimes decrease in this distance band. When moving further from the stadium, both types of crime decrease suggesting that those who engage in criminal behavior seem drawn toward the stadium and this provides a corresponding offset in crime some distance from the stadium.

Similarly events held in the Arena correspond with increases in reported total, violent, and property crime within one-half-mile of the Arena, but when moving to the one-half to one-mile distance band, violent crimes increase and reported property crimes decrease. This suggests that the nature of criminal activity differs across the two venues: whether this has more to do with the immediate environment of the two venues, the Stadium has low-concentration parking, whereas the Arena generally has more concentrated parking, or whether the opportunities for various criminal activities differ across the events held in the two venues is clearly an avenue for future research.

The empirical evidence in this chapter contributes in two ways to the debate concerning public subsidies for Stadiums and Arenas. First, perhaps because economists continue to find that realized net benefits of a new stadium are considerably less than predicted, predicted quality-of-life improvements are increasingly used to justify stadium subsidies. In at least one case, a stadium proposal was specifically justified because of an expected *decrease* in crime after the stadium opened. Specifically, in 2004, the city of Arlington, Texas, debated and ultimately passed a referendum to subsidize a new stadium for the NFL Dallas Cowboys with $325 million. During the debate stadium proponents distributed fliers stating that the proposed location of the new stadium was the neighborhood with the highest number of 911 calls, suggesting that the new stadium would reduce reported crime and therefore reduce policing costs within the city. Whether crime actually fell after the stadium opened has not been investigated to date. Second, if the result found here is not idiosyncratic, shifts in crime patterns during stadium events have implications for the social benefit of the new stadium and should be incorporated in the estimated social costs and benefits of the new stadium.

References

Baumann R, Engelhardt B, Matheson V, Ciavarra T (2009) Sports Franchises, Stadiums, and City Livability: An Examination of Professional Sports and Crime Rates. Working Paper 0913, College of the Holy Cross, Department of Economics.

Card D, Dahl GB (2011) Family Violence and Football: The Effect of Unexpected Emotional Cues on Violent Behavior. Quaterly Journal of Economics 126(1):103–143.

Carnibella G, Fox A, Fox K, McCann J, Marsh J, Marsh P (1996) Football violence in Europe: A report to the Amsterdam Group. The Social Science Research Centre.

Depken CA, Wilson DP (2004) Wherein Lies the Benefit of the Second Referee in the NHL? Review of Industrial Organization 24(1):51–72.

Dunning E., Murphy P, Williams J (1986) Spectator Violence at Football Matches: Towards a Sociological Explanation. The British Journal of Sociology 37(2):221–244.

Guttmann A (1998) The Appeal of Violent Sports. In Why We Watch: The Attractions of Violent Entertainment, ed. Goldstein JH. Oxford University Press: New York, NY.

Jones, JCH, Stewart KG, Sunderman R (1996) From the Arena into the Streets: Hockey Violence, Economic Incentives, and Public Policy. American Journal of Economics and Sociology 55(2): 231–243.

Messner SF, Blau JR (1987) Routine Leisure Activities and Rates of Crime: A Macro-Level Analysis. Social Forces 65(4):1035–1052.

Orbach BY (2009) Prizefighting and the Birth of Movie Censorship. Yale Journal of Law and the Humanities 21:251–304.

Osborne E (2005) Performance-Enhancing Drugs: An Economic Analysis. Unpublished manuscript, Wright State University.

Paul R (2003) Variations in NHL Attendance: The Impact of Violence, Scoring, and Regional Rivalries. American Journal of Economics and Sociology 62(2):345–364.

Preston I, Szymanski S (2003) Cheating in Contests. Oxford Review of Economic Policy 19(4):612–624.

Rees D, Schnepel K (2009) College Football Games and Crime. Journal of Sports Economics 10(1):68–87.

Roberts J, Benjamin C (2000) Spectator Violence in Sports: A North American Perspective. European Journal of Criminal Policy and Research 8(2):163–181.

Silverman B (1986) Density Estimation for Statistics and Data Analysis. Chapman and Hall: London, UK.

Zani B, Kirchler E (1991) When Violence Overshadows the Spirit of Sporting Competition: Italian Football Fans and Their Clubs. Journal of Community and Applied Social Psychology 1(1):5–21.

About the Contributors

Vassiliki Avgerinou is an Assistant Professor of Sports Economics in the Sport Management Department of the University of Peloponnese (Sparta, Greece). Her research interests focus on the economics of hooliganism, the economic impact of sports events, attendance demand for professional sports, and competitive balance.

Marcel Battré studied International Business at the University of Paderborn (Germany) and Universidad Carlos III de Madrid (Spain). His specialization is strategic and business management. Since 2008, he has worked as a research assistant at the University of Paderborn. His research areas are personnel economics and sports economics.

David J. Berri is a Professor in the Department of Economics and Finance at Southern Utah University. He received his PhD in Economics from Colorado State University. His current research focuses on the economics of sport, specifically the topics of consumer demand, competitive balance, and worker productivity.

Stephen B. Billings is an Assistant Professor of Public Policy and a Research Fellow in Real Estate at the University of North Carolina at Charlotte. He received his PhD in Economics from the University of Colorado. His research interests include the relationship between tax incentives, public investment, and the location of economic activity, the spatial pattern of crime, and how local government impacts residential development patterns.

Ross Booth is a Senior Lecturer in the Department of Economics, Faculty of Business and Economics, at Monash University (Australia). His main research interest is the economics of professional team sports leagues, especially the Australian Football League. His research has been published in books (*International Sports Economics Comparisons*, *Handbook on the Economics of Sports*, *Economics of Sports Leagues: An International Perspective*, and *The Games are Not the Same: The Political Economy of Football in Australia*) and in Australian journals. Since 1988, Ross has complemented his academic interest in sports economics with football commentary on the Victorian Football League for ABC TV.

R.T. Jewell (ed.), *Violence and Aggression in Sporting Contests: Economics, History and Policy*, Sports Economics, Management and Policy 4,
DOI 10.1007/978-1-4419-6630-8, © Springer Science+Business Media, LLC 2011

Robert Brooks is Associate Dean in the Faculty of Business and Economics and Professor in the Department of Econometrics and Business Statistics, Monash University (Australia). His main research interest is in applied econometric modeling of a broad range of financial and economic data, including data of relevance to sports economics. Previous research includes an analysis of test cricket strategy and performance and an analysis of stock market reaction to the Sydney Olympic Games announcement.

Dennis Coates is a Professor of Economics at the University of Maryland, Baltimore County. He is the Book Review Editor for *Journal of Sports Economics* and on the editorial boards of *Journal of Sport Management* and *International Journal of Sport Finance*. He is the editor of the Springer series of which this book is a part. His research in sports economics focuses on the impact of sports on the economy of a city, state, and region.

Trevor Collier is an Assistant Professor of Economics at the University of Dayton. He received his PhD in Economics from Southern Methodist University in Dallas, TX. His research interests include productivity analysis, the economics of public policies, and the economics of sports.

Craig A. Depken II is an Associate Professor of Economics in the Belk College of Business at the University of North Carolina at Charlotte. He received his PhD in Economics from the University of Georgia. He has published on a wide range of topics in the areas of sports economics, public choice, industrial organization, and real estate economics.

Christian Deutscher studied economics at the University of Bonn (Germany). Since 2007, he has worked as a research assistant at the University of Paderborn (Germany), where he finished his doctoral thesis in 2010. His research focuses on sports economics and personnel economics.

Stefanos G. Giakoumatos is an Associate Professor of Statistics and Quantitative Methods at the Technological Educational Institute of Kalamata (Greece). He is also a Vice-President at TEI and Chairman of the Department of Local Government. Before becoming an academic, he worked as a statistician for the National Statistical Service of Greece. His research interests focus on Bayesian analysis, applications of Markov Chain Monte Carlo, time series analysis, sampling design, and applications of statistics in social sciences.

Janice A. Hauge is an Associate Professor of Economics at the University of North Texas. She received her PhD in Economics from the University of Florida and an MSc degree from the London School of Economics. Her research focuses on industrial organization, utility regulation, and sports economics. Currently, her work centers on empirical analyses of the effectiveness of broadband policies and initiatives both within the USA and internationally.

R. Todd Jewell is a Professor of Economics and department chair at the University of North Texas. He received his PhD in Economics from the University of California at Santa Barbara. In addition to the economics of sports, he has also published in the areas of the economics of immigration and health economics.

Andrew L. Johnson is an Assistant Professor in the Department of Industrial and Systems Engineering at Texas A&M University. He obtained his PhD from the H. Milton Stewart School of Industrial and Systems Engineering at Georgia Tech. His research interests include productivity and efficiency measurement, warehouse design and operations, material handling, and mechanism design.

Afsheen Moti received an MS in Economic Research from the University of North Texas in May 2011. While a graduate student at UNT, she was a research assistant and teaching fellow. She currently holds the position of Senior Analyst at Enterprise Spectrum in Dallas, TX.

John Ruggiero is the Edmund B. O'Leary Professor of Economics at the University of Dayton. He received his PhD in Economics from Syracuse University. His research expertise is in the area of performance analysis using nonparametric frontier estimation and regression-based approaches. He is the author of *Frontiers in Major League Baseball: Nonparametric Analysis of Performance using Data Envelopment Analysis*, a Springer book in this series on sports management.

Ryan M. Rodenberg is an Assistant Professor in the Department of Sport Management at Florida State University. He earned his law degree from the University of Washington in 2000. Prior to entering academia, he served as Associate General Counsel at sports marketing firm Octagon in Washington, DC. Sports law analytics is his primary research focus.

John Solow is an Associate Professor of Economics at the University of Iowa. He received a PhD in Economics from Stanford University. He has published articles in the areas of sports economics, industrial organization, and the creative economy, and his research interests include sports economics, antitrust law and economics, and public policy. He has worked at the Federal Energy Administration and the Electric Power Research Institute, and he has served as a consultant to the US Departments of Energy and Justice.

Peter von Allmen is a Professor of Economics at Skidmore College in Saratoga Springs, NY. He received his PhD in Economics from Temple University. His primary research area is sports economics, focused mostly on compensation schemes and incentives. He has also published in the areas of family labor supply and post-secondary pedagogy. In addition, he is the co-author (with Michael Leeds) of *The Economics of Sports*, now in its 4th edition, and *Economics* (with Michael Leeds and Richard Schiming).

Index